FIDEL CASTRO: THE RAPE OF A NATION

EXPOSING THE TRUE CHARACTER AND INNER FEELINGS OF A RUTHLESS DICTATOR

DR. RAFAEL R. PEDRAJA

Trafford
PUBLISHING

Order this book online at www.trafford.com/07-1708
or email orders@trafford.com

Most Trafford titles are also available at major online book retailers.

Note for Librarians: A cataloguing record for this book is available from Library
and Archives Canada at www.collectionscanada.ca/amicus/index-e.html

ISBN: 978-1-4251-4142-4

*We at Trafford believe that it is the responsibility of us all, as both individuals
and corporations, to make choices that are environmentally and socially sound.
You, in turn, are supporting this responsible conduct each time you purchase a
Trafford book, or make use of our publishing services. To find out how you are
helping, please visit www.trafford.com/responsiblepublishing.html*

*Our mission is to efficiently provide the world's finest, most comprehensive
book publishing service, enabling every author to experience success.
To find out how to publish your book, your way, and have it available
worldwide, visit us online at www.trafford.com/10510*

www.trafford.com

North America & international
toll-free: 1 888 232 4444 (USA & Canada)
phone: 250 383 6864 ♦ fax: 250 383 6804
email: info@trafford.com

The United Kingdom & Europe
phone: +44 (0)1865 722 113 ♦ local rate: 0845 230 9601
facsimile: +44 (0)1865 722 868 ♦ email: info.uk@trafford.com

10 9 8 7 6 5 4 3 2

Dedication

I dedicate this book to the memory of my dear parents, Jesus M. and Ursula, who had to leave Cuba at an advanced age because of the repression of the Castro dictatorship, and to the memory of my in-laws, Mario and Elsa Ochoa, who also left their beloved country for the same reasons. Furthermore, I dedicate this book to the many victims of the Castro regime who have given their lives fighting the cruel Communist dictator. Additionally, this book is dedicated to the myriad of courageous prisoners of conscience who, just for expressing their views in a non-violent manner, have suffered, and continue to suffer, abuse, torture and misery at the hands of an inhumane and brutal ruler.

Acknowledgements

I must admit that this book turned out to be a more ambitious undertaking than what I first envisioned. Thank you, Gladys, my dear wife, for your patience, encouragement and support during this effort. Thank you, Ralph and Amy, my beloved children, for your helpful comments pertaining to the sequence of subjects and chapters in the initial typed manuscript. And special thanks to my son-in-law, Mike Burnham, for skillfully typing my hand-written manuscript.

Testimonials

"A balanced and thorough history of Cuba; its political and economic life and its descent from a state working toward full democracy to its plundering by Castro. Thank you for writing this informative and sorrowful book."

— HUGH DUNBAR, COUNTY COMMITTEEMAN AND ACCOUNT EXECUTIVE

"This needed to be told so that Cuban American children/grandchildren, whose parents/grandparents lived through these torture-filled times, never forget how great Cuba was, how Cuba is today, and how Cuba was transformed to its current day misery. This needed to be told so Americans of all backgrounds learn not to embrace a dictator, or his regime, who has broken the will of freedom of its people for nearly 50 years just 90 miles away from American shores."

— RICHARD ROSEN, BUSINESS EXECUTIVE

"This book is very clear, revealing, informative and expertly researched. Dr. Pedraja in *Fidel Castro: The Rape of a Nation* exposes vividly the propaganda machine that Castro has used to make inroads in the liberal circles of the USA."

— DR. ANDRÉS CORNEJO, M.D. AND CUBAN ÉMIGRÉ

"Straighforward, hard-hitting, like a good exposé should be. Dr. Pedraja uses a lot of words to describe Castro, all of which I liked; two that quickly come to mind are 'psychopath' and 'skunk.'"

— ROBERT T. GROVE, TRADER/BROKER

TABLE OF CONTENTS

Introduction

THIS BOOK IS about repression, suffering, torture, murder, lies, infamy, deception, brutality, humiliation, manipulation, hate, misinformation, treason, perversion, cowardice and everything else that is evil. A tyrant by the name of Fidel Castro Ruz represents one of the worst humans in history. He has the ominous distinction of joining the group of conscienceless, savage, bloody dictators who have been the scourge of humanity, including Hitler, Stalin, Mussolini, Pol Pot, Mao Tse-Tung, Ceaucescu and Saddam Hussein among the most notorious.

Many readers may be asking themselves, "Who is the author of this book and what were his motives behind it?" These are logical questions, especially when the writer is unknown to the vast majority of readers. Undoubtedly, the book is not written by a famous person. It is written by, of all professions, a food scientist with political inclinations and a profound interest in political science. In spite of being a scientist, I never wanted to be portrayed simply as a man wearing a white smock enclosed within the four walls of a laboratory.

My motives behind this book are very clear. I want the world to know the truth about Fidel Castro, including the damage and suffering he has inflicted upon the population of a noble country through deceptive means. I would also like to put an end to the distortions propagated by many liberals and left-wing radicals about the real intentions and the disastrous results of the Communist revolution in Cuba. In addition, I want to send a wake-up call to those who ignore, accept or promote the ever-present danger of self-destruction represented by extremists, whether they are Communists, Fascists, Nazists, anarchists, terrorists, or hold to any other variety of malicious ideology.

During the short republican existence of Cuba, beginning on May 20, 1902, until it fell to Communism on January 1, 1959, the island had made significant progress in spite of its sporadic political turmoil, typical of a nation in its formative years. In its 57 years as a republic, Cuba excelled in many areas, including its cultural development, legal system, constitutional rights, sports activities, agricultural and industrial progress, education, labor laws, public health and hygiene, transportation, arts, music and news media communication (newspapers, radio and television).

Cuba's main shortcoming was its intense political discord. Most prominent was the unexpected military coup d'état of March 10, 1952, under the leadership of ex-President and retired General Fulgencio Batista y Zaldívar, then a senator, against the duly-elected President Carlos Prío Socarrás. The coup occurred only three months before general elections were scheduled and for which, ironically, Batista was one of the three presidential candidates aspiring to replace Prío.

Amid the Batista regime that followed, the main woes of the republic were not related to the economy, which was thriving at an accelerated pace. Instead it was attributed to the political infighting and restlessness caused by the doggedness of Batista to stay in power, and by the reluctance of the democratically-minded opposition to negotiate and reach a political settlement. In spite of seven years of a politically destructive atmosphere under Batista, free enterprise was flourishing, and Cuban capital investment and private businesses were on the rise.

Throughout this restless time, the people who were somewhat oblivious to politics and those who did not participate in violent or conspiratorial acts against the government were left alone to go about their business. They simply tolerated the status quo and, as much as possible, led a normal life. However, under the Communist tyranny in Cuba that followed, all aspects of every human life would be affected and controlled by the regime.

The progress made during the years as a republic came to an abrupt end just a few months after Castro took the reins of government and began a precipitous march toward Communism. Initially the "26th of July Movement," founded by Fidel Castro to promote the armed revolution against Batista, was projected to the world as a pro-democracy organization with the sole intent of bringing freedom of expression, justice and the reestablishment of the democratic Constitution of Cuba, originally enacted in 1940. It was based on free elections under a multiparty system, and championed private enterprise, respect for human rights, equal opportunity regardless of race, religion or sex, and many other components of a free society.

All of these tenets, which Castro repeatedly vowed to respect while promoting the revolution against Batista, were blatantly discarded by his imposed Communist regime. Castro suffocated what appeared at the onset to be an act of redemption for all past political sins in Cuba. He skillfully and maliciously manipulated the brightest, the bravest and the fittest to establish a totalitarian Communist state in an effort to satisfy his implacable thirst for power and fame. His well-planned design was known only to a handful of close collaborators. Once he felt secured in power, Castro began to purge the revolutionary leaders, both civilian as well as military, who did not approve of turning the revolution to Communism. Many of these leaders were executed, jailed or forced into exile, if they were lucky enough to escape from Cuba. Some were so frustrated with the Communist takeover or embarrassed by their unsuspecting involvement in it that they committed suicide.

Castro, as I will prove through an analysis of his acts and behavioral trends, is a psychopath with a political agenda bent on destroying the aspirations of others while satisfying his own selfish ambitions. His mannerisms were very similar to Hitler's and Mussolini's, and his never-ending harangues, spewing hatred against the United States, often lasting over four hours, fit the mold of a mentally deranged bully. Castro adopted Marxism-Leninism as his political ideology early in life. Like all Communists, he uses fear, lies and deception as his main weapons of domination. The assertion by liberal elements in the United States and elsewhere that Castro was pushed into Communism at the hands of the Soviet Union will be shown to be false.

Castro's godless Communist tyranny, now in existence for over 48 years, has robbed those who had legitimate material possessions (i.e., a house, a farm, a shop, a manufacturing plant or some other kind of business). But what is even more perverse, he has stolen from the young people of Cuba the opportunity to reach their maximum potential, to develop a free-thinking mind, and to enjoy life in all of its fullness. Castro has trounced the legitimate and natural aspirations of several generations of Cubans by using a discredited political system as a vehicle to exert his will. As Aleksandr Solzhenitsyn said so well in his article entitled "Communism at the End of the Breshnev Era" published in the *National Review* on January 21, 1983: "Communism is the denial of life, it is the fatal disease of a nation and the death of all humanity."

Solzhenitsyn was the winner of the Nobel Prize for Literature in 1970 and one of the most outstanding Russian writers of the 20th century. He wrote, among other essays and books, *The Gulag Archipelago,* in which he describes the abuses and tortures committed under the Stalin rule of the Soviet Union, and was an avowed anti-Communist. During the Stalinist era he was sentenced, without a trial, to eight years of hard labor for his role as a dissident, which he served in various labor camps. After Stalin's death he was exiled to the West in 1974, and then settled with his family in the United States. He was openly critical of the persecution and killing of Soviet Union writers, the censorship imposed by Communism and the torture of dissidents held in inhumane jails and forced labor camps. His suffering under Communism parallels that of Cuban dissidents and writers under the barbaric rule of Castro. We could not find a better exponent of what Communism really is than Solzhenitsyn to describe and denounce the pitiless and grotesque rule of Castro in Cuba.

Over two million Cubans have left the island since the Castro takeover. They include rich, middle class and poor; black and white; and adults and children of all ages. After the initial massive exodus during the early years of the Castro dictatorship, Cubans have continued to leave, in spite of the severe travel restrictions imposed upon them. They have used all kinds of transportation, including hijacked planes, fishing vessels, boats, makeshift rafts and artifacts of different sorts – a testimony to the desire of mankind to be free.

Thousands of people searching for freedom have died in the effort to escape, before or after leaving the Cuban shores. Many were victims of the rough seas or faulty vessels. The majority of the refugees have settled in the United States; others have gone to countries in South and Central America, as well as to Europe. A truly cross-section of the population has fled Cuba; among them athletes,

artists, intellectuals, industrial and commercial workers, farmers, business people, members of the revolutionary armed forces, economists, physicians, scientists, teachers, lawyers, librarians, journalists, government employees, students,
high-profile figures such as the first revolutionary provisional president, cabinet
members, diplomats, and revolutionary leaders who were at one time closely
allied with Castro. The vast majority of exiled Cubans have made a significant
contribution to the United States by practicing their professions, opening businesses, working in factories, shops, healthcare facilities, corporations and government offices. Many have reached political positions of relevance, either by
being elected to public office or nominated to important government posts.

According to many observers and sociologists, Cubans have exceeded expectations in regard to their full integration into the American society. We
are indeed grateful to this great country that welcomed us and gave us the opportunity to share in its bounty and freedom. We deeply hope that some day
Cuba will join the free nations of the world when the long nightmare it has suffered under the Castro tyranny comes to an end. We wish that some misguided
Americans, who do not feel comfortable with the democratic system we enjoy
in this wonderful land, will come to realize that the United States is the most
generous and just country on the face of the earth. We look forward to the moment when the historic friendship between Cuba and the United States will be
reestablished after the fall of Castro, a demagogue, a despot and one of the most
vicious tyrants of our time. May God help us in this noble endeavor.

1

A HISTORICAL AND GEOPOLITICAL PERSPECTIVE OF CUBA

"This is the most beautiful land that human eyes have ever seen."
— CHRISTOPHER COLUMBUS

I THOUGHT IT appropriate to describe some important facts about Cuba, particularly for those readers who are not totally familiar with the island and its historical and geopolitical perspective. Cuba in the pre-Castro era was justifiably known as the Pearl of the Antilles. Today it is sad to say that it has become a pearl lost in a sea of poverty, oppression and despair.

The Cuban territory consists of a long, narrow island which lies on an east-west direction in the northern part of the Caribbean Sea.

Map of Cuba Showing Its Current Provinces

The latitude of Cuba is comparable to that of Mexico City, Mexico; Honolulu, Hawaii; the Philippines; Calcutta, India and Canton, China. The island is bathed on the north by the Canaries Ocean current and on the south by the Equatorial Ocean current. Both ocean currents join just north of Cuba to form the great

1

Gulf Stream. This oceanographic phenomenon contributes significantly to the pleasant, mild climate of the island practically all year round. Cuba is in the so-called Trade Wind Belt. The winds come most of the time from the northeast in the summer and from the southwest in the winter. The sea breeze moderates the heat of the noon and afternoon hours. The island is so narrow that the temperature is promptly equilibrated within the width and length of the territory. Humidity is relatively high all year round. Winters are somewhat dry, clear and with moderate temperatures, which generally vary between 60°F and 75°F. The summers are warm with temperatures rarely exceeding 85° F. Since there is not a great annual variation in temperature, many tourists came to enjoy the blue skies and temperate, clear waters on the beaches of both coasts.

Cuba as a nation had tremendous opportunities and resources for growth. It also had a privileged geographical location in this hemisphere that was already paying dividends for its economical development up until the advent of Castro. Cuba has a length of 760 miles and an average width of 25 miles. The coast line is 2,500 miles long. There are several important harbors which are deep and protected by nature's geological formations. The ports of major renown include Havana, Santiago de Cuba, Nuevitas, Guantanamo, Manzanillo, Baracoa, Santa Cruz, Jucaro, Trinidad, Caibarien, Cienfuegos, Sagua la Grande (Isabela de Sagua), Cardenas, Mariel, Matanzas and Nueva Gerona on the Isle of Pines. Cuba has an area of 44,164 square miles, about the same size as the state of Pennsylvania or Louisiana and is about three times the area of Switzerland. The northern coast of the island is only 90 miles south of Key West, Florida, making Cuba the nearest to the U.S. in distance of all Latin American republics, with the exception of Mexico. This proximity to the U.S. gave Cuba a significant strategic and economic advantage. To the south of Cuba lies the Isle of Pines, which is only 33 miles from the main coast and a part of the Cuban national territory now occupied by the infamous Castro and his thugs.

Cuba was discovered on October 27, 1492, by the Genovese explorer Christopher Columbus, sailing to find new horizons on behalf of the Queen of Spain, Isabella the Catholic, who was his protector and sponsor. At his arrival on the Cuban shores, he exclaimed, with admiration: "This is the most beautiful land that human eyes have ever seen." He knew indeed how to judge beauty. The King of Spain assigned the colonization of the island to Captain Diego de Velázquez who, with several ships and an expeditionary force of 300 men, landed in Cuba in 1511 at a port north of Baracoa, Oriente. Thus Baracoa, on the northeastern coast of Cuba, became the first village founded by the Spaniards in Cuba.

The Spaniards, in an attempt to exploit the riches of Cuba, promptly imported black slaves from Africa as early as 1517. Africans continued to be brought to Cuba until the year 1886, when slavery was officially abolished. Many prominent Cuban intellectuals were openly against slavery and promoted the liberation of the slaves. The native Indians in Cuba (Aborigines) were few, and they were given such harsh treatment by the Spaniards that they were practically extinguished over a short span of time. The African slaves also received severe handling, but they were physically more resistant than the original Indian inhabitants. With time, the treatment of the slaves was somewhat softened. Slavery was one of the major aberrations of humanity in the history of civilization. Today a cynical form of slavery is practiced by the Castro-Communist dictatorship, which attempts to control the lives and souls of every Cuban residing on the island by using repression and fear.

At the beginning of the Cuban rebellion against Spanish rule in 1825, there were already several generations of native Cubans. They were direct descendants from the influx of Spaniards who, since the beginning of the colonization, came to Cuba to find new horizons from the limited opportunities available in Spain and other European countries. Many also came as adventurers looking for excitement and riches, while others came as members of the military forces and administrative personnel. The black slaves and their children also became part of the general population, and many joined the cause of the Cubans, who conspired and fought for their independence from Spain. They were, of course, considered to be Cubans as well. Antonio Maceo, a member of a heroic black Cuban family, gained admiration and respect from all segments of society, Cubans as well as many Spaniards. He rose to the rank of General in the Cuban revolutionary army in its fight against Spanish domination. He was killed by the Spaniard troops during an ambush in 1896. This was a huge loss to the war of independence; nevertheless, the Cuban fighters recovered from this setback and continued to fight against Spain.

After many years of struggle, Cuba finally obtained its independence from Spain in 1898 with the help of the United States. This forged a lasting link of deep friendship between the two countries until the Castro takeover. The Cuban revolutionary war against Spain was a long and bloody conflict. José Martí, born of modest Spanish parents, was considered the missionary of Cuba's independence. He was revered in Cuba in the same way that George Washington is in the United States and Benito Juarez is in Mexico. At a young age he was imprisoned for his stand against the Spanish despotism and was deported to Spain, where he studied law and philosophy. Martí traveled to several countries in an effort to maintain ties with Cuban émigrés who had fought against Spain in past wars. He organized and coordinated the last unified Cuban revolutionary movement against Spain's regime. Martí collected funds and united the many patriotic elements within Cuba and in exile to launch what became the final armed struggle to remove the Spanish yoke from Cuba. Shortly after returning from exile and landing an expeditionary force in Cuban territory, he was killed during a battle with Spaniard troops on May 19, 1895. Martí was not a soldier; however, he was willing to offer his life on behalf of the cause he loved so much. He was a man of profound depth and intellect.

Martí was a dreamer, a patriot, a teacher, a writer, a philosopher, a sociologist and a dedicated and creative individual of unlimited energy and mental resources. He was considered one of the greatest prose writers of Spanish America. As a poet he was a precursor of the "Modernism Movement." He dreamed of a democratic Cuba. He was the antithesis of a tyrant. Against all kinds of adversity he inspired a country and became a legendary figure in the annals of Cuban history. What a stark difference from the selfish and hateful monster that imposed a disastrous Communist dictatorship in today's Cuba.

Castro has desecrated José Martí's ideology in a perverse attempt to tergiversate the legacy of the most honored and beloved hero of Cuba. The tyrant has no limits on his unscrupulous methods and actions. On his direct order, the Communist revisionists have redesigned Cuban history as a step to establish a new ideological and cultural structure based on Marxism-Leninism. The ultimate purpose of this malevolent strategy is, of course, to impregnate the minds of new generations with the seeds of their fanatical and irrational creed and to erase all vestiges of Cuba's best traditions. To achieve this aim they had to break up the roots of Cuban national history and distort the facts beyond any imaginable recognition.

This process began early in the conversion to Communism. Many Cuban patriots were eliminated from the history books because of their conservative, democratic or pro-entrepreneurial ideas; others because of their family lineage. In the case of José Martí, however, it would have been counterproductive to remove him from the pages of Cuban history. His image and philosophy were ingrained in the minds of all Cubans since their early childhood. He was adored by all generations and even given the designation as "the Apostle of Cuba." Instead, with distinct malice, Castro admonished the Communist revisionists to rewrite Martí's path to democracy, freedom and human rights. They began the task of twisting his thoughts to fit Socialism and the hate they felt toward the United States. Castro and his cohorts were terrified at the true thinking of Martí, who had written extensively about his abhorrence for tyrants, his democratic and freedom of expression ideals, his search for liberty, his advocacy for human rights and his repulsion of Socialism, which was in the midst of being expounded at that time in Europe by Karl Marx and others.

José Martí spent many of his exiled years in the United States, where he wrote extensively in the New York newspaper *Patria,* as well as in other publications, while organizing and promoting the cause of Cuban freedom. He expressed on many occasions his admiration for the U.S. and his gratitude for the support he cultivated here for the Cuban independence movement. Two different quotations from Marti confirm this. In a letter to the *National Opinion* newspaper, Caracas, Venezuela, on January 21, 1882, he wrote: "Here lies the secret of the prosperity of the United States: They have opened their arms." His other remark is of profound meaning because it reflects his faith in the democratic system of the United States. In a letter to the Director of the *New York Herald,* on May 2, 1895, shortly after he began the independence war in Cuba, he said: "It is not certainly in the United States where men will dare to find seeds for a tyranny."

Martí's thoughts about Socialism were clear and concise from the early stages of this misleading philosophy enunciated during the middle part of the 19th century. He denounced Socialism as a tyranny and he foresaw it as the future slavery of men. As such, he was a prophet in his time. While Martí predicated love, Marxism predicated hate. It is understandable why he could not accept Marx's ideology. Martí was a spiritual leader and never accepted the materialistic and atheistic doctrine advanced by Marx and his followers. Marti wrote about the dangers of Socialism and dictatorial systems. Examples of his thoughts on the subject are recorded for history in his diaries, written articles, lectures and letters to his friends, family and co-revolutionaries. Consider the following written in a letter to his friend, Fermín Valdés Dominguez, on May 3, 1884:

> The Socialist idea, among others, has two dangers: one is its outlandish foreign teachings, misleading and incomplete, and the other is the hypocritical anger and rage of the ambitious who under disguise aspire to rise in the world by riding high on the shoulders of others while pretending to be the frantic defenders of the have-nots.

Again, writing about Socialism and oppression, he wrote in his diary during a journey from Montecristi, Dominican Republic, to the Haitian Cape on his way to Cuba on March 3, 1895, the following insight:

> An authoritarian society is, of course, the one based on the concept, sincere or feigned, of human inequality, under which it is demanded obedience to the social obligations from those whose rights are denied, for the principal benefit of the controlling power and the pleasure of those who negate them: a mere reminder of a barbarian state.

Martí was an advocate of the universal right to private property. In an article he wrote in the New York newspaper *Patria* on November 1, 1892, he stated: "It is proper to defend and guard the richness gained by personal effort." Many other writings by Martí could be cited pertaining to his ideological repulsion to Marxism-Socialism. The examples given above are offered to emphasize the tragic and profane lies of Castro in his efforts to destroy the heritage of what once was a glorious, proud and prosperous nation. The vision of Martí transcends the pages of history and defines the tragedy of the Cuban calamity under Castro with a crisp objectivity that makes it seem that he is still here with us at this sad moment. He would never have thought that this would be the fate of his beloved country.

All of the above quotes of José Martí – translated from Spanish into English by the author – were found in an extraordinary book containing a compilation of many of Martí's thoughts, entitled *El Pensamiento Martiano (The Thoughts of José Martí)* by Adalberto Alvarado, Gonzales Printing, Miami, Florida, 1985.

At the official end of Cuba's War of Independence, known in the United States as the Spanish-American War, and the ensuing transition of government functions on January 1, 1899, the President of the United States appointed General John R. Brooke as temporary governor of the island. General Leonard Wood succeeded him in December 1899. In May 1902, the provisional government was ended and Cuba was delivered to a constitutional government, democratic in character and having an elected President and two legislative bodies (the Senate and the Chamber of Representatives). The country became free and independent. This independence and freedom lasted until the dreaded takeover of Cuba by Communism on January 1, 1959.

Cuba, before Castro totalitarianism, had enormous sea traffic with many ports throughout the world. Air traffic, both commercial and passenger, was also heavy during that time. Many international airlines flew to Cuba either as an end destination or as a mid-point with other countries. The proximity of Cuba to the United States placed Cuba in a privileged position. The cost of freight and accessibility to the most powerful country in the world was indeed a blessing to the island. Cuba was a leader among all Latin American republics in volume of trade with the U.S. It had a thriving economy, a high level of education, an advanced healthcare system, and a dynamic industrial and agricultural development. Cuba also had the highest standard of living of all Latin American countries. The only aspect that needed restoration to normalcy was the political situation. Given Cuba's talent resources, diversity of political parties and intellectual climate, this could have been resolved with the fall of Batista through the reestablishment of a democratic government. Castro, acting as a pawn of the Soviets, purposely sabotaged all of those altruistic efforts based on his frantic desire to be the only one in control.

There was no need for the political and economic upheaval that was brought about by Castro and his cohorts after Batista was overthrown. Cuba was unfortunately destroyed by a Communist experiment. This was not the intended purpose of the revolution fought by the Cuban people and the many honest revolutionaries. They had all joined in the cause for what they believed would be the establishment of a democratic society. The Cuban people were betrayed, and what seemed to be a bright opportunity for redemption was miserably squandered. Castro had blatantly lied about his intentions, as he repeatedly promised to restore a democratic system to the island.

The conversion of Cuba to Communism was performed under false pretenses by Castro, masked as a defender of freedom, democracy and human rights. When Cubans woke up to the reality of his true intentions, it was already too late. He had, in the course of less than two years, complete control of the printing press, the rebel forces, the labor unions, the cultural and educational institutions, the radio and television stations, and all the means of production and distribution throughout the country. All free enterprises were forcibly confiscated without compensation, including small family businesses. He abolished all political parties except the Communist Party, called the Popular Socialist Party (PSP), which at that time was a very small nucleus of the population and a discredited organization. He then publicly declared himself a Communist, although this was already known by his actions. The Cuban people were trapped with practically no recourse. The curtain had fallen. The republican era came to an abrupt end.

We will demonstrate without a scintilla of doubt that Castro was always a Communist disguised as a "nationalistic reformer," a title given to him by the *New York Times* liberal journalist, Herbert L. Matthews, during the early stages of the insurrection against Batista. After Matthews interviewed Castro in January 1957, at his camp in the Sierra Maestra Mountains, he began to broadcast to the world the glory of the revolution. He wrote many favorable articles in defense of Castro and grossly exaggerated the strength of the rebel group in the Oriente Province. He made Castro an international hero and contributed enormously to the popularity, growth and success of the rebellion. Matthews, along with other not less famous apologists for Castro, blasted Batista and falsely pictured Cuba as a very impoverished country with no social justice whatsoever. They foolishly or intentionally served to enhance the myth of Castro as a savior and reformist. In March 1962, after Castro's onslaught on free enterprise, freedom of the press and human rights, his promotion of subversion, of leftist movements in Latin America, and his allegiance with the Sino-Soviet block against the United States, Matthews began to see the light and criticized the role of Castro's furious anti-American campaign and the danger of his international activities. It was too little too late. The damage was already done.

The leftist apologists of Castro during the early years of his regime, and those who still maintain that he was forced to embrace Communism and the Soviet Union by the policies of the United States, were completely out of touch with the reality of the situation and Castro's true designs for the revolution. Nothing could be more distorted and further from the truth than that assertion. The truth is that the United States, in spite of repeated early offers of economic help to the new revolutionary government of Cuba, was, and continues to be, the scapegoat for all failures of the Communist dictatorship imposed upon the Cuban people. Cuba, contrary to the derogatory pronouncements from the deluded liberals and all other Castro defenders, was not the impoverished country they mischievously or ignorantly portrayed. They were, and some still are today, ominously attempting to justify Castro's irrational behavior and profound hatred for the United States.

It is not that I favor suffocating criticism or muffling the thoughts of people with views different than mine. On the contrary, I firmly believe that responsible and constructive ideas in any field of endeavor should be encouraged under our democratic prerogatives. Nevertheless, there is a limit beyond which the good of the nation can be seriously damaged by the destructive and corrosive advocacy against the fundamental principles under which the American republic was created. It is baffling to me why these unsavory left-wingers discredit their own country, especially while visiting or lecturing in other countries. In so doing, they show no respect for the values we care so deeply about.

We should all be proud of the United States, the beacon of liberty, opportunity and justice that illuminates the whole world. The history of Cuba is yet to be completed, and we still have much to learn from the lessons of this great nation where we live.

2

The Spectrum of World Communism and Castro's Ambitions. An Eye Witness.

"The spreading of Communist falsehoods and hatred became a powerful weapon in an attempt to weaken, undermine and penetrate the free world."

Communism: A Historical Review

WITH THE DEFEAT of Hitler and Mussolini in the mid-1940s, the despicable and brutal Nazism and Fascism systems became discredited. Communism was on the rise. Joseph Stalin, as supreme leader of the Soviet Union, was at the apex of his totalitarian control of Eastern Europe. The agreements signed at the Yalta Conference by the Big Three Allied Leaders (Churchill, Roosevelt and Stalin) gave too much territory to the Soviet Union. A big chunk of Europe was transferred into the unscrupulous hands of Stalin during that historic conference held in Crimea in February 1945. One of the conditions for ceding such vast territory to the Soviet Union was based on the promise of Stalin to grant independence and to permit the holding of free elections in the newly liberated nations. Needless to say, those promises were never fulfilled. On the contrary, all opposition parties were eliminated and the Communist Party took over the reins of government in the various Eastern European countries under Soviet dominance. Britain and the United States were too generous and credulous. This is just one more example proving that Communists, no matter what the circumstances, cannot be trusted.

The immediate result of the Yalta Conference was that Poland, Hungary, Romania, Bulgaria, Yugoslavia, Czechoslovakia, Albania and East Germany became satellites of the Soviet Empire, which already had hegemony over Latvia, Estonia and Lithuania since 1940. Russian troops were stationed in each satellite country to crush opposition and to keep the people in line. Many industrial

9

plants and equipment were stripped and shipped to the Soviet Union. Russia began to shield the Soviet Union and the satellites from the non-Communist world. The "Iron Curtain," as Churchill described the Soviet policy, was erected. The so-called Marxist-Leninist "proletarian paradise" had been enormously extended and protected from democratic influence. In reality, it turned out to be a brutal, enslaving system of exploitation of the human race.

What could be expected of Stalin and his ruthless behavior? He had been a brutal, bloody and cruel dictator. He had slain millions of Russian peasants during the collectivization of agricultural lands. The bloody purge under his regime extended throughout the country, many more millions were to die, including those who perished in the forced labor concentration camps known as the "gulags." All resistance was quashed with no compassion. His paranoia was such that he coldly executed many prominent politicians and elite members of his military apparatus. He was constantly obsessed by the ghost of faltering loyalty on the part of his closest associates and of potential plots to eliminate him. Anyone suspected of disloyalty, including members of his own family and his collaborators, were summarily executed on the spot. A few were lucky enough to flee the country while they were being hunted like wild animals. His own daughter, Svetlana, fled Russia and came to live in the United States. Stalin pretended to be a genius in every field of endeavor. He desperately wanted to create adulation around him. He practiced the personality cult to the hilt. In all of this there is a tremendous similarity to what Castro has been doing during his total control of the Cuban scenery for the last unprecedented forty-eight years. Megalomaniacs have many things in common.

Communist Tactics: Spreading Lies and Hate

Communism had determined that to reach its target and succeed, a systematic, well-designed indoctrination campaign was essential. The spreading of Communist falsehoods and hatred became a powerful weapon in an attempt to weaken, undermine and penetrate the free world. To accomplish this training and proselytism, the Communists founded the Lenin School of Political Warfare in Moscow, the Far Eastern University in Peiping (now Beijing) and the Psychological Warfare Schools in Prague and other Communist countries. The graduates of those schools served to spread the venom all over the world. The United States became a prime target of such schools. The Soviets desperately wanted to influence and subvert American opinion. Parallel to the indoctrination campaign, the Reds had developed a formidable military and espionage apparatus, not only to suffocate internal dissent, but also to intimidate the non-Communist nations.

During the 1940s and 1950s the Communists made significant inroads in the United States with their espionage and subversion campaign. Some American intellectuals, including scientists in sensitive positions, became tools of the Communist conspiracy. They not only were actively promoting Communist ideas, but additionally got involved in espionage activity. They passed atomic secrets to Soviet agents. Some of these individuals went to trial and were convicted, while others fled to the Soviet Union. Even some prominent, high-post government officials in the United States were duped by Communists and tended to favor the Soviet Union in matters connected with security and the sharing of atomic secrets.

The propaganda machine of the Communists was so extensive, deceiving and intensive that many young scholars began to embrace Marxism-Leninism as their political doctrine solely on the mischievous premises that Communism was creating equality and destroying capitalism for the benefit of the poor classes. In fact, Communism led by the Soviets was using violence, deceit, terrorism, espionage, persecution and brutal force to abolish human rights, religious freedom, democracy, free enterprise, free expression and individual determination from the countries under its domination. Counter to their claims, poverty, scarcity and blight were running rampant in the "workers' paradise." The economies of the countries under Communism became a disaster. The state enterprises failed because of lack of incentives, low productivity and mismanagement. The quality of goods and services was very poor. Under Communism there is no competition; people have to accept whatever is produced because there are no alternatives or choices. The state failed miserably as a substitute for private enterprise. Slave labor did not produce results. Under Communism, rhetoric is abundant, results are meager. The irony of all of this is that the chieftains of Communism live in luxury, at least until they fall in disgrace with their own comrades.

The Fall of the Soviet Empire

The United States led the democracies of the world to stop the expansion and aggression of Communism. The "cold war" began its course after World War II and lasted until the Soviet Empire disintegrated and collapsed under the weight of its own sins, with the final dismantling of the Union of Socialist Soviet Republics (USSR) in December 1991. Twelve separate independent republics emerged from the split; namely, Russia, Moldavia, Turkmenia, Azerbaijan, Tajikistan, Georgia, Uzbekistan, Ukraine, Armenia, Kazakhstan, Byelorussia and Kirghizia.

The historical, unprecedented and monumental defeat of Communism in the Soviet Union and Eastern European countries in a practically bloodless popular revolution taught us an unforgettable lesson: we should never be pessimistic, there is a lot of good in this world, and evil never prevails.

We shall never lose sight of the positive accomplishments of many outstanding people who had the mental energy, faith and fortitude to defeat the forces of evil. Three prominent leaders of our time played a pivotal role in the demise of the despotic Soviet imperialism: Lech Walesa, Ronald Reagan and Pope John Paul II.

Walesa led the Solidarity workers movement in Poland through a valiant struggle. Solidarity began as an independent workers union in the shipyards of Gdansk where Walesa was an electrician. After an uphill battle, it became a powerful social labor instrument with a mass following. Walesa suffered persecution and incarceration during the process. His courageous efforts brought down the Communist puppet regime in Poland in 1989. This was the beginning of the end of Communism in the Eastern European countries. It served to spark a wave of non-conformity which was in the making for years under dictatorial puppet regimes. Additionally, from 1989 to 1990 Czechoslovakia, Romania, Hungary, East Germany, Bulgaria, Yugoslavia, Albania, Estonia, Latvia and Lithuania got rid of the Communist stranglehold. Then, as cited before, the Soviet Union was dismantled from within. Democracy had won an epic victory that turned the tide of a corrupted and hellish system in an unanticipated way. For his extraordinary achievements, Walesa won the Nobel Peace Prize in 1983 while Poland was still under the Communist dictatorship and later, after the fall of Communism, he was elected President of Poland.

President Ronald Reagan, through his steadfast stance against Communist perversion, made it extremely difficult for the disease to advance. His famous reference to the Soviet Union as "the evil empire" resonated all over the world and opened many eyes. It gave nightmares to the Moscow gang. Reagan's determination and leadership made it impossible for the Reds to reach, let alone surpass, the United States development and deployment of advance deterrent weapons, drawing them to the brink of economic disaster.

The Strategic Defense Initiative (SDI) sponsored by Reagan to counter Soviet nuclear capabilities, and his assertion that Communism was destined to the ash heap of history, made Moscow realize that indeed they had a formidable and determined foe on the other side of the Atlantic. The Kremlin raised its level of concern. Additionally, the repression of freedom to maintain the slavery within the USSR and satellite countries was proven counterproductive, as boldly denounced by President Reagan. His unforgettable words when he stood before the ominous Berlin Wall resounded as the ultimate call for freedom: "Mr. Gorbachev, tear down that wall." Reagan's masterful handling of Gorbachev during the crisis that ended with the falling of the Soviet Union was typical of his firm, optimistic and persuasive personality. The masses responded and the wall was torn down. Indeed, it took a strong president to accomplish this monumental task.

Pope John Paul II was a pilgrim in our midst. He traveled through many countries, including Communist-dominated nations, proclaiming the rights of self-determination, freedom of worship and individual rights for the human race. His message of respect for human dignity carried an inexorable power. His image and his religious, spiritual and moral projection gave the underdog an immense inner strength and hope. He openly challenged the legitimacy of the Communist regimes. He gave encouragement to dissidents in Communist countries, including Lech Walesa in Poland and Vaclav Havel in Czechoslovakia. His visits to Poland in 1979 and 1983 became events of major historical proportions. He was the embodiment of hope for the suffering population. In spite of the atheistic position of the government in Poland and the fact that children were taught there was no God since their early upbringing, the Polish people never abandoned the Christian faith. The Pope's visits reinvigorated the faithful and elevated the aspirations of the struggling populace.

The Pope supported the Solidarity movement and gave encouragement to Walesa to continue his efforts for social justice and democracy. The striking workers began to carry posters of the Pope as a peaceful weapon of resistance to the abuses and lies of the Communist regime. The scenery was moving, defiant and patriotic. The Communists were confounded. They did not know how to react. The demonstrations were massive. The fear of the Polish was gone. The Communist cowards knew right then and there that their time was running out and began to retract. The Pope indeed was armed with a clear and powerful vision, and his words "Be not afraid" resounded all over the world as a challenge to Communist oppressors. Walesa became unstoppable.

Background of the Author

I began attending public school in my hometown of Sagua La Grande on the north coast of the central province of Las Villas. My parents moved to Havana, the capital of Cuba, when I was in seventh grade, where I continued my public school education. In 1947 I graduated as Eminent Alumnus (Summa Cum Laude) from the Superior School of Arts and Trades (Technological School) of Havana, earning a BS degree in Industrial Chemistry. As a result of this achievement, I received an award of $100.00, presented to me by the Mayor of Havana, Mr. Nicolás Castellanos.

From 1947 to 1952 I was a full-time student at the University of Havana, where I entered the Faculty of Agronomical and Chemical Engineering and was active in student politics. I had the privilege of being elected class delegate every year, and later Vice President of the student body of the faculty. I was President and founder of the independent group called "University Committee for the Advancement of Agrarian Affairs" (Comité Universitario de Superacíon Agraria). I was also a member of the "University Anti-Communist Front." In spite of being involved in campus politics, I was a good student, a conservative and a very respectful individual. At the University of Havana I earned a degree in Sugar Chemistry and Technology (equivalent to a Masters of Science) and a degree in Agronomical Engineering (which included Food Science and Technology) at the doctoral level (PhD).

I had a lot of admiration for my professors and for the University as a first-class cultural institution. In fact, I spent some of the best years of my life at the University of Havana. I must admit that I don't recall any of my professors, within the University ambient, ever expressing or advancing individual political beliefs or ideologies. They kept their teaching to the subjects of their respective philosophical, scientific or technical expertise. They did not attempt to shape the political formation of the students, and that was commendable, unlike some professors of left-wing persuasion that we have here today in the United States of America at colleges and universities, and even in grade schools.

Knowing Castro

During my student days at the University of Havana I had the unfortunate occasion of meeting Fidel Castro. He was a student at the Law Faculty and a little over two years my senior. I never had much to do directly with him because we were in two different schools within the large and sprawling university campus which had over a dozen faculties (Education, Civil Engineering, Architecture, Agronomical and Chemical Engineering, Law, Odontology, Medicine, Veterinary Medicine, Chemistry and Physical Sciences, Social Sciences, Philosophy and Letters, Commercial Sciences, Pharmacy, Political and Diplomatic Sciences) and in excess of 15,000 students. Additionally, we were in two radically opposite ideological camps.

I ran into Castro only casually during student political activities and can say with certainty that he was no friend of mine. However, I began to learn first-hand about his personality and his political maneuvers. He was a leftist and I was a conservative. I guess I followed the same political ideology of my father, of whom I was very proud. I was a staunch anti-Communist, which I continue to be up to the present time. I remember that during those early days Castro was an anti-establishment radical and was invariably attacking the imaginary "Yankee Imperialism," following the teachings of his far-left mentors.

At that time Castro already had the "Communist bug" impregnated in his brain and his demonstrated, uninhibited psychopathic behavior. He was a rabble-rouser, an agitator and a student gangster. Castro had been inspired and trained by Communist activists since his early youth, in spite of his education in private Catholic schools from the very beginning of his schooling days through his graduation from high school. The pro-Communist inclination of Castro during his University days was well known to most students, particularly those participating in political affairs within the campus. The rumors of his indoctrination by a special Soviet emissary to Cuba, whose sole mission was to train selected students in Marxism-Leninism, turned out to be a fact. It was not a secret that Castro had close ties with Communist elements both inside and outside of the University environment.

It has been reported and reaffirmed by other authors and by close friends and former associates of Castro that he had manifested early sympathies for absolutist, authoritarian personalities of fascist ideologies, such as José Primo de Rivera, founder of the Spanish Falangism (an ultra-right organization), Hitler, Mussolini and Juan D. Perón (strong man of Argentina during the 1940s, 1950s and 1970s), founder of "Peronism" which was reminiscent of German Nazism and Italian Fascism. On the other extreme he expressed admiration for Vladimir Lenin, the founder of the Communist Party and leader of the Bolshevik Revolution of 1917. These were his heroes. We can surmise from his idolatry of these leaders the type of political monster he was destined to be in later years. He was capable of being either a Fascist or a Communist. The Communist influence over Castro was evidently more powerful than the right-wing totalitarian sway. Castro's authoritarian bent and his infatuation for one-man rule was put into practice the very moment he took power in Cuba.

Free Education in Cuba

My complete education in Cuba, from kindergarten beginning in 1934 until my graduation from the University of Havana in 1952, was completely free, with the exception of some books and materials that had to be purchased, particularly at the technical school and university level. Cuba had an excellent public school system, as stipulated by the Constitution, and it was never affected by political changes in the country during those years of republican existence. I was no exception; millions of young Cubans had the same experience of free schooling.

Free education in Cuba was not the invention of Castro. As a matter of fact, under Communism there is really no free education. Children and adults have to pay by working free for the government as "volunteers" in the sugar cane fields and other menial jobs, or by serving in the brigades or the militias and performing work assignments, among them spying on their neighbors and taking part in acts of repudiation against dissidents. Before Castro, private schools were also available as a choice at a reasonable cost for those who could afford it and preferred it. Many of the private educational centers were under the administration of religious orders (predominantly Catholic), while others were laical in nature. However, regardless of whether they were laical or religious, they all had to follow a curriculum similar to the public schools in accordance with the requirements established by the Ministry of Education. Private schools also offered scholarships to some students who could not afford to pay tuition. At the University of Havana, an autonomous institution before Castro, only students whose parents had a relatively high income had to pay tuition (although the fee was very nominal; believe it or not, only sixty dollars a year in the 1950s).

Castro's Embrace of Communism

It was during the early 1940s that the Communist indoctrination movement influenced Castro to accept Communism as his preferred ideological motivation – never mind the brutal and repugnant nature of the system. Even under the tragic circumstances surrounding the malignant Communist doctrine and the bloody and merciless backdrop of this sinister system of slavery, Castro embraced it with candor. This gives you a measure of his true character and intentions. He entered the University of Havana in 1945 when Communism was flourishing. However, he did not become a card-carrying Communist during his student and immediate post-graduation years. Although he was already acting like a Communist, he did not openly declare that he was one of them, nor did he join the Communist Party – called the Popular Socialist Party – the name adopted by the Party in 1943 to make it more palatable to the population. Castro knew that the Cuban people overwhelmingly had a firm dislike toward Communism.

The Communist Party at its peak was less than four percent of the registered voters in Cuba and was a discredited organization. Its leaders were leading the life of the bourgeois, having luxury cars, private chauffeurs, bodyguards, elegant residences, servants and other privileges while pretending they were defenders of the working and the poor classes. They were siphoning money from labor unions they controlled, the newspaper they published, the money they accepted from industrialists and politicians, and the funding they received from Moscow. At one time they had an alliance with General Bastista during his term as the constitutionally-elected president from 1940 to 1944. In fact, they had backed Bastista during the presidential campaign. As a recompense for their support, they were given positions in the government, including cabinet posts – Ministers without Portfolio – to two top leaders of the Party; namely, Dr. Juan Marinello and Dr. Carlos Rafael Rodríguez. A few months after the revolutionary takeover, the latter, believe it or not, was appointed by Castro to be his chief economic advisor and a member of his cabinet. Dr. Rodríguez was incorporated into the new Communist Party founded by Castro and became an influential member of its National Directory. Later on, when Castro appointed himself as President, he named Carlos Rafael Rodríguez as his Vice President.

Other members of the old Communist Party were rehabilitated by Castro and given important positions. They were also put in charge of the Confederation of Cuban Workers against the wishes of its legitimate revolutionary leaders. This organization became an instrument of the government and was used for purposes of party recruitment, indoctrination and training in anti-dissident activities. The labor unions have been instrumental in getting the people out, forcibly, to fill the plazas every time Castro speaks before the so-called "pro-revolution" rallies, or march through the streets in support of "revolutionary causes." The old Communist Party joined the Castro revolution against Bastista in 1958, at the very end of the insurgency process, when it was evident that the revolution was on a roll and Bastista's military forces were retreating.

Castro surmised that the old Communist Party leaders could be used to help him with their experience in organizing labor unions and agitation campaigns. Castro, of course, had already accepted, long before the triumph of the insurgency, the role of being the man selected by the international Communist conspiracy to lead the revolution and conversion of Cuba into a Communist state. He had, from the beginning of his campaign against Bastista, an inner circle of Communist elements, who closed ranks even more during his planning at a training camp in Mexico in 1953. Among his inner circle of associates were his own brother Raúl, already known as a youth Communist activist, the Argentine soldier of fortune, Ernesto "Che" Guevara, and the veteran of the Spanish civil war, Colonel Alberto Bayo.

The old Communist Party in Cuba had no future. Moscow had its doubts about its effectiveness as the organization to make serious inroads in the political scheme existing in Cuba. In the absence of an organized substitute and to avoid a vacuum, they continued to use the Party as a propaganda machine. Building for the future, the Soviets during the 1940s and 1950s began to recruit, train and breed a new generation of young, promising leaders to penetrate the student groups, the labor unions, the women's organizations, the teachers' associations and other civic, political and cultural groups.

Castro's Communist Training by a Soviet Agent

Cuba became a center of Communist propaganda in the Western hemisphere, and particularly in Central and South America. The Moscow activities were accelerated beginning in 1943 when Cuba, under the presidency of Batista, recognized the Soviet Union. The Soviets immediately proceeded to establish an oversized diplomatic mission in Havana. A Soviet agent, G. W. Bashirov, was assigned to Havana to be in charge of youth recruitment and indoctrination. This emissary had previously served in Spain to recruit young Spaniards for the training and infiltration of various organized groups. He was fluent in the Spanish language. To disguise the purpose of his presence in Havana, he established a private residence at No. 6 Second Street in the plush suburban section of Miramar. As a secret Soviet agent, he was kept away from the Soviet Embassy building. The Soviets did not want to raise any suspicions about young people going in and out of the Embassy with regularity.

Among the young Cubans who frequently visited his residence was Fidel Castro. Others known to visit the Bashirov residence were Alfredo Guevara (no relation to "Che" Guevara), who was an advisor to Castro and known as an overt Communist during my days at the University of Havana, and later was designated Minister of Culture when Castro took over the government; Antonio Núñez Jimenez, who became Castro's first director of the National Institute of Agrarian Reform and was later appointed president of the National Bank; Luis Más Martin and Flavio Bravo, who became leaders of the old Communist Party youth and later on occupied positions in the Castro regime; and the famous prima ballerina Alicia Alonso, who stayed in Cuba after Castro took over and occupied several art-related positions within the new Communist order. She was a covert Communist before Castro's revolution.

The activities of Bashirov and his disciples were traced and documented by Dr. Salvador Díaz Versón, a respected journalist and statesman during the pre-Castro era. He was director of the Cuban Military Intelligence Service under the centrist presidency of Dr. Carlos Prío Socarrás (the president deposed by Batista in March 1952). Dr. Díaz Versón was also president of the Inter-American Organization of Anti-Communist Newspaper Journalists, an organization with over eight hundred members as of May 1960. He had compiled the most extensive archives of Latin American Communists. It is said that he had over 250,000 cards and profiles of Latin American Communist activists, including an extensive dossier on Fidel Castro.

I remember, at the University of Havana and elsewhere in Cuba, they used to say that if you wanted to know who was a Communist in Cuba, all you had to do was ask Dr. Díaz Versón. He had the facts. According to him, the students of Bashirov, including Castro, also received a stipend to subsidize their activities among youth circles, including the Federation of University Students (FEU). This Federation was, since the 1930s, politically active and became a powerful organization which was both feared and respected by politicians. It played an important role in the deposition in 1933 of General Gerardo Machado, who became a dictator after his first term as elected president. The FEU opposed the second presidency of Bastista (1952-1959) and became involved initially against the establishment of a Communist regime during the first months of the Castro rule, but it was promptly muffled and manipulated by Castro's goons at the University. It is significant that, during the early days of 1959, immediately after Castro triumphantly entered Havana, the archives of Dr. Díaz Versón were raided and destroyed by Castro's militias.

I had the good fortune of incidentally meeting Dr. Díaz Versón one Sunday evening while I was walking on busy Neptuno Street in the heart of Havana's commercial district. I recognized him and stopped to shake his hand. I introduced myself and told him how much I admired him and his stand against Communism. I asked him, as a young university student, what words of wisdom he would have for me. He rapidly snapped back, as I remember, with words like this: "I know you are concerned with the Communist infiltration at the University. Be honest and forthright in your political beliefs. Never, ever trust a Communist. They are out there to cause misery, distortion and pain, and to rob your mind and personal determination." This brief encounter happened in the year 1948 and I was so impressed that I would never forget it.

The Communist Conspiracy and Castro's Role

For those who still believe that Castro was pushed into Communism by the attitude of the United States toward the revolution, remember that a Communist system is not something that can be improvised on the spur of the moment. Communism is established through a well-planned political stratagem. In the case of Cuba, it was being cleverly hatched long before Castro took over. The Communist conspiracy had purposely elevated Castro to the category of a hero. They had found in him the vector for the conversion of Cuba. The Kremlin had all but discarded the old Communist Party (PSP) and their discredited leaders, knowing full well that they could not execute the change. They desperately needed to establish a beachhead in a strategic location in the Western hemisphere. They also knew that the Cuban people would have rejected an outright Communist attempt to take over the island. Castro knew that, too. They had to come in through the back door using false pretenses. In a sly maneuver,

Moscow had already thrown its weight behind Castro. They were extremely careful to not raise any suspicions from the United States. Castro had cleverly kept his Communist inclinations under the disguise of a leftist, but still a pro-democracy-leaning leader. Any similarities with other known leftist leaders are purely coincidental.

Castro cunningly decided to play along with the Moscow directives and wait for the proper time to show his true colors so as not to compromise his political ambitions. He continued to act as a fellow traveler. Meanwhile, after graduating from the University and following the Communist strategy to the letter, he joined the relatively new Party of the Cuban People (Orthodox) like many other leftists did, seeing an opportunity to use the Orthodox Party as a wedge to introduce Communism into Cuba under a different banner. The ultimate aim was to gradually seize control of this new party, which was rapidly growing in popularity. The Orthodox Party was considered to be on the center to the left of the political rainbow. Although it was infiltrated by neo-Communists, the vast majority of its members were not Communist sympathizers. Among the membership was a good segment of the middle and wealthy class. Many young, idealistic non-Communists joined the Orthodox Party in the late 1940s and early 1950s. Its leader, Eduardo (Eddie) Chibás, from a wealthy and well-educated family, was an attractive, dynamic person with a persuasive message based primarily on restoring honesty in government. He was eloquent, passionate and somewhat strident. Some of his critics, including this author, thought Chibás was a demagogue because of his style and frequent diatribes. In spite of his controversial personality, his popularity had soared since his unsuccessful run for the presidency in 1948, when he had only about 16 percent of the popular vote.

Chibás had become a crusader for clean government. His message began to be very appealing to many. He was considered to be a truly viable presidential candidate for the elections scheduled for June 1952. This possibility never materialized. He got involved in an on-going, heated dispute over accusations he made regarding public funds allegedly stolen by the Minister of Education of then-President Carlos Prío Socarrás. Unable to prove the charges, he dramatically shot himself in the stomach in August 1951 during his popular weekly radio broadcast after shouting that this was his last call for honesty. He died days later after undergoing extensive surgery, a truly emotional and unexpected end for the troubled leader. The Cuban people were shocked and disconcerted over the tragic incident. A political vacuum had been created.

After Chibás' death, Castro thought that his chances to become a leading figure in the Orthodox Party had grown. Bear in mind that Castro was clearly a power seeker and a first-class opportunist. He pushed his way to become a candidate in the province of Havana for a seat in the House of Representatives in the general elections of 1952. However, Castro's ambitions were going to be dealt a severe blow. The elections would never happen. The Batista coup d'état interrupted the election process. Nevertheless, this was proven in the long run to be a blessing in disguise for Castro. Batista inadvertently had created the proper climate for Castro to thrive and accelerate his plan to convert Cuba into a Communist state.

The Impact of the Batista Coup D'état

It is significant to underline that, in spite of the contentious political atmosphere, the republic had made significant strides in many fronts over the years, such as educational, industrial, commercial and agricultural development; arts, science, healthcare, social services, sports and other areas, but it was lacking in governmental integrity. Many people, rich, middle class and poor, had gravitated toward Chibás. In their minds, he was the solution to the country's ills. Chibás had emerged as the "Mr. Clean" of politics. The enthusiasm he had created was dampened by his death. A mantle of consternation and disillusionment had covered his ardent supporters. Taking advantage of the somewhat disconcerted political atmosphere in Cuba and the weakness of the pro-democratic but embattled regime, on March 10, 1952, Batista took power in Cuba in a surprising military maneuver concocted with the support of high- and middle-ranking army officers.

I was in the last year of my career at the University of Havana. Needless to say, I was disappointed with the fragile course of events. There was confusion and uncertainty among a large segment of the population over the bloodless, but forceful, change of power. Batista broke the continuity of the constitutional succession of government only three months before the general elections were to take place. Batista himself was one of three candidates aspiring to the presidency. He was far behind in the polls. I remember that in the morning of that fateful day I rushed to the University of Havana campus, only to see it surrounded by army forces equipped with high-powered weapons. I joined with the students who were protesting the coup and making a lot of noise. Hours later we realized our helplessness, and decided to abandon the campus and go home. It was crazy to do what we did, but as young idealistic people, we weren't thinking of the consequences. We had no weapons. Our reaction was only to show inconformity with the situation. The soldiers were restrained and evidently did not want to cause any harm to the students. After a brief period of suspension of classes and closing of the campus by University officials in protest for the overthrow of the constitutional government, classes resumed and we were able to graduate in September 1952.

3

My Professional and Political Credentials

"Statistics indicate that Cuba before Castro was the most advanced country in Latin America and the most unlikely to fall under Communism."

A Pre-Castro Journey Through Cuba: The Potential of the Republic

FOLLOWING MY GRADUATION from the University of Havana, I accepted employment early in 1953 as a sugar industry auditor for a private consulting firm, which was under contract by the sugar cane planters to inspect and supervise the cane sugar yields at sugar mills throughout the island. Sugar yields entered into the formula for the payment of the sugar cane delivered to the mills. Among other tasks, I also checked the accuracy of the cane weighing stations and the reliability of the methods of analysis used by the sugar mill laboratory to determine sucrose (cane sugar).

During the exercise of my duties I had a golden opportunity to travel to many regions of the country and observed first-hand the beauty and prosperity of Cuba. I will never forget the neat, clean and orderly small towns with bustling public markets and shops, the nice local hotels and restaurants, the abundance of fresh vegetables and fruits sold at family-owned stalls, the butcher shops with plenty of supplies, the theaters (no matter how small the town, they all had a movie house), and the never-missing central park where families gathered on Sunday evenings to socialize and listen to the music of the local municipal band playing from a center stand. It was customary on such occasions for young women to walk in an inner circle around the park while young men would walk in an outer circle in the opposite direction. Occasionally eye contact would be made with a member of the opposite sex and an exchange of subtle smiles would indicate a certain measure of attraction. This signal eventually could bring about the beginning of an amorous relationship. Older people, mostly parents and relatives, would sit outside and around the circling space on chairs provided by the municipal authority. These were indeed innocent times.

In the course of my traveling throughout the island, I passed by many farms on both sides of the road and stopped at villages and towns while traveling by car, bus or rail. I saw the toiling of farmers and farm hands plowing, sowing, raising and harvesting crops, attending to the sugar cane plantations or nurturing livestock. I admired the beauty of the countryside, the mountains and valleys, the breathtaking long rows of palm trees almost touching the sky. I had the opportunity to converse with both small and big ranchers and farmers, and detected an aura of prosperity and faith in the future, an affirmation of individuality and entrepreneurial thrust. Just about everybody thought that the political quagmire would eventually settle down by peaceful and democratic means.

Based on my pleasant experience during my travels, I reflected on the richness of Cuba's agriculture and the grit and dedication of the people. As a former student leader, I was very active in the defense and promotion of agrarian advancement. I was ecstatic, for the beauty of the country indeed surpassed any other experience I ever had before. Of course, during the phases of my early boyhood and student life, I enjoyed times at farms and factories. In fact, I was born in a small town. The section of the town I lived in was on the outskirts of the city, near a river surrounded by farms. We had a large lot in which we had fruit trees, a vegetable garden, goats, fowl and an occasional pig. However, I never saw so many diverse places as during the country-wide travel I was engaged in to attend to my technical assignment. It is coincidental that the last sugar mill in which I served as an auditor during my journey was the Covadonga Sugar Mill in the immediate vicinity of the Bay of Pigs where, in April 1961, so many heroic Cuban fighters died in a failed attempt to liberate Cuba from Communism.

Cuba – by any stretch of the imagination – was not the impoverished country portrayed by its detractors with the intention of justifying the Castro revolution. I was fortunate to see, study and experience the reality of the country before the Castro debacle. Cuba was a rich and educated country blessed by its natural resources and by the determination and nature of its people. Cuba was endowed with a rich and fertile soil, mineral resources, a growing fishing industry and an accelerated industrial development. Statistics indicate that Cuba before Castro was the most advanced country in Latin America and the most unlikely to fall under Communism. Yes, there were pockets of poverty in Cuba, like we find in practically every country of the world, including the mighty United States and many advanced European nations, but not nearly to the extent asserted by the exaggeration of the Castro apologists. There is far more poverty and distress in Cuba today than before the Communist dictatorship imposed by Castro. The proof is that Cuba before Castro was not known as a country where mass exodus occurred.

My First Trip to the United States: A Dream Fulfilled

I spent nearly five months on my technical auditing journey for the duration of the cane sugar milling season, which ended in June 1953 at the onset of the rainy season. In spite of my attachment to family and country, I had a dream to come to the United States and further develop my career. Succeeding in my profession became an obsession for me. I saved enough money during my tenure as a sugar chemist auditor to enable me to finance my trip. I obtained a temporary visa and entered the U.S. on September 4, 1953. I flew to Miami, Florida, and from Miami to Chicago, Illinois, the same day.

In Chicago I had a good friend from technical college, Jorge Laborde, who had left school in Havana and later enlisted in the U.S. Army, subsequently serving in the Korean War. On a visit he made to Havana in 1951, Jorge encouraged me to come to Chicago where he had made his home. He truly impressed me. Jorge was on a furlough, wearing the uniform of the U.S. Army, when we met at the Nautico Club by the sea. As part of the amenities offered by the private club, they had a beautiful, well-maintained beach. I remember that the club president was Dr. Rafael Díaz Balart, Sr., a respected and distinguished businessman. He had previously given me a free permanent pass to the club (since I could not afford the membership dues) so I could enjoy the facility with my fiancée and her family, who were members of the club. Needless to say, I appreciated his generosity.

At this point let me give an incidental observation about the Díaz Balart family. After Batista came to power in 1952, Dr. Rafael Díaz Balart, Sr., was appointed to Batista's cabinet as Minister of Transportation. His children were Rafael, Mirta and Lincoln. I had met his sons, Rafael and Lincoln. Rafael Díaz Balart, Jr., was subsequently named Sub-Secretary of the Interior Ministry. The Díaz Balarts were honest government officers doing their best under difficult circumstances. Their political ideology brought them around the Batista circle of friends. Mirta happened to marry Fidel Castro in 1948 while he was a student at the University of Havana. A few years later after having a son, their marriage ended in divorce. In 1953, after the Moncada Army Post attack (concocted by a small opposition group led by Fidel Castro and consisting mostly of university students, including his brother Raúl), the survivors were captured and given 15 years in prison by a court. After serving less than two years, Castro and company were granted a pardon by Batista. The Díaz Balart family was instrumental in obtaining the amnesty. It should be noted that, throughout his tyrannical mandate, Castro has been incapable of pardoning any of his adversaries who had been sentenced by kangaroo courts to lengthy jail terms or executed by firing squads, in spite of many pleas from mothers, fathers, wives, sons, daughters and other relatives of the condemned. Many of his victims were rebel army members accused of betraying the revolution because they did not accept Communism.

The Díaz Balarts went into exile in the United States and the descendants of this honorable family carved out a successful life in America. Two grandsons of Dr. Rafael Díaz Balart, Sr., became congressmen from the state of Florida, namely, Lincoln Díaz Balart and Mario Díaz Balart, both of whom are strong supporters of the cause for reestablishment of freedom and democracy in Cuba.

During those days Cubans openly admired the Americans, and my friend Jorge was the center of attention at the club that evening. He had a multitude of people surrounding him, anxious to shake hands and talk to him. I felt very proud of my friendship with him. Finally we were able to break away from the crowd and sit at the bar for a drink. Two years later, in 1953, my good friend introduced me to Chicago and advised me about opportunities for chemists in this big industrial city. By that time he had already been honorably discharged from the Army and was working as an editor for the magazine *Popular Mechanics*. It did not take me too long to find a job in my profession. A week after my arrival I began to work as a chemist, and later as a microbiologist, for the Borden Company in Elgin, Illinois.

Previous to my first trip to the United States, I had read extensively about the history and technological advance of the colossal neighboring country to the north. To me it was like reaching Mecca. I was not disappointed by what I saw and experienced. I returned to Havana in December 1953 to spend Christmas with my relatives. On January 23, 1954, before my return to Elgin, I married my sweetheart Gladys, whom I had met during my university days. We both came to the United States shortly after our marriage. This time we had obtained permanent visas to stay indefinitely in the U.S.

The following year, 1955, I duly registered in the Selective Service System and was classified 5-A. I was never called to duty, but willingly complied with my obligations to the country. A few years later, after the required residence time, Gladys and I became proud citizens of the United States. We consider that event as one of our greatest achievements in life. My wife and I came to realize that, perhaps by coming from another country and being given the opportunities and privileges offered so generously by this nation, we can truly appreciate the magnanimity of the United States of America. We kept returning to Cuba every year to visit our relatives, particularly during the Christmas season.

Visiting Cuba at the Onset of the Revolution

Gladys and I happened to be in Cuba during the Castro takeover on January 1, 1959. We witnessed the turmoil following the Batista departure. He had resigned and escaped in an airplane in the wee hours of the morning of January 1st. The transport aircraft left the air base in Camp Colombia, Havana, with the Dominican Republic as its destination. A group of his closest aides departed with him. We evidenced the ensuing demonstrations of public support for the revolution and heard scattered firearm shots in the streets of Havana. Public euphoria was visible everywhere. The rebel forces were attempting to mop up remnants of Batista's armed supporters. Some store windows were smashed as vandals took advantage of the confusion and lack of law enforcement. Parking meters were destroyed and the coin contents emptied. Other acts of violence were executed by the lawless elements of society. Some Batista sympathizers were caught by mobs and beaten on the streets or in their place of hiding.

Finally, after a few days, order was restored and calm prevailed. The Havana International Airport was reopened and we were able to leave Cuba and return to Chicago. Little was known at that time of Castro's plans to convert Cuba into a Communist tyranny with the support of the Soviet Union. Even his closest allies of democratic persuasion thought Castro had emerged as a liberator, forgetting his turbulent leftist past. They believed his repeated vows to fully reestablish the model Constitution enacted in 1940 and to respect freedom of the press, private enterprise, human rights, and to hold free elections within a reasonable time. The cream of Cuban intellectuals, entrepreneurs and democratic minds supported Castro during, and immediately after, the struggle to oust Batista. A great segment of the population was blinded by his promise of redemption.

The Betrayal of the Revolution

Castro's popularity soared beyond any imaginable expectation. There was a frenzy and adulation for him. His acting ability helped convey this type of feeling to his adoring masses. Under the circumstances, no one dared to challenge his authority or decisions. He had thrown a spell over the populace and practically owned Cuba lock, stock and barrel. It did not take long for many of his political allies and the Cuban people to wake up to reality. When the honeymoon was over, it was very embarrassing and hard for many to admit that they had been duped and betrayed. A vicious Communist dictatorship began to develop under their eyes. It was heartbreaking to know that it was too late to reverse the nightmare. Very rapidly Castro gained absolute control over the press, the economy, the means of production and distribution, the educational system, the military, the labor unions, the student associations and everything else that exists in a free society. He, in fact, gutted the country and its cultural, social and educational institutions. The integrity of the Cuban civil society had been shredded. The country was delivered on a silver platter to Communism, then under the aegis of the former Soviet Union.

Castro took advantage of his immense and fanatical popularity to use the well-developed network of public communication vehicles, already existing in Cuba as the product of a progressive capitalistic society, to undertake a massive and constant brainwashing campaign to sell his nefarious Socialist agenda. The irony of this is that he began to do it while these communication facilities were still in the hands of their lawful owners. He used the radio, television and printing press as a means to convey his almost daily harangues against the institutions that existed before he gained power, and to castigate the United States for all of the perceived ills affecting Cuba. At the very onset of his regime, on January 1, 1959, he confiscated the three newspapers that were favorable to Batista, namely, *Alerta, Pueblo* and *Ataja*. They were turned over to pro-Communist elements.

During 1960 he forcibly confiscated the rest of the newspapers, many of which were critical of Batista, such as *Avance, Prensa Libre, El Crisol, El Pais, Excelsior, El Mundo, Información, Zig Zag* (a humorist weekly journal), *Bohemia* (an openly pro-Castro weekly magazine), *Diario de la Marina, The Havana Post, Mañana* and *Diario Nacional*. The number of good quality newspapers and magazines we had in Cuba was amazing. Even Batista never dared to close or confiscate a newspaper, although they were, with some restrictions, critical of his regime. The Communist Party newspaper *Hoy* was the only national newspaper that was closed twice, once during the presidency of Dr. Ramón Grau San Martín (1944-48), and then during the presidency of Batista (1952-58). In both cases the two reasons for shutting down the newspaper were (1) the publication of articles negating and attacking the principles of the democratic Constitution of 1940 and (2) the declared illegality of the Communist Party.

To dig deeper into the hidden agenda Castro had for the revolution and his faked projection as a populous leader with a democratic inclination, I cite what he told the newspaper reporters in a press conference he held at a stop in the city of Camagüey on January 4, 1959, while he was on his way to Havana on the victory caravan (the *Información* newspaper, Monday edition, January 5, 1959, Havana):

> You, the journalists, have to help us in the most difficult part of the revolution, which is the maintenance of the peace. We will in turn help the press, firstly by helping to maintain the achievements you have obtained and the sacred freedom of expression, and secondly by facilitating the ample exercise of your work. This is not a favor but the application of our principles of justice.

It didn't take Castro too long after he made that declaration to completely wipe out the free press, proving once more the lies he fabricated to gain the initial support of the press and of the Cuban people. The confiscation of the printing press was followed by the takeover of all the radio and television stations. All of the means of communication came under the control of the state and were used for propaganda purposes by the Communist oligarchy.

Immediately after Castro took over, the bulk of the Batista military officers and army personnel, along with high- and middle-ranking civilian members of his government, were taken prisoner and judged by improvised rebel army kangaroo courts. Thousands were found guilty of alleged crimes and summarily executed before firing squads. They were tried under the so-called revolutionary laws. No formal system of justice was followed. It was a brutal spectacle where the judge, the prosecution and the defense were all members of the revolutionary forces.

America became the whipping boy of Castro. Every dictator in history had to have an illusory victim, a target to blame or to hate. By doing so, they divert public opinion from their own failures and frailties to a common enemy of their own creation. It is a technique used by demagogues to rally public support by exacerbating the worst instincts within the minds of individuals while blocking their sense of rationalization. Castro had the training to instill such unbridled emotions in the masses and he used it masterfully to indoctrinate his followers. His hatred for the United States was, and continues to be, part, not only of his psychopathic behavior, but also of the Communist strategy to discredit this great nation. Castro has allied himself with world terrorists and with the leaders of rogue nations in a common bond against America.

My Visit to Cuba in 1960: A Sad Experience

Although I was visiting Cuba at the time of the overthrow of Batista on January 1, 1959, my truly first encounter with the Castro regime came about in May 1960 when I traveled to Cuba to present two scientific papers before the Third National Congress of Agronomical and Sugar Industry Engineers. I had been invited and committed a year in advance to present my scientific works. I was a research chemist for the Griffith Laboratories, Inc., Chicago, Illinois (a leading manufacturer and supplier of ingredients, seasonings, meat curing materials, antioxidants, spices and other functional agents to the food industry). I knew the organizers of the conference. They were dedicated professionals and included several of my former university professors. I already knew that the dark shadow of Communism was lurking over the horizon and it had already begun to contaminate the scene. In spite of that prior knowledge, I still wanted to visit Cuba and see for myself what was going on. My parents and siblings had already warned me in some indirect and discreet way of the "dubious changes" taking place. They had to be very careful about how they expressed themselves either by mail or telephone. They were afraid of the government tampering with communications.

For this trip I did not take the family with me. I thought the climate in Cuba was already in a state of confusion. Under the circumstances it would not have been proper to visit Cuba accompanied by my son Ralph, who was four years old, and my wife, who was pregnant with our daughter Amy Ann. I went on this trip with a feeling of uncertainty, but I was anxious to visit with my relatives, my fellow professionals and friends, and talk to them about political matters they would not dare to reveal through letters or telephone conversations. Censorship had evidently been in place. I was compelled to have a hands-on impression as to what was really happening in Cuba. I wanted to find out how it was affecting my relatives and what I could do to help.

After my arrival I was not totally surprised by the many negative comments I received about the path of the revolution and the bizarre developments occurring in the country. I had been following the news in the United States about the resignation and exit of prominent members of the revolutionary government, many of whom were heroes of the rebel army and the civil resistance movement against Batista. These included Commander Pedro Díaz Lanz, Chief of the Air Force; José Miró Cardona, Prime Minister; Manuel Urrutia Lleó, Provisional President; Commander Huber Matos, Provincial Armed Forces Chief; Faustino Pérez, Minister for the Recovery of Stolen Property and National Coordinator of the 26th of July Movement; Commander Humberto Sorí Marín, Minister of Agriculture; Commander Manuel Artime, holder of a top post at the Bank of Agriculture and Industrial Development; and Luis Conte Agüero, Secretary General of the Orthodox Party and founder with Castro of the 26th of July Movement.

Incidentally, the grade of "Commander" was the highest rank in the rebel army. Later, after Castro consolidated his power and established the Communist state, the military was reorganized under the conventional armed forces nomenclature, elevating as a reward most of the still-existing commanders to the rank of general, including Castro himself.

I knew of Castro's systematic hostility against the United States, and his growing antipathy towards private enterprise and whatever "free press" was still remaining in Cuba. I found that some of my university friends had already left the country or had disappeared from the scene, the majority of which were initially sympathetic to the revolution or had positions in the new government. Others still there told me about the sad reality of the Socialist approach of the Castro regime and the fact that they had lost faith in the outcome of the revolution. The prevalent joke was that the revolution was like a watermelon, green (the color of the rebel army uniform) on the outside and red on the inside. There was no mention anymore of elections or restoring a democratic government with freedom for the various political parties with diverse ideologies to participate in the process. Before the revolutionary government there were about a dozen political parties, the majority of which opposed Batista. The clamp on the free press was already in place and progressing at an accelerated pace. Castro's anti-United States outbursts continued at a crescendo with no reason at all. It was evident that a Communist society was being planned and executed by Castro.

I was disenchanted with what I saw and heard, however, I was not foreseeing anything different. My observation was that the process was proceeding faster than anticipated. I felt frustrated, but hopeful that somehow the trend was going to be stopped and reversed by the nonconformity of the democratic forces still remaining in Cuba. The initial hope was for the rebirth of a democratic nation. The path taken by Castro was negating such hope.

I presented my two papers at the Congress: (1) Edible Fats: Mechanism of Their Natural Oxidation, Rancidity and Antioxidants; and (2) Agents, Factors and Mechanisms Intervening in the Curing of Meats; Function of Myoglobin and Hemoglobin in These Processes. I noticed that only a few of those attending the convention had a blind pro-Castro tendency and a certain aversion and cynical attitude toward anything coming from the United States. However, the vast majority of those I talked to were either opposed to, or concerned with, the current state of affairs and the Socialist trend of the revolution. After I presented my papers, I had nothing but accolades from friends and many of the delegates. I had ample conversations with some people who still honestly believed that the things going on were not by design but the product of an overly nationalistic fervor. They were expecting that Castro and the revolution were going to adopt a moderate position after the younger, immature, impulsive and more radical elements within the government slowed down. They theorized that the leftist tendencies were finally going to be tempered or neutralized by the level-headed conservative elements still remaining in the Castro government. They added that the moderates had the support of still-standing religious groups, student bodies, industrial and commercial organizations, and other civic and cultural institutions within the mainstream of the population, all of which had supported and participated in the insurgency against Batista. All of this proved to be wishful thinking, a battle against the impossible.

Soon the hope of the faithful was going to be crushed. Brutal force was in the mind of Castro to achieve his end game: the delivery of Cuba to Communism. Anyone attacking or opposing Communism was labeled as anti-revolutionary. The case was made that everybody had to support the revolution. No one, absolutely no one, could oppose the dictates of the revolution. Castro had the last word on every issue, and those who disagreed with him would fall by the side and be excluded from the new society. His Leninist tactics were already being put into practice.

During my conversations with the more radical, pro-revolution adepts, I noticed that either they had been brainwashed or they had a pre-revolution leftist inclination, because they expressed, in no uncertain terms, their willingness to go all the way with Castro's directives, even to the extent of accepting a Communist system. They were blinded, fanaticized by Castro's truth twisting and incessant pounding against the United States, private enterprise, the free press and everything else that was part of a capitalist system or that stood on his path of destruction. Castro created a false nationalistic fervor even among many who had never been sympathetic to Communism. It was a sad and pathetic sight. Many initial supporters later regretted their foolishness. They took off their blindfolds as they gradually realized that they had been duped. I met many of them here in the U.S. in the years that followed and they admitted they had been dead wrong.

Over the course of my visit I never stopped praising the United States' democratic ways, the opportunities I found, the friendly treatment I received, and the support given to me to succeed and advance in my career. I went out of my way to explain to people, left or right, the climate of freedom and the opportunities available, particularly for technical and scientific professionals, in the United

States. I may have gone too far in expressing my views in a candid manner. I never expected that my euphoric appreciation for what the United States represented to me was going to create, later on, some problems for me. I honestly thought that returning to Cuba on a special trip to make a contribution to the scientific community was going to be appreciated as a gesture of good will. I had given my word to the organizers of the Congress that I was going to deliver the lectures in spite of the circumstances, and I did as planned. It did not take me too long to feel a complete frustration over the state of affairs after I analyzed the situation as an eye witness. The system was brutal and this was only the beginning of worse things to come.

An Unexpected Delay at Departure Time

The day came when I was ready to leave Havana after my visit and rejoin my family in Chicago. I was deeply saddened to say good-bye to my Mom and Dad, my brothers and sisters, in-laws and friends. I knew that I was leaving a country which was destined for the worst, unless there was an internal uprising or some sort of miraculous change of course. I was dejected by the existing situation and extremely concerned with the fate of my immediate relatives left behind. I had to find a way to extricate them from the hell that was gripping Cuba. Later on I did manage to get them out of Cuba with the exception of a sister, her husband and their two children. Their oldest child was of military age and could not leave the country, so they all reluctantly opted to stay.

Many relatives came to the airport to bid me good-bye. They were all looking at me through a glass wall (called the "fish bowl") separating the passengers from the airport visitors. As I approached the ticket counter, a customs officer sitting at a desk at the entrance to the gateway stopped me and began asking me questions. The first question was about the purpose of my visit to Cuba. I explained about the Congress and my visit with relatives. I was asked how much money I had left with me, and I replied about $215. He immediately impounded the money. When I asked why my money was being taken, he said it was because I had to declare all the money I brought with me when I entered the country. I told him that at my arrival no one had asked me about it. All they had done was inspect my luggage and briefcase. He rapidly snapped back that it was the law, and I said, "What law?" He quickly replied, "The revolutionary law of the Fatherland." His face at that time was denoting anger. I had no choice but to relinquish the money, although I told him that I needed some cash to take a taxi home once in Chicago. He reluctantly let me keep ten dollars, although he insisted that I may not need it. At the time I did not know exactly what he meant.

However, this was not the end of the ordeal. He continued the interrogation, asking me whether I had any connection with the U.S. government. I explained that I was a chemist for a private company in Chicago. He then followed up with a question that I was not expecting at all – whether I had any ties with the CIA. At this point I was completely perplexed and worried. I had known of trumped-up charges against innocent people who had been imprisoned or executed as counter-revolutionaries. I, of course, replied with a rotund "No!" without hesitation. At his request I opened my briefcase, and he went carefully over the contents: my passport, newspaper clippings about the conference, pictures taken during the sessions, copies of my scientific papers, slides, the Congress program, a speaker ribbon and other documents pertaining to the event. I was then escorted to a small room by two guards and asked to remove all of my clothes. They searched them thoroughly, and then scrutinized my wallet and briefcase again. Finding nothing of a compromising nature, I was told to get dressed. They released me and I proceeded to the gate, where they checked my flight ticket. I was very lucky that the plane had been held for about one hour for departure. I believe I was the only passenger on the completely full flight to be submitted to such an extensive and humiliating inspection.

As I was taken to the gate, I looked through the separating glass wall and saw the worried and nervous expressions on the faces of my relatives. When they realized that I had been released, they broke into smiles and cheers as they bid me good-bye. What a relief for everybody! As I entered the plane disheveled, suit and shirt rumpled, my tie hanging untied from my collar, the passengers applauded. Evidently word had spread about my detention, perhaps by an attendant or a passenger who saw me being detained. It was an outrageous experience. I had never before been through such a traumatic situation. As unpleasant as it was, I had one satisfaction left inside me: I had learned firsthand the true, harrowing process developing in Cuba under Castro's rule.

As the plane took off, I breathed a sigh of relief. I completely and irrevocably realized that Cuba had been lost to Communism and that a repressive regime was already in place. Upon further reflection, I believe that someone had tipped the airport authorities of my scheduled departure, and that my pro-United States conversations with pro-Castro elements, and possibly undercover agents, had raised some doubts about my mission in Cuba. Bear in mind that the Castro propaganda was aimed at rejecting anything having connections with the United States. Otherwise, why had I been picked for questioning among over one hundred passengers on that fateful flight to Miami? It was an experience I would never forget for the rest of my life.

Participating in Politics: A Patriotic Duty

As a political enthusiast I have kept track of the developments in Cuba. Over the years I talked to many Cuban exiles, including professionals, political and ex-rebel military leaders, workers, students, artists and entrepreneurs – people from all walks of life – to get information about their tribulations under the Communist regime. I was active with Cuban patriotic exile organizations and developed ties with anti-Communist Eastern European exile groups. I have spoken before many political, cultural, civic and educational groups to explain the Cuban ordeal and the danger of Communism in Cuba, Latin America and in other parts of the world, and to reveal the lies and falsehoods of Communism and its inhumane and disastrous results.

I engaged in politics as a gesture of appreciation for the opportunities I found in this marvelous country. Parallel to that I fully dedicated my life to my family and my career. Politics was the nature of my inner impulse. My father was active in politics in our native town in Cuba. I guess I took after him. I must make it clear that the only thing I got out of politics was the satisfaction of participating in the democratic process and advancing my conservative ideas. Of the two major parties I chose the Republican Party, which I perceived as the farthest from the left of the political spectrum without falling into extremes.

It is encouraging that, to counter the liberals and radical leftists trying to justify Castro's conduct, there are a host of conservative thinkers and fair-minded individuals – among them journalists, commentators and leading public personalities – who understand, and have never lost sight of, the adversities the Cuban people are suffering under the Communist oppression. These men and women are great Americans and patriots. I am most grateful for their contribution to the cause of freedom and democracy. They continuously strive to advocate, inspire and strengthen the political persuasion of many generations based on the principles under which this nation was founded.

In the political arena I was very active supporting Republican candidates at all levels: county, state and national. In 1990, I was elated to be appointed to a blue ribbon Advisory Committee by then-Republican Cook County Chairman Dick Siebel. The committee's function was to advise the chairman on party issues and strategies. Among the nineteen distinguished members of the committee were former Governor William Stratton and Donald Rumsfeld. What an honor to be included among this group of prominent Americans. Incidentally, I had met Rumsfeld previously at my home on October 17, 1964, when he was running for reelection to the United States House of Representatives. My wife and I had hosted a coffee meeting in our home in Skokie, Illinois, attended by a group of neighbors and friends to back his candidacy. Afterwards he sent us a letter of thanks for our hospitality and support. Needless to say, we kept this letter as a prized memento.

Contrary to what would be expected from individuals brought up in families of different wealth levels as far as political inclination is concerned, my origin was from a humble, closely knit, working family struggling to make an honest living. We were nine siblings and we all, at one time or another, helped in the family business. My parents, of necessity, required that their children participate in the business, part-time or full-time, to help financially and to instill work ethics necessary for personal development and character. This was done without sacrificing our educational years. As I mentioned before, I attended public school all of my life, and so did my siblings. I also helped in the family food service business during my spare time. I never owned a car until I came to the United States and earned the money to buy one.

I used to walk to school, sometimes long distances, or take public transportation when I had the money to pay for it. I remember that my mother used to put coins below a cup in the dining room hutch so I could pay for my bus or streetcar ride. In spite of our modest financial means when we were young, I was, and continue to be, a conservative, and became a professional with a dignified status. On the other hand, Castro came from a wealthy family and was spoiled by the riches of his father and the money he received from him. While attending the University of Havana, he drove a luxury car as a gift from his father. He never had to earn a living or help his family during his student days. The only job he held before the revolution was a short stint as an attorney with a law firm in Havana after he graduated from Law School. Yet he turned out to be a hooligan, a university gangster, a terrorist, a Communist and a perverse dictator. There is a lesson to be learned in this contrast of profiles. You don't have to be rich to be a conservative, and you don't have to be of modest means to be a left-wing agitator.

A guiding light of my life has been a concern for humanity. I am not just sailing along steering my own ship. I like to look at every possible facet surrounding the immense sea of our universe and the spiritual being of my existence. That is why I have branched out in my career to reach beyond one specialty, and why I have participated in politics, searched different philosophical avenues and ventured modestly into painting, poetry, history and other subjects. This book, which I have been writing for the past five years, is the fruit of the resolve I have imposed upon myself to expose the emptiness of character and the moral aberration of a repulsive dictator. Furthermore, if you study and understand conservatism, you have to come to the conclusion that conservatives are compassionate and have a deep feeling for the well-being of the human race, a dedication to individual freedom and self-determination.

The following poem, which I wrote about fifteen years ago, metaphorically suggests my conservative view on the dignity of mankind. People should not be subjected to sub-human conditions as they exist in Cuba today.

JUDGMENT DAY

It is cold, damp, quiet
Forces brewing in the dark
Muscles bristling without rest
The tense incense of defiance
Dresses sharply for the fest.

Darkness conquers the Earth
The space is filled with fire
Sounds of desperation, agony of souls
Decay and obsolescence stand in judgment
An eerie feeling transcends.

Waves of uncertainty are felt
Mysterious forces shake the universe
Horror and fright carve bodies and minds
A spark of light suddenly strikes
Signaling the end of a long, long night.

Attempts at mending are made
Carriers of faith deliver the plight
The ethereal jury does not compromise
The verdict:
Stamp out misery, injustice and blight!

My Professional Career

I am a firm believer in self-improvement, self-determination and hard work to achieve individual goals. On a parallel track to my political activities, I continued the enhancement of my profession through dedication to my career and my desire to succeed. I conducted extensive research in the areas of analytical chemistry, microbiology, food science, new product development, processing technology, industrial hygiene, nutritional and quality systems at the various institutions, companies and corporations I served, either as a bona fide employee or as an independent consultant. To compliment these areas I wrote numerous scientific and technical papers, many of which were published in scientific journals and trade magazines. I also achieved recognition as a Certified Nutrition Specialist, PhD level, granted by the Certification Board for Nutrition Specialists, founded by the American College of Nutrition. For several years I wrote a monthly column called "Nutrition and the Diet" in the Chicago newspaper *La Voz Panamericana* (*The Panamerican Voice*) for the benefit of the Spanish-speaking community.

During my professional career extending over 50 years, I held uninterrupted employment as a chemist, microbiologist, food scientist, consultant and technical-administrative executive with several corporations and institutions. I worked in many areas of the food industry, i.e., functional food ingredients, flavorings, fishery products, meats, beverages, bakery products, fruits and vegetables, dairy products, preserves, food coatings, dressings and sauces, nutrition, quality systems, industrial hygiene, food safety, regulatory affairs and management. I was designated by the U.S. Department of Commerce - National Marine Fisheries Service as a member of the U.S. delegation to the Codex Alimentarius Commission – Committee on Fish and Fishery Products of the Food and Agriculture Organization of the United Nations. At that time I was the Vice-President Research, Development and Quality Assurance of Booth Fisheries Corporation (a division of Sara Lee Corporation). I have held membership in the following professional associations: American Chemical Society, Institute of Food Technologists, American Association of Cereal Chemists, American Dairy

Science Association, American Society for Microbiology, American Association for the Advancement of Science, American Association of Official Analytical Chemists, Chicago Nutrition Association, Certified Nutrition Specialists, and the New York Academy of Sciences.

I always felt good about transmitting my knowledge to others. I delivered many dissertations and scientific papers at symposiums, seminars, workshops, professional organizations and universities in the U.S. and abroad. These included the Institute of Food Technologists, the American Association of Cereal Chemists, the Association of Official Analytical Chemists, the American Institute of Baking, the National Restaurant association, the University and Hospital Food Service Directors Association, the American Shrimp Canners and Processors Association, the National Food Processing Association, the Dairy and Food Industry Supply Association, the National Shrimp Breaders and Processors Association, the New England Fisheries Development Foundation, the Virginia Polytechnic Institute, the National Fisheries Institute, the National Marine Fisheries Service, the Food Processing Magazine, the Frozen Food Council of Georgia, the Seafood Expo, the University of Puerto Rico, the Louisiana State University, the Environmental Management Association, the American Sanitation Institute, the Research and Development Association for Military Food and Packaging Systems, the Illinois Environmental Health Association, The Soap and detergent Association, the Food and Drug Administration, the Food and Agricultural Organization of the United Nations, the Atlantic Fisheries Technological Conference, the International Trade Center, and the American Society of Heating, Refrigeration and Air Conditioning Engineers.

Over the years I have served on many technical committees in the food industry. I was elected Chairman of the Quality Assurance Division of the Institute of Food Technologists for 1987-88. From 1971 to 1991 I was honored to be a judge of the Food Processing Awards sponsored by the Putman Publishing Company. And for many years I was a lecturer at the Food Processing/Chemical Processing Magazines Seminars held in many cities throughout the United States. In addition, I have been listed in several biographical publications, including *Who's Who in America, Who's Who Among Men and Women of Science, Community Leaders and Noteworthy Americans, Dictionary of International Biography, Who's Who in the Midwest,* and *Men of Achievement.*

My international experience was complemented by having the opportunity to travel to many countries on company assignments, or as a consultant for the Food and Agricultural Organization of the United Nations, or by direct invitation of institutions in various countries for lecturing and training purposes. Among the countries I visited are Norway, England, Italy, Canada, Puerto Rico, Nicaragua, Costa Rica, Uruguay, Peru, Mexico, Ecuador, Chile, Jamaica, India, Malaysia, Singapore and Hong Kong.

Politically, I have lectured in the United States about the menace of Communism and the Cuban tragedy under Castro before civic organizations such as Lions Clubs, the Daughters of the American Revolution, the American Federation of Small Business, the Women's Republican Club, the Cuban Bar Association in Exile, Eagle Forum, the Cuban Patriotic Council, Rotary Clubs and others.

Throughout my career I have received many awards, diplomas and certificates of recognition from governments, academic institutions, trade organizations, publishing enterprises, professional associations and a Presidential Achievement Award authorized and signed by President Ronald Reagan, which represents to me a great privilege and honor. I was very impressed by a Certificate of Appreciation I received from Louisiana State University in September 1975 which reads: "In grateful recognition of outstanding contributions to agricultural programs in Louisiana and invaluable support of research programs dedicated to an improved quality of living for all our people." I am very proud of all of the awards conferred on me and I prize them immensely.

I also made some inroads into entrepreneurial ventures. Among them are the design and completion (until operational) of a small sausage and ham processing plant in Nicaragua, including the development of the formulas and the design and selection of packaging materials; the development of a line of frozen fishery dinners in Uruguay, which were distributed in the United States by a company I founded with an Uruguayan partner, Worldwide Quality foods, Inc.; the creation of an analytical laboratory, Sci-Tek, as a subsidiary of Sara Lee Bakery, which performed chemical, microbiological and nutrition analyses for the food industry. I became the Executive Director of the laboratory while serving as head of Quality Assurance and Regulatory Affairs for the Sara Lee Company. After 25 years of executive tenure at two of its divisions, I retired from Sara Lee Corporation in 1992. I then proceeded to establish my own consulting company, Dr. Rafael R. Pedraja and Associates, Inc., continuing to serve the food industry for many years. In 1993 my consulting company formed a business partnership with Northland Food Laboratories, Inc., a Manitowoc, Wisconsin-based, analytical chemistry, microbiology, and nutrition services multi-laboratory. I served for two years as its Executive Vice President with responsibilities for business development, regulatory affairs and scientific advisory while I maintained my independent consulting business.

I would like to impress on many aspiring individuals that in a free climate, as we are fortunate to have in the United States, if you strive hard, fulfill your obligations as a citizen and search for opportunities to advance, no matter what your profession or trade is, there are no impediments to move forward and succeed. This is the nature and temper of America, the greatest country in the world.

The reason I have cited some aspects of my professional activities is not for self-aggrandizement or any other selfish motive, but for the readers to know where I am coming from. It establishes the credentials to support my credibility and the integrity of my thoughts and character. I have not written this book because of a personal vendetta. Such a thing would not enter my mind or inspire my soul. People should judge the contents based on the facts presented by an individual who has been observing and analyzing the events and way of life in Cuba since early youth. I left Cuba on my own volition, as I explained earlier, six years before Castro grabbed power. My family in Cuba was of modest middle class and did not lose any meaningful material wealth or possessions as a result of the revolution. What they lost was their physical and spiritual tranquility, their freedom, the resources to get the necessary food staples and other essential living needs, and, what is most important, the respect for their dignity as human beings. We are thankful that we were able to rescue our parents and other close relatives from the paws of Communism before it was too late to get them out.

4

FACTS ABOUT CUBA
BEFORE THE REVOLUTION:
THE ECONOMY, LABOR LEGISLATION,
EDUCATION, PUBLIC HEALTH, CULTURE
AND SPORTS

*"Cuba was at the top of Latin America in prosperity and under
Castro has become one of the poorest countries in the region."*

Discerning the Truth

CASTRO'S TAUNTING OF America as an exploiter of Cuba's resources for its self-ish benefit has no validity whatsoever. His rhetoric against the United States has gone beyond any human comprehension. On July 26, 1959, in another of his hours-long harangues before a throng of people in the Plaza of the Revolution (previously known as the Civic Plaza) in Havana to celebrate the anniversary of the foundation of the 26th of July Movement, he viciously attacked the U.S. Among other scathing remarks, he said:

> The United States is the sworn enemy of all Latin American countries and of the progress of people all over the world. Cuba is today facing United States imperialism, a rapacious and exploiting imperialism which has lost some of its rapacious claws here in Cuba.

The venom coming out of his mouth from the very beginning of his power grab was indicative of the profound hatred he had, and continues to have, for America. He did his best to pass it on to the Cuban populace through his con-stant, repetitious tirades.

The myth of U.S. imperialism falsely raised by Castro has served as fodder for the liberal media and other left-wing apologists. I will summarize some facts about pre-Castro Cuba in an effort to dispel the cloud of lies and innuendos he has spread over the true role of the United States in the economic development of Cuba. The economic data I am citing are based on reliable reports, studies and statistics from diverse sources, including U.S. Department of Commerce Reports, *Investments in Cuba*, Washington, D.C., U.S. Government Printing Office, 1956; U.S. Department of Commerce Reports, *U.S. Investments in Latin America*, Washington, D.C., U.S. Government Printing Office, 1957; U.S. Department of Agriculture Economic Research Service, *Agricultural and Food Situation in Cuba*, Washington, D.C., U.S. Government Printing Office, 1926; Wyatt MacGaffey and Clifford R. Barrett, *Twentieth Century Cuba*, American University, New York, Double Day and Company, Inc, 1965; The Economic and Technical Mission of the International Bank for Reconstruction and Development, *Report on Cuba*, 1951; Secretariat of the Commission for Latin America, *United Nations Economic Study of Latin America*, Mexico, 1958; Juan Clark, *Cuba: Mito y Realidad (Cuba: Myth and Reality)*, Saeta Ediciones, Miami, Florida, 1990; and Mario Lazo, *Dagger in the Heart: American Policy Failures in Cuba*, Twin Circle Publishing Co., Inc., New York, New York, 1968.

Additional sources are the works and publications of distinguished Cuban economists and scholars who, incidentally, were opposed to the Batista regime but, nevertheless, recognized the advances made by Cuba during the decades prior to Castro's advent to power. These individuals include Dr. José Alvarez Díaz, who held the post of Minister of Finance during the presidency of Dr. Carlos Prío Socarrás; Dr. Aureliano Sánchez Arango, who was Minister of Education, also under Prío's presidency; and Dr. Felipe Pazos, ex-President of the Cuban National Bank during the first eleven months of the Castro government. These three personalities went into exile after the Batista coup d'état in 1952, and then went into exile again during the initial phases of the Communization of Cuba. Some of the observations made in this book about the economy and other topics in Cuba before Castro include my own thoughts, notes from my studies at the University of Havana, and my subsequent field experiences as a professional.

The Economy

Let's begin to reveal the real economic situation in Cuba during the pre-revolution era and separate it from the much-distorted picture of poverty and despair painted by Castro and parodied by his backers in order to justify the tyrannical regime. Cuba, in the 1950s, had a standard of living higher than almost all of the Latin American republics, a large part of the European continent and all of the republics of Africa and Asia. In Oceania, only New Zealand and Australia had a higher per capita income than Cuba. In 1956 per capita income in Cuba was $339, while Chile was $296, Colombia $287, Brazil $217 and Mexico $202, with lower figures for the rest of Latin America. The Cuban economy was so strong that, by 1957, the per capita income had risen to $379. In fact, 1957 was the most prosperous year in Cuban history.

Unfortunately, when the political violence on both sides increased, the economy declined. If Batista had heeded the advice of level-headed politicians and intellectuals to hold free and honest elections, the disaster caused by the Castro revolution could have been avoided. Batista was blinded by power and an evanescent search for glory. On the opposite side there was a Communist conspiracy determined to convert Cuba into a slave state, as well as a satellite of the Soviet Union. Regrettably, this was a well-guarded secret within a very small circle of Castro's intimates. The overwhelming majority of the good people who supported the revolution were victims of one of the greatest political swindles ever known. It didn't take too long after the triumph of the revolution for Castro to take off his mask. The rape of a nation had begun.

Another misleading fallacy about Cuba, the assertion that the Cuban economy depended only on the sugar trade, was false. It is a fact that the sugar factor was a significant contributor to the economy. Statistics reveal that sugar represented 80% of the exports, while contributing only 25% of the overall national income. The American spirit of private enterprise and know-how contributed enormously to the development of Cuba into the most industrialized nation in Latin America. Of course, the hard-working, creative, intellectual and industrious nature of the Cuban people facilitated the achievements within the free enterprise system prevailing during the republican era. The United States gave an additional impetus to the growth of Cuba by buying its sugar at higher-than-world market prices, especially after World War II.

As a personal experience with the American entrepreneurial spirit, I recall visiting as a student a model foundry in my hometown of Sagua la Grande on the north coast of the central province of Cuba. This enterprise was founded by Mr. McFarland, an American who fell in love with Cuba and invested in the country. The McFarland Foundry, as it was known, was engaged in the construction and retooling of heavy equipment for the sugar industry and employed hundreds of workers all year round. Many examples can be given of the benefits Cuba had by being closer to, and having strong and healthy commercial and industrial relations with, the United States.

It must be emphasized that Cubans, in general, never had any animosity against Americans. The working relationship between Americans and Cubans was excellent at all levels. Proof of that is that the somewhat disrespectful term of "gringos" was rarely heard in Cuba when referring to Americans. To us they were simply "los Americanos." Furthermore, to shatter the myth of U.S. ownership of the Cuban economy, it is noted that only seventy-five thousand out of a working force of two million people were employees of American companies.

A vast number of selfless American educators, artists, agronomists, engineers, businessmen, economists and scientists gave time and energy to help Cuba develop into a free and democratic country. They truly loved Cuba. Many established themselves in Cuba, had families and partook of the Cuban culture and environment. The revolution, supported by a large majority of the Cuban population, was not addressed to "Yankee Imperialism" because it simply did not exist in Cuba.

Since the 1930s Cubans were increasingly assuming ownership over many enterprises, and sugar was not an exception. By 1958 Cuban entrepreneurs owned 121 sugar mills out of the 161 existing at that time. The mills in the hands of Cuban industrialists produced 62% of the total sugar production. The sugar industry was certainly not the monopoly of the Americans, as Castro and his apologists proclaimed. Cuban professionals held most of the administrative and technical positions in the sugar industry, and I was a witness to that assertion. The personnel were very capable and contributed to the high productivity and effective technical and accounting system existing in this vital sector of the Cuban economy.

In 1958 the U.S. investments in Cuba were $861 million, less than 14% of the total capital investments in Cuba. The banks in the hands of Cubans reached 61% of all the private deposits. By 1956 Cuban national income had attained levels which gave the Cuban people one of the highest standards of living in Latin America. The dichotomy between the very rich and the very poor, quite common in many Latin American countries, was not so evident during the pre-revolution era in Cuba. In fact, during the 1950s the imbalance was increasingly being erased. Castro, in adopting the socio-economic patron of Communism, led the country into a debacle. Communism had failed to deliver prosperity to the people under its enslaving system. At his advent to power, Cuba had a standard of living superior to that of the Soviet Union and its Eastern European satellites. The great wealth of Cuba was a subject of surprise to the Russians, Poles, Czechs and other Eastern Europeans who came to Cuba as advisors during the very early stages of the revolution before the free economy had been completely gutted by Castro-Communism. I am not suggesting that Cuba was a paradise with no problems or shortcomings. However, it cannot be said that Cuba was an underdeveloped country as depicted by its leftist detractors to distort the facts and make excuses for the Castro rule. Even though the revolution had begun its destructive path, Cuba still looked like a paradise to these early visitors from the captive nations.

The Economic and Technical Mission of the International Bank of Reconstruction and Development stated in its 1951 *Report on Cuba*:

> The general impression of members of the Mission from their observations during traveling all over Cuba is that living levels of the farmers, agricultural laborers, industrial workers, storekeepers and others are higher all along the line than for corresponding groups in other tropical countries and in nearly all other Latin American countries.

Before Castro took over, Cuba's food supply was abundant. A U.S. Government report described Cuba as among the better fed people in the world. As far as the per capita consumption of calories is concerned, Cuba was well above the minimum required for sustainment and occupied the 26th place in the world in this category.

For decades Cuba was self-sufficient in meat, dairy products and poultry. By the 1950s Cuba was exporting beef. The climate conditions and the pasture consisting of native grasses amenable to cattle all year round made the country ideally suitable for livestock breeding. Additionally, the cattle experimental stations and the initiative of ranchers led to the development of new, improved and adaptable breeds from imported cattle lines crossed with native stock. The quality of Cuban beef was good and the price was kept at a reasonable level. Furthermore, there was a high consumption of beef by the population. The industry was mostly in the hands of the Cubans. The income from livestock was the second in the agricultural field, surpassed only by sugar.

The advent of the revolution and its state-controlled economy ruined the livestock industry in Cuba. The ranchers were robbed of their property, only to see it pitifully mismanaged and ruined. There is a scarcity of beef in Cuba under the Communist system, and it has been rigidly rationed for years. While Cubans are longing for beef, the Communists, as usual, blame the shortage on the U.S. trade sanctions. They would not admit that it was their incompetence and the elimination of private enterprise that actually caused the wreck of the livestock industry in Cuba.

It is easy to visualize the complete contrast to the conditions existing in Cuba today under the miserable state-controlled Socialist economy, where people suffer from scarcity of foods and malnutrition. In pre-Castro Cuba there was never a necessity to establish food rationing. Today the population is subject to a strict rationing of common food staples, such as meat, fish, milk, rice, flour, coffee, cooking oil, eggs, canned goods, baby foods, beans and even sugar. All of these items and others are dispensed by means of a rationing card at the state-owned stores. Non-food items are also under severe limitation. Common products like clothing, shoes, underwear, toothpaste, cosmetics and a myriad of other basic household goods are scarce. When some of these items appear on store shelves, people run to the government stores trying to get there before they are depleted. They have to take a place in long lines and wait for hours to have access to the products, oftentimes finding to their chagrin that, when they finally enter the store, the merchandise is already gone. Out of desperation and necessity, some people with enough money have to buy items on the black market at much higher prices. The black market in Cuba is rampant and, in most cases, controlled by goons with connections to people of influence in the official Communist hierarchy. There is extreme corruption at all levels under the mantle of the so-called people's revolution or, what is commonly and ironically called by the populace, the "robo-lution" (robo means theft or robbery in Spanish).

Pre-Castro Cuba, by any standard, was not a third-world nation in the commonly-used term which defines backward countries. By all measures, Cuba was far ahead of most nations in Latin America and many developed countries in Europe. Cuba was among the top countries in the number of cars, radio-receivers, telephones, television sets and refrigerators per inhabitant. By 1958 Cuba was number one in Latin America in the number of television sets, one for every twenty inhabitants. In this category it was only exceeded in our hemisphere by the United States. In fact, it also had television programs transmitted in color, which was quite an advancement at that time.

From the 1930s to the end of 1958, Cuba honored its foreign debt with a high degree of compliance. This spotless record enabled the Cuban currency to reach one of the highest values in the world, on a par with the dollar by 1950. Cuba also had a high ranking in the consumption of steel. Likewise, it was the leading country in Latin America in usage of electrical power, number 33 among 124 world countries in this category. These were impressive credentials for a small country and an indicator of the progress made by Cuba in its dynamic path of development.

Several reports highlighted the fact that Cuba's transportation system and domestic markets were the most highly developed in Latin America. By the end of 1958, Cuba had 7,224 kilometers of paved roads. The east-west central road was 1,144 kilometers long and it facilitated communication throughout the length of the narrow island, reaching all of its six provinces and providing access to the most remote places, either directly or through converging smaller and well-paved provincial roads. Cuba had over 18,000 kilometers of railroad lines extending throughout the entire length and width of the country, reaching practically every city and village. The extensive railroad system placed the nation among the thirteen most developed countries in the world in this class.

Before the Castro takeover, there were 2,340 establishments in the industrial sector generating about half of the total national product. The commercial activity was not left behind. Over 38,000 large, medium and small private businesses had been created, and this growth continued at an incremental pace up to the end of 1958. The Cuban entrepreneurial spirit was very ebullient and creative. These businesses included apparel shops, appliance and furniture stores, restaurants, cafeterias, bars, catering services, liquor stores, groceries (bodegas and supermarkets), bakeries, fish markets, butcher shops, private schools and academies, books and school supplies, newspapers and magazines, printing presses, radio and television stations, pharmacies, medical and dental offices, orthopedic supplies, law offices, health clinics, insurance agencies, realtors, barbershops, beauty shops, laundries, automotive services, gasoline stations, automobile showrooms, department stores, paint shops, hardware stores, agricultural equipment and supplies, theaters, souvenir shops, glassware and ceramic shops, fruit and vegetable stands, transportation, bicycle shops, social and cultural clubs, hotels, warehouses, cold storages, baseball stadiums, sports arenas, gymnasiums, fine jewelry shops, professional baseball leagues and other professional sports, night clubs and a myriad of other enterprises.

Among the industrial establishments were sugar mills, crude oil refineries, construction companies, mining (nickel, copper, manganese, iron, non-metallic minerals, etc.), real estate, textile mills, chemicals, soaps, detergents, cosmetics, coffee processors, tobacco products, flour mills, banks and other financial institutions, rice processing, textiles, breweries, rum and other alcoholic beverages, soft drink plants, food processing plants, alcohol distilleries, glass containers, livestock, slaughter houses, tanneries, poultry and eggs, dairy products, fisheries, fruits and vegetable processing (grapefruit, oranges, limes, avocados, tomatoes, lima beans, black beans and other beans, peppers, eggplants, cucumbers, okra, bananas, pineapples, mangoes and other fruits and vegetables), pharmaceuticals, paper and paperboard, cement, ham and sausages, copper wire, aluminum foil, steamship lines, maritime terminals, aviation, railroad lines and energy plants (electricity and natural gas).

All of these businesses and industrial establishments, whether Cuban- or American-owned and regardless of size, were forcibly taken over during 1960 and 1961 with no compensation or indemnity. The free enterprise system came to an abrupt end. On May Day 1961, Castro proclaimed to the world "the birth of a patriotic, democratic and Socialist revolution." He further declared that "the means of production were in the hands of the working class." The Sovietization of the country had been accomplished under a blitz that confounded the unprepared and defenseless population. The entire country was taken aghast. The state was in control of all of the physical and human resources of the country. A slavery order was in place under an overwhelming military and police force. Protests, dissent, rebellions and insurgencies were brutally suppressed.

The commercial and industrial establishments under private control together employed over two million people and constituted the heart of the Cuban economy. They were thriving businesses for the most part. Before the revolution, Cuba was on a fast-growing pattern in spite of the political crisis. The Castro revolution was the negation of all the progress made by Cuba during its republican era. There was no rational justification for the obliteration of a dynamic socio-economic mechanism that was providing an exemplary reflection of what a successful free enterprise foundation can achieve. The only change needed in Cuba was the restoration of a free and honest electoral process leading to a rightful democratic government. This was the purpose of the struggle against Batista and what the people expected. No more, and no less.

After the takeover of the businesses and the appointment of ill-prepared "interventors," many of the commercial establishments were closed and boarded up. Others were closed after the merchandise was depleted. State-owned stores were created and a strict rationing system was established. Under these circumstances, the exodus of Cubans continued.

The Success of Cuban Exiles in Business, Finance and Politics

To demonstrate the caliber of Cuban émigrés, thousands of them achieved high executive positions in the business and financial world. Many established their own businesses, mostly in the United States, although some in other countries. Typical examples of successful Cuban executives and entrepreneurs can fill many pages, but let me briefly cite a few. Roberto Goizueta achieved the position of Chairman and Chief Executive Officer (CEO) of the Coca Cola Company before his premature death. Carlos M. Gutierrez became the Chairman and CEO of the Kellogg Company. He later resigned his position with Kellogg to accept the nomination of Secretary of Commerce by President George W. Bush at the beginning of his second term.

Jorge Más Canosa founded MasTec, a telecommunication services company which, through hard work and dedication, he developed into a multi-million dollar enterprise. Mr. Más Canosa was also very active in the anti-Castro movement and founded The Cuban American National Foundation, a powerful, independent, non-profit organization. He was instrumental in the creation of Radio Marti, a public service station that transmits special programs to Cuba to educate the people on the meaning of freedom and democracy. Radio Marti is widely heard in Cuba, in spite of the jamming of its transmissions by the Castro government. Unfortunately, Más Canosa died at the peak of his business and civic career without the opportunity to see a free Cuba, for which he fiercely dedicated much of his very productive life.

Maria Elena Lagomasino has succeeded in the business world in a big way. She came to the United States with her parents at the age of 11 when they fled from Communism in Cuba. She studied hard, worked diligently and climbed the corporate ladder, holding key executive positions with Citigroup Bank, Chase Manhattan Corp Private Bank, and J. P. Morgan and Company. She later became CEO of Asset Management Advisors LLC, overseeing over ten billion dollars in assets under management and 200 employees in 11 offices. She has also served in a variety of important ad-hoc committees. For instance, in 2005 she helped the Bush Administration in its efforts to secure funds for Central American disaster victims, and in 2006 she was appointed to serve on the Secretary of State's Advisory Committee on Transformational Diplomacy. Ms. Lagomasino was selected as "Woman of the Year" (2007) by the widely circulated *Hispanic Business* magazine.

Among the most distinguished Cuban émigrés in United States politics is an outstanding member of the U.S. Senate, a person who hails from my hometown of Sagua la Grande, Las Villas Province, U.S. Senator Mel Martínez. He was designated by President George W. Bush on January 7, 2007, as General Chairman of the Republican National Committee. Senator Martínez left Cuba at a very young age, fleeing from the atrocities of Castro-Communism. He advanced in the political arena, becoming a cabinet member, the Secretary of Housing and

Urban Development, in the first term of President George W. Bush. He was later elected to the U.S. Senate in his home state of Florida.

Other noteworthy Cuban-born public servants who came to the United States at an early age, escaping from the oppressive Castro regime, are Ileana Ros-Lehtinen, Lincoln Díaz Balart, Mario Díaz Balart and Bob Menéndez. They all finished their education in the U.S., practiced their respective professions and successfully entered politics.

Congresswoman Ileana Ros-Lehtinen (R-FL), an educator by profession, was the first Hispanic woman and first Cuban American elected to the U.S. Congress. She has been a trail blazer, being also the first Hispanic woman to be elected to the Florida State House of Representatives. She went on to be elected to the Florida State Senate. In 1989 she was elected to the U.S. House of Representatives, and has returned to Congress since winning the post by overwhelming majorities. She has been an effective legislator, serving her Congressional District with distinction, working incessantly for the good of South Florida and the nation. She is also a strong voice for the advancement of human rights in oppressed nations and has consistently denounced the Castro dictatorship in her native Cuba.

Congressman Lincoln Díaz Balart (R-FL) practiced his law profession in Miami before being elected to the Florida legislature in 1986. In 1990 he was elected to the Florida State Senate, and to the U.S. House of Representatives from Florida's 21st Congressional District in 1992. He was the first Hispanic in U.S. history to be named to the powerful House Rules Committee. He has been a stalwart defender of the U.S. national security, a severe critic of the oppressive Castro-Communist regime, and a watchdog for the best interests of his district and the state of Florida.

Congressman Mario Díaz Balart (R-FL) is an effective and dedicated legislator. He is respected by his constituency and admired by the Cuban Community for his stance against the Castro tyrannical system.

U.S. Senator Bob Menéndez (D-NJ) was previously a member of the U.S. House of Representatives. He is a Democrat with an anti-Castro record, for which I commend him. In line with the majority of his party, he is of liberal inclination on other issues. He is respected for his merit in ascending – by popular support – to such a prominent position in his state of New Jersey.

Labor Legislation

Labor legislation in Cuba was very advanced and far ahead of other American countries. Many labor laws protecting the workers were enacted as early as 1933 through a good number of laws, decrees and additional resolutions. All of the principles of the laws were adopted in the Constitution of 1940. The model Constitution added principles and provisions which strengthened the rights of the workers. It established that work is an inalienable right of the individual and that the state should employ all resources at hand to provide occupation to all those in need of same, to assure to every laborer, manual or intellectual, the necessary economic conditions and an appropriate standard of living. Just to cite an example out of many that could be mentioned, the labor laws were so advanced that as far back as 1934 they established that salaries for women may not be contracted at rates lower than those in force for men doing the same or equivalent work. It was many years after 1934 before other developed countries adopted similar legislation. All labor laws were strictly enforced by the Ministry of Labor.

The labor laws contained provisions for payment of social security, maternity and accidental benefits, overtime, minimum wages, paid vacations and restrictions for dismissal of workers. Before the revolution, Cuban workers, according to statistics of the International Labor Organization, received 66.6% of the gross national income, compared to 57.2% for Argentina, 47.9% for Brazil and 70.1% for the United States.

Education and Literacy

Cuba had made enormous progress in the field of education. In the mid-1950s, 80% of the population was literate. In literacy, education and national income invested in education, Cuba was the leading country in Latin America. The Castro regime has manipulated and distorted the education statistics beyond any recognition to make it appear that Cuba was a retrograde country and that the revolution was the salvation of Cuba. The same thing has been done with other aspects of the country's development during the pre-revolution era. The fact is that pre-Castro Cuba had an extensive system of public, primary and secondary education. It had three public universities, three private ones and numerous public high schools, technical and vocational schools. All of the public educational institutions were at no cost to the students. Many of the technical schools were at the college level. Private education was available and it was rather extensive. Among these were schools, colleges, academies and universities, mostly administered by religious groups, and others laical in nature. Attending grade school was mandatory for all Cuban children. The curriculum at all public and private schools was the same, in conformity with the Ministry of Education norms and based on a precept of the Constitution of 1940.

Numerous public vocational-polytechnic schools throughout the country supplied lodging, meals and sometimes even clothing to the students, all free of charge. Agricultural schools subsidized by the government in every one of the six provinces were available at no cost. The schools owned their own land and livestock and were adequately supplied and equipped with all the necessities for teaching the farm trades. The admission requirement was an eighth grade certificate and an examination, if the number of applicants exceeded the school's capacity. Admission was preferential to students from farm families. The schools worked on a three-year plan, the graduates receiving a certificate of Master Farmer.

Normal Schools (college-level) were available in each province for the development of Kindergarten and Grade School Teachers, respectively. The entry requirement was an eighth grade certificate and a scholastic exam in cases where applicants exceeded the required capacity of the school facility. An ample curriculum was taught which included mathematics, science, psychology, literature, geography, history, the arts, teaching methodology and other subjects. It was a four-year plan, after which the graduates were granted a teacher's certificate. At the same level, in each province, there were Home Economy Schools granting a degree of Master of Home Economy upon graduation. All of the Normal Schools were public and free of charge.

High Schools (institutes of secondary education) existed in practically every city throughout the country. They required an eighth grade certificate for entrance and had a five-year plan to prepare students to enter university-level education. There were also private schools, many operated by religious institutions, which had high school level education.

Technical Schools, in some cases called Schools of Arts and Trades, had a curriculum similar to a High School, but also encompassed the teaching of a technical career. Such careers would include industrial chemist, master mechanic, master electrician and master constructor. Evening classes were available for students who worked during the day. These schools were at the college level and had an intensive four-year plan. Graduates would be admitted to a university to advance their careers in different branches of engineering at the PhD level.

There were public Commerce Schools (college-level) in all the provinces. Admission required an eighth grade certificate. After completing a four-year plan, the students received a degree of Public Accountant. Most of the graduates went to work for banks and other businesses, while some established their own accounting services. There were also private Commerce Schools, both secular and religious, which conferred the degree of Public Accountant equivalent to the degree extended by the public accounting schools.

Excellent public art schools teaching painting and sculpturing were available in all six provinces. Havana had the famous San Alejandro National School of Fine Arts, which graduated well-recognized painters and sculptors. A goodly number of them exited Cuba after Castro and excelled in their artistic achievements in the United States and other countries. The art schools were under the advisory umbrella of the National Council of Culture, a prestigious institution whose main function was to review, promote and advance the development of the fine arts in Cuba.

There were also evening public schools to learn languages (predominantly English), telegraphy, stenography, typing, sewing (seamstress) and other light trades. The entire public school system was free, whether it was high school, normal school, technical school, commerce school or any other specialized school.

The advances in the field of education resulted in Cuba ranking at or near the top among Latin American and European countries. Cuba ranked first among Latin American countries in the percentage of national income invested in education. It was said that it was less expensive and more feasible to obtain a college education in Cuba than in many countries in our hemisphere, including the United States. The graduates from Cuba's colleges and universities proved their capabilities and values not only during the practice of their professions in pre-Castro Cuba, but also when thousands fled the brutal Castro tyranny and settled in the U.S. and other countries. Exiled professionals in many fields have occupied important positions in their respective careers, including scholars, chemists, biochemists, microbiologists, agronomists, physicians, bankers, financiers, engineers, architects, economists, lawyers and administrators, in private and public institutions. Medical doctors have done an outstanding job in hospitals, clinics, research institutions and private practice.

The medical profession in Cuba had outstanding doctors even before the start of the 20th century. As early as 1881 a Cuban physician, Dr. Carlos J. Finlay, discovered that the dreaded, and often fatal, yellow fever was conveyed by the mosquito. Finlay's theory served to eradicate the disease in Cuba, which became the first country to get rid of the deadly malady. His advanced study was corroborated in 1900 by an American medical team under the direction of Major Walter Reed, an army surgeon who headed the Yellow Fever Commission. He and his team traveled to Cuba in 1898 during the Spanish-American War to conduct a research study on the transmission of the disease. Many American soldiers were dying as a result of being infected by the tropical infirmity. The experiments conducted by Dr. Reed using human volunteers proved Dr. Finlay's early postulates. It was confirmed that the mosquito bite transmitted the disease by carrying the virus, and that it was not contracted from person-to-person contact or by infected clothing. Dr. Finlay's discovery saved thousands of lives. There is much to be said about the work of Major Reed, who made a great contribution to accelerate the fight to conquer the epidemic yellow fever scourge. As a result of these pioneering efforts, the first vaccine against yellow fever was developed in 1927. It is appropriate to note how Cuban and American scientists worked together through historical events for the well being of humanity. There are many other salutary examples showing how our relationships in many other fields have proven to be of mutual benefit to both countries. It is sad to see how a Communist tyranny full of hatred has poisoned the good relations that existed between the United States and Cuba.

The progress in education attained by Cuba during the republican era was exceptional and was not deterred in the least by the mood and temper of the political affairs until the arrival of the devastating and largely unexpected turn of events which took place after January 1, 1959. Castro's despotic rule perverted and destroyed the orderly and well-structured educational system it inherited. The path of destruction covered all phases of Cuban life.

While describing the subject of education in Cuba before the revolution, I can't fail to mention the ordeal teachers and scholars had to go through during the terror and turmoil which took place during the Communist takeover. They were forced to teach the school children and older students about the benefits of the revolution during classes; otherwise, they would be harassed and threatened to be fired by members of the militias, who attended classes as observers to monitor their behavior. Many teachers opted to give up their profession rather than surrender their principles of justice and freedom. They refused to abide by the Marxist-Leninist ideology that they were being compelled to accept and teach. This began to happen only a few months after Castro took over. It shows how well planned was the conversion to Communism.

Agents of the old Communist Party now allied to Castro were called "milicianos" (militias). They used the organized Communist Youth Movement to infiltrate the schools and openly challenge the teachers when they stuck to their standard teaching subjects, which they considered their primary responsibility. School teachers, college and university professors by the hundreds fled Cuba to find a new life elsewhere, many coming to the United States.

One specific example, out of hundreds of similar cases, was that of my wife's younger aunt, Dr. Eva Ochoa-Somoza. Let me describe her nightmarish experience because it touched so close to home. Eva was a dedicated teacher for sixteen years. At the time of the revolution, she was hopeful that the country would have a better future under a truly democratic system. She had the disappointment of her life when, only months after the toppling of Batista, she was subjected to all kinds of humiliating experiences and vilification. She had two younger daughters, 14 and 4 years old, respectively. Her husband Tony was the administrator of a private health clinic, Our Sacred Heart, located in a suburb of Havana. She was relocated, along with other teachers, to another province to join the so-called alphabetization campaign of the revolution.

Under the circumstances, Eva had no recourse but to accept the transfer; otherwise, she would have been fired. It wasn't easy for her to gain her position and advance in her career. She decided to take the new assignment which was to be, according to the promises of the education committee, only temporary. She rearranged her life to be sure that her children were properly attended to during her absence. Her husband and relatives pitched in to help with the children. During her assignment she was told to teach the basics of Communism, the evil of "Yankee Imperialism" and the purpose of the revolution; that is, to participate in an indoctrination program for children. She wasn't happy at all and resigned after her many years of service. From there on, she was harassed and persecuted. Her older daughter was also submitted to harassment in school by gangs of students who favored the revolution and had innocently joined the Youth Committee for the Defense of the Revolution.

Before the revolution, Eva and her family led the life of a typical, quiet, comfortable and religious middle-class family. They were happy and had the essentials to enjoy a normal and peaceful existence. They had even saved enough money to buy a car. They were not active in politics; however, like good citizens, they were always hoping for the best for Cuba. The Castro revolution turned their lives upside down, like it did for millions of people. They began to formulate a plan to leave Cuba. Their children were sent first to the United States in November 1961 through the underground Operation Peter Pan (which is described in more detail in Chapter V). Later the following year, she was able to leave Cuba and join her children. Meanwhile, her husband remained in Cuba because he was not allowed to travel with her. This separation, which fortunately was only temporary, added more pain and suffering to the lives of Eva, her husband, and other relatives left behind. The shadow of Castro's misadventures continued to lacerate the body and soul of Cuban families.

Eva arrived in the United States in February 1962, realizing the dream of joining her two loving daughters. However, the family would not be complete without her husband Tony. Meanwhile, the private clinic where he was administrator was confiscated by the government and he lost his job. He was unable to find employment because he had been marked as antagonistic toward the revolution. Following a series of acts of sabotage against the clinic by anti-Castro groups, although he was no longer associated with the health institution, Tony was accused of being connected to the disruptive actions and was detained for a week without any material proof of the charges. After intense and abusive interrogations, he was finally set free, but not before they confiscated his wedding ring, his wristwatch, his wallet and money. This was petty theft. Were these people the ones that were going to restore honesty and justice to Cuba? Hypocritically, these hoodlums are the same ones who cry "Fatherland or Death" at the drop of a hat.

Tony never gave up. He began to work at menial jobs off and on to sustain himself until he could find a way to leave the country and join his wife and daughters. Many times he had to depend on help from relatives or friends to survive through very trying times. He was relegated to an outcast by the Communist system. After several months he managed to get an exit permit to leave Cuba and, in August 1962, he joined his wife and two daughters in the United States. This was a miracle! Finally he had rest from his anxiety and constant worries about reuniting with his family. According to Eva, it was the happiest day of their lives. Later Tony found a good job in Miami and his wife had made inroads in returning to her beloved teaching career.

Through a magnificent effort, hard work and dedication, Dr. Eva Ochoa-Somoza rose again in her brilliant career as an educator in spite of the hurdles she had to overcome. She adjusted to a new country and a new language with admirable dexterity. She laboriously performed her duties in various schools in Dade County, Florida, beginning as an auxiliary teacher and then as a regular teacher, a specialist teacher for the handicapped, an assistant school director, a director of education programs, and other positions of responsibility. She excelled in the field of bilingual education and special learning systems, and traveled to many cities in the United States to lecture and train other teachers, including lectures at many colleges and universities. She went to Lima, Peru, at the invitation of scholars who heard about her new approaches to bilingual education and reading skills. In Peru she installed the first Spanish Lecture Laboratory in Latin America, which was acclaimed as an innovative tool by the Peruvian teachers. For her dedication, hard work and merits she received many awards and commendations throughout her career. She was the co-author of the book series *Mil Maravillas (One Thousand Marvels)* and *Campanitas de Oro (Golden Bells)*, published by Macmillan Publishing Company and designed for the teaching of reading. She retired from the Department of Education of Dade County after twenty-one years of professional service.

There are many other examples of exiled Cuban educators who demonstrated their values, proudly earned during the Cuban republican era, by gaining positions at schools and institutions of higher learning in the United States. The greatness of America cannot be tarnished by the malignancy and diatribes of its enemies. America is a country which opens the doors of success to those who come yearning for liberty and opportunity. It is a country that deserves our respect, admiration and loyalty. It can be said that in America, if you put your mind to it, you can be anything you want to be.

Public Health and Social Welfare

Cuba had a very extensive and varied healthcare system. There were both public and private hospitals. The public health facilities were free. There were many fine national, provincial and municipal hospitals available to the general population. Diseases and injuries of all natures were treated by well-trained doctors and nurses, including surgery and recuperation treatment. There were private hospitals maintained and operated by social clubs (associations) in which any person or family could hold membership for a very low cost. In the 1950s the dues were as low as three to five dollars a month. The benefits included medical care for the entire family. Many of these associations also had recreational facilities and evening schools at a separate site available to all members. The health services provided were of first-rate quality, and medications were included. Additionally, there were many private clinics offering complete medical services to members for a very reasonable monthly fee. The University of Havana owned and administered an excellent, large hospital in Havana, the Calixto Garcia Hospital, which offered free healthcare services. It can be said that regardless of the healthcare facilities chosen by individuals or families, they were well equipped with very competent medical staffs. Homes for the aged (nursing homes), either public or private, were available but not common. It was customary in Cuba for the family to take care of the elderly in their homes unless special circumstances occurred.

At the municipal level there were many first aid centers or mini-clinics called "Casa de Socorros." They were spread over various sections of Havana and throughout many other cities all over the island, and provided medical assistance to patients afflicted with minor ailments and injuries. After receiving initial emergency care, if the condition was serious, the patient was promptly rushed by ambulance to a full-service hospital for further attention. The first aid centers were staffed at all times with a general practitioner physician, a nurse and a pharmacist. The medical attention and medications dispensed were free. The facilities were open 24 hours every day of the week. They serviced mostly low-income people or those in need of immediate attention.

Under the revolution the public health system is in disarray. The government propaganda machine and the leftist parrots in the U.S. press herald the free healthcare existing in Cuba, projecting to the world a totally different scenario. The fact is that the hospitals in Cuba are in a state of crisis, the majority of which are not even meeting the minimum sanitary requirements. The medical attention is deplorable and the physicians are poorly paid. They are limited to prescribing the medications in stock because oftentimes the drugs available are not necessarily the ones required for treating the specific diseases of the patients. Potable water is often unavailable and the food served is of poor quality. The families of the patients have to bring certain basic staples to supplement the inadequate supplies of the hospital. Reports and references about Cuba published in the U.S. press and elsewhere oftentimes cite, as if they were credible, bogus statistics released by the regime about the low infant mortality, the high life expectancy and other egregiously manipulated indexes to propagandize the "advances" attained in Cuba under Socialism.

The only hospitals which are well-equipped, supplied and staffed are reserved for the high-ranking military personnel and the privileged top-level civilian members of the regime that comprise the elite class, referred to as "mayimbes" or "pinchos" in the slang language of the population. Incidentally, these luxury hospitals are used as showcases for the foreign press and important visitors. These special hospitals are also available to foreigners who can afford to pay exuberant charges in dollars for medical services. The common people are kept away from these healthcare facilities. The apartheid system applied to elegant recreational resorts is also applied when it comes to the health of the less fortunate citizens.

These facts about the sad state of affairs of the healthcare situation in Cuba have been reported and documented by physicians who had the good fortune of escaping the country. Physicians are also poorly paid and prohibited from engaging in private practice. Sometimes, out of necessity, they treat patients underground and face serious risks. At other times they double-up as taxi drivers or take on other menial jobs to make ends meet and sustain their families. It is another sorry and shameful paradigm of the "Socialist Paradise" established by Castro and his cadres.

Culture

During the republican era that ended on January 1, 1959, Cuban painters, sculptors, writers, poets, novelists, musicians, composers, singers, dancers, actors and actresses projected an expression very typical of the Cuban culture through their notable creations and performances. Cuban artistry reached high levels of international recognition. I will mention only a few of the many praiseworthy individuals who left the country, fleeing the Castro revolution. Ernesto Lecuona was a famous pianist and composer. His music served as the theme for several Hollywood films. He traveled the world performing at concerts and special presentations and was acclaimed as a musical genius. Osvaldo Farrés was a notable writer of songs and a composer of popular music. His creations were sung by the most popular singers of his epoch in Cuba and all Latin America. Some of his songs were played as background music in American films. Miguelito Valdés, a singer and musician, was considered the king of the Cuban conga. He had his own orchestra and traveled the world as an exponent of Cuban popular music. Dámaso Pérez Prado, of international fame, introduced the mambo song and dance to audiences across the world.

Celia Cruz, also known as the Queen of Latin Music, was a leading performer of the Afro-Cuban song, the salsa, and other well-known styles of music. She was unquestionably among the greatest in the history of Latin music. Celia was already famous in Cuba when she defected shortly after the Castro takeover. When her mother died in Cuba, the Castro government refused to issue a visa to allow her to attend the funeral. Celia then vowed never to return to her native land until Castro was ousted or died. Needless to say, she had an intense dislike for Castro and his oppressive Communist regime. She was the pride of the Cuban exiled community and won many awards throughout her illustrious career. Celia left Cuba searching for freedom and found it in the United States, where her artistry, personality and charm made her larger than life. Her dream of returning to a free Cuba and receiving the love of her people in person never came true. She died in 2003, a tragic and painful event which shook the music world.

Olga Guillot was a superb singer who demonstrated her grace and talents in many scenarios on the continents. Maria Conchita Alonso displayed her acting endowment and grace as a Hollywood star. Rick Sánchez became a top newscaster on national television. Arturo Sandoval is an extraordinary trumpet player and the central figure in a film about the life and tribulations under the Castro totalitarian rule. After his defection, he has amply succeeded in the United States. Israel "Cachao" López, a bassist and one of the mambo music leaders in Cuba before Castro, defected to the U.S. and performed in several clubs. One day he was found by actor Andy García in a relatively obscure San Francisco club where he was displaying his magnificent talent. Andy, a lover of Cuban music, took him under his wing and helped him to remake his career at an advanced age, sort of a "second coming" of Cachao. Andy García himself came to the United States with his family at age 5, fleeing from the Communist malaise affecting Cuba, and reached stardom in Hollywood. Who can forget his brilliant acting in the film *Godfather III?* He also became a director and film producer. He made a successful film, *The Lost City*, which depicts the tragic ordeal of the Cuban people under Communist totalitarianism. It relates to his own experience and his beloved devotion to his native country.

Cristina Saralegui is a talented and famous TV personality in the Spanish entertainment world and an exponent of the Cuban culture. She fled Cuba when she was very young and developed her career in the United States. Presently she is a celebrity in her own right. She has been for many years a hostess of a TV show broadcast in the U.S. and many Latin American countries. She has excelled not only in television but has expanded into other ventures, such as the popular publication *Cristina, The Magazine (Cristina, La Revista)* and a line of household items. She is a champion of the Cuban creativity which existed before the country was buried by the Communist cataclysm.

Gloria Estefan, an extremely popular star in the world of pop music, came to the United States as a child when her parents fled Cuba. She unfolded her triumphant artistic profession as a brilliant bilingual singer. She is famous not only in the U.S. but all over the world. Her also famous Cuban exiled husband, Emilio Estefan, founded the very popular group *The Miami Sound Machine*, with Gloria Estefan as the leading vocalist. Emilio is a successful entrepreneur with multifarious talents. Gloria and Emilio are immensely popular in the Cuban community of Miami. Their achievements have earned them many awards.

Among the most distinguished exiled Cuban artwork masters in painting and sculpturing is an unassuming artist with extraordinary talents, Eladio González. He left Cuba in 1967, fleeing from the suffocating Communist tyranny which has restricted and censored artistic expression not conforming to the Socialist ideology. Eladio went to Madrid, Spain, and then to Paris, France, for a brief period before settling in Chicago in 1968. He is a graduate of the prestigious San Alejandro National School of Fine Arts in Havana. I had the pleasure of meeting him many years ago, and have followed his career with great interest and delight. He has been acclaimed by critics as a genius, a truly creative artist, and has excelled both as a sculptor and a painter.

Eladio masterfully blends abstract and reality in many of his works, projecting an image of elegance and fascination, unique to his creative prodigy. He has exhibited in major cities in the U.S. and abroad. He frequently exhibits in his adopted Greater Chicago medium. The Chicago Press Club, the Grand Salon of Illinois, the Hyde Park Art Center, the Collins Fine Art Gallery, the Art Institute of Chicago and other exclusive exhibit halls have displayed his fine art pieces. Cubans are proud of Eladio González as an exponent of the excellence of émigrés who had to abandon a country where human rights and freedom of expression have been trampled.

I could go on and on naming prominent Cuban émigrés who have excelled in their respective categories of the performing arts and other artistic manifestations, recreating a spectrum of the culture that existed in the Cuba I knew during my younger years. All of the aforementioned celebrities have one thing in common: they escaped Cuba searching for freedom. Their names have been erased from the pages of Cuban publications and history as if they never existed. They are labeled as traitors of the revolution because they did not accept the abominable oppressor. They were all welcomed in the United States and, through their determination, they achieved their goals. This is the country that is maligned by the likes of Castro, Chavez, Ahmadinejad and other thugs. What a disgrace to humanity to have these satanic and delusional characters spewing hatred on a noble country that, over the years, has opened its doors to the downtrodden of this world.

There is more to say about the Cuban culture before the onset of the Communist tyranny. There were a significant number of public libraries, museums, exhibition halls, art fairs, book fairs and a diversity of cultural institutions at all levels. The means of communication were ample, there was a robust growth in the graphic press, most notably newspapers and magazines. The daily newspaper circulation reached 101 copies per 1,000 inhabitants, occupying the thirty-third place among 112 nations and exceeded in Latin America only by Uruguay. The newspapers and magazines had quality writers and columnists. Hundreds of radio stations throughout the island and numerous TV stations served to continually inform the public about important national and international news and contributed to the cultural education of the Cuban people. In Havana there were about twelve major newspapers which circulated throughout the entire nation. There were also provincial and municipal newspapers which extended the graphic communication to the most remote villages in the country. In addition, there were schools for those who aspired to enter the journalistic profession, as well as schools for learning radio and TV broadcasting.

Several cultural institutions, parallel to the good system of education, contributed significantly as components to the intellectual progression of Cuba's cultural advancement. Among the most important organizations engaged in a variety of cultural activities were the Lyceum Lawn and Tennis Club, the Pro-Musical Art Association, the Philharmonic Orchestra, the National Ballet Patronage, the Plastic Arts Patronage, the Performing Arts Theater, the Opera Patronage and the University Theater. These private and public institutions promoted artistic events by inviting renowned national and international artists or artistic groups to perform before audiences in their respective genres or, in the case of painters and sculptors, to display their art in fairs and exhibits. There was an intense intellectual activity not only in Havana, but also in the capitals and major towns of the various provinces.

Sports and Games

A claim that the revolution had developed the practice of sports in Cuba is another fallacy of the Communist regime propaganda machine. The truth is that Cuba was already a very advanced country in many competitive sports. From the beginning of the republic in 1902, Cuba had progressively cultivated a sports climate that led to an active and successful system of developing athletes in many different competitive games without the need for governmental control and manipulation. Personally, like many other kids and young people, I played baseball in sandlots, grassy lots, public parks, sports parks, school fields and even in not-very-busy streets. The government didn't have to tell us where to play, how to play and what to play, nor were we forced to participate in any sport. It was a voluntary effort done for the purpose of having a good time. It all developed naturally with coaching from our elders, our parents, older brothers, friends or relatives and school trainers. We had the freedom to choose our own destiny. This is a divine privilege which has been lost in Cuba under Communist rule.

Generally, baseball in Cuba was not just a game. It was really a passion and our number one national pastime. U.S. major league baseball was extremely popular in Cuba. We followed the games on radio, TV and in newspapers. Many American players became household names in Cuba, including Babe Ruth, Lou Gehrig, Dizzy Dean, Red Ruffing, Bob Feller, Stan Musial, Ted Williams, Phil Ruzzuto, Pee Wee Reese, Yogi Berra, Jackie Robinson, Tommy Lasorda, Whitey Ford, Roy Campanella, Don Zimmer, Johnny Podres and Joe DiMaggio. In Cuba there were various organized amateur, semi-professional and professional baseball leagues and organizations. Baseball was also played in high schools, colleges and universities. Many local teams in towns all over Cuba, not necessarily attached to any organized group, would play each other under loosely and informally arranged conditions on any field available. They always found volunteers to serve as umpires. In amateur baseball, the Cuban selection was invariably the champion of the Amateur World Series from the 1940s through the 1950s against teams from the United States, Mexico, Venezuela, the Dominican Republic, Costa Rica, Panama and other countries.

From 1911 to the late 1950s and early 1960s, self-made Cuban baseball players were already displaying their skills in the U.S. big leagues. As pioneers in the sport I can cite Rafael Almeida and Armando Marsáns, who were signed by the Cincinnati Reds in 1911. Over the decades a host of fine players who had developed in a free Cuba were scouted and recruited to play in the U.S. major leagues. Among many we can mention are Adolfo Luque, Mike González, Tomás de la Cruz, Conrado Marrero, Willie Miranda, Sandalio Consuegra, Napoleón Reyes, Mosquito Ordeñana, Luis Tìant, Tony Taylor, Camilo Pascual, Witto Alomá, Minnie Miñoso, Bert Campaneris, Roberto Ortiz, Cookie Rojas, Tony Oliva, Tony Pérez, Mike Cuellar, Andy Etchebarren, Edmundo Amorós, Joe Azcúe, Orlando Peña, Diego Seguí and José Cardenal.

There were also many young people who came to the United States fleeing Communism with their parents and developed their baseball prowess in this country. Among them are José Canseco, Rafael Palmeiro, Tino Martínez and Luis Gonzáles, four superstars among the American-bred crop. Special mention should be made of Martín Dihigo, who played professionally in Cuba, Mexico and the U.S. Negro leagues during the decades of the 1930s and 1940s. He was recognized as one of the outstanding pitchers of all time, and he was also a good hitter. For his extraordinary record of achievement he was inducted into the professional Baseball Hall of Fame in all three of the aforementioned countries, the only player in the history of baseball to achieve that feat. He, along with many others, was an exponent of the high caliber of baseball played in Cuba before Castro-Communism took possession of the island nation.

Boxing was another natural development in Cuban sports. It evolved from street fracases to the formal boxing rings in a big way before the revolution. Boxing was popular across the island, although the main arenas were located in Havana, the capital of Cuba. It was sort of a second preference in overall popularity among competitive sports in Cuba. There was amateur boxing, which included golden gloves competitions, and professional boxing. The latter produced world-recognized names, including ex-featherweight world champion Kid Chocolate (1930s), ex-welterweight world champion Kid Gavilan (1950s), middleweight of world renown Kid Tunero (1940s), heavyweight contenders Onelio Agramonte (1940s) and Niño Valdés (1950s), ex-welterweight world champions Benny Paret and Luis Manuel Rodríguez (early 1960s), among many notables who made it big in Cuba, the U.S. and Europe.

Other sports practiced in Cuba included basketball, swimming, track and field, tennis, racquetball, jai-alai, softball, fencing, javelin, wrestling, sailboating, rowing, car racing, horse racing, gymnastics and bicycling. Table games such as dominoes, chess, cards and ping pong were also popular. In the ambit of chess, José Raúl Capablanca was world champion from 1921 to 1927. He was known for his highly refined technique and has been recognized as one of the greatest champions of all time. In fencing, Ramón Fonst was a gold medalist. Many more accomplishments can be cited of other Cuban sports figures who excelled before the onset of Communism in Cuba. Numerous athletes, while still active, exited after 1959 and continued to shine in the United States in their respective sports careers.

Professional sports in Cuba, like all other private enterprise activities, were totally suppressed by the state after Communism was imposed upon the Cuban people. Athletes aspiring to take advantage of their God-given talents had to manage through various means to leave the country. They have done it in droves, which is another indication of the failure of a suppressive, abusive and morally corrupt regime.

The embarrassing spectacle of seeing Cuban athletes searching for asylum in free countries where they have gone to compete has led the dictator to find ways to contain the bleeding. When Cuban sports teams travel to participate in international competitions, they are accompanied by a large contingent of security guards, many disguised as coaches and trainers. They restrict the movement and outside contacts of the athletes to prevent them from fleeing the sports facility or the place where they are lodged. In spite of such precautions, many athletes have found clever and daring ways to outmaneuver this vigilance and escape to freedom, requesting asylum in the host country or the American embassy.

Never in the history of pre-Castro Cuba did athletes have to be guarded during international events held in foreign countries. They were free to tour places, walk the streets, meet with admirers and move at their will within the normal rules of conduct established for participants in such events. When the athletes return home now, they must display obedience and adulation to Castro, so they fake it to the best of their ability. Out of necessity they have to be in his good graces to maintain the meager rewards given to the ones who return victorious. It is an artificial life full of uncertainties and could be compared to giving a dog some treats when it behaves. Such is the odious and perverse system established in Cuba. Otherwise, you become an outcast, an anti-social, an undesirable dere-lict. All of this is part of the miserable existence brought about by the inhumane order forcibly controlling the bodies and minds of the Cuban population. It is like living a surrealistic nightmare. It is not easy to show happiness on the out-side while inside the suffering and anxiety is searing your guts. There is a limit to what the human person can tolerate. Therefore, an intense and latent desire exists in not only the athletes but practically an entire population to break away from slavery.

The country is in shambles under Communism, the economy is ruined, the culture is destroyed, civil liberties are non-existent, the rule of law is in the hands of a dictator and poverty is widespread. Cuba was at the top of Latin America in prosperity and under Castro has become one of the poorest countries in the region. Thousands of political prisoners languish in filthy jails and many have died over the years of abuse, torture, diseases, starvation or execution by firing squads. Only fools and idiots can think that the system will change by lifting the U.S. embargo and establishing relations with the abominable regime.

5

THE COMMUNIST CONVERSION.
CASTRO'S TREASON.
DEFECTIONS, PURGES AND EXECUTIONS.

"From the very early stages of the revolutionary government, important civilian and military members of the regime began to feel uneasy about the pronouncements of Castro and his overly antagonistic attitude against the United States, as well as his alliance with the leaders of the old Communist Party."

The Road Map: Castro, Master of Deceit

IT IS CLEAR that the road map to Cuba's course to Communism had been secretly hatched well in advance of the triumph of the revolution. The facts presented earlier in this book revealed a crystal clear motive for the Soviet's involvement and interest in the entire conspiracy and for the role that Castro played as a partner. It was not surprising how Castro fooled his many fervent supporters. He had an uncanny ability to disguise his true feelings. He cleverly used his known acting adroitness to his advantage. It is well documented that a good segment of the Cuban business community generously contributed financially to the 26th of July Movement and other anti-Batista organizations. Many wealthy and middle-class people participated in conspiracy missions and the ensuing armed struggle.

The revolution against the Batista regime was not the result of a "peasant uprising" as some leftist American journalists misleadingly described it. Rather, it was a movement whose backbone consisted of a large proportion of well-educated upper- and middle-class citizens. It also included students and workers who were opposed to the political stranglehold of Batista. They thought it was an insult to their intelligence to have a government imposed by force and which disrupted the constitutionality of the nation. They clamored for democracy, honest elections, freedom of expression and the elimination of political corruption. It was a given that the free enterprise system was going to be maintained. There was nothing wrong with the progressive capitalistic foundation of the republic. This important sector of the Cuban economy was never a target of those joining the various revolutionary groups. The old Communist Party, already in disarray, was not a factor in the anti-Batista current.

Those who knew Castro's early leftist posture as a student leader, and later as a member of the left-wing of the Orthodox Party, had been willing to forgive him for what they wishfully thought were errors of an overly-aggressive and zealous young man. Perhaps in the fervor to reestablish a democratic government in Cuba, it never crossed their minds that he was a consummate liar who had never abandoned his early Communist formation. Or maybe they were not totally convinced that he was a fellow traveler. Batista and his followers had denounced him as a Communist. They knew the facts as they had access to intelligence files, but who within the populace was going to have faith in their words? Castro had the backing of many mature intellectuals and seasoned democratic politicians who were opposing Batista. He had cleverly, during the insurgency campaign and the very early days of his government, made repeated statements in which he declared that he was in favor of democracy, although from the very beginning he could not completely hide his true intentions. Castro had given interviews during this process to several sympathetic U.S. journalists, among them Herbert L. Matthews (*New York Times*) and Jules Dubois (*Chicago Tribune*), flatly denying that he was a Communist. Furthermore, he said that he was determined to fully restore the model and advanced Constitution of 1940 (which had set the basis for a solid democratic foundation) and was planning to hold free elections by January 1961. Castro repeatedly denied, while in the Sierra Maestra Mountains, any desire for power or to occupy a high office in the provisional government. Of course, he was knowingly lying through his teeth.

The Ordeal of Ex-President Carlos Prío

A major contributor to Castro's movement was the ex-President of Cuba, Dr. Carlos Prío Socarrás. According to prominent former ex-Castro supporters, Prío had made a $100,000 contribution to finance the Castro expedition on the Granma boat from Mexico to the southeastern shores of the Oriente Province. Eighty-three rebels disembarked on December 2, 1956, with disastrous consequences – only twelve survived after landing, Castro, his brother Raúl and "Che" Guevara among them. The rest were killed or captured by Batista's troops. Castro and the other survivors managed to regroup and took refuge in the dense forest of the Sierra Maestra Mountains. From there they began to gain strength to continue the fight against the Batista regime.

Dr. Prío had enthusiastically given his backing to the revolution. He was pivotal in uniting the various factions opposed to Batista into a joint effort to dislodge the dictatorial regime. He returned from exile to Cuba in 1959 shortly after the defeat of Batista by the rebel forces. He became increasingly dissatisfied with the way the revolution was turning and began to criticize the suppression of liberties and the elimination of private enterprise. He was promptly menaced and subjected to persecution. Prío, in spite of his long and important role in the political process in Cuba since the 1930s, had grossly misjudged Castro. He was no exception, as many other prominent and distinguished democratic Cuban leaders made the same mistake. He was reluctant to leave Cuba this time because he wanted to keep fighting to reverse the course of events. However, forced by the suffocating circumstances, Prío went into exile and established his residence in South Florida, where he continued his opposition to the Communization of his country. Later on, feeling dejected, depressed and betrayed by Castro, he committed suicide and became another victim of the treachery of Castro. This tragic occurrence, and countless other similar incidents, is part of this sad chapter in the history of Cuba. In Chapter XI it will be shown that the betrayal of Castro even extended to members of his own family.

Hatching the Communist Conspiracy: The Betrayal

As demonstrated by the developments occurring from the first days of the revolutionary government installed by Castro, it was clear that all along he was setting the table for the delivery of Cuba into Soviet hands. He carefully played his cunning role as an ambivalent maverick. His apologists of the left, mainly the foreign journalists, preferred to call him a "nationalist reformer." Castro was, in fact, stalling until the Soviets were ready to enter the picture at the proper time. He was avoiding an early crisis from the mostly moderate and conservative elements he picked for his first cabinet, the presidency and other top posts. He deliberately maneuvered to present a pro-democratic front to satisfy the expectations of the people and maintain his popularity. In addition, he was careful not to create a head-on collision with the United States too soon, although he could not refrain from blaming and assailing his neighbors to the north for all the perceived political and economical ills of Cuba. Clearly Castro's plans were to force the United States out of its relations with Cuba while he completed the takeover of all aspects of the economy, the Communization of the country and the entry of the Soviet Union into Cuban affairs as a benefactor of the revolution.

During the initial changes indicating the Socialist path he was taking, there were public demonstrations in many cities throughout the island opposing the move to alter the Cuban society and to deviate from the true objectives of the revolution. The demonstrations were brutally repressed. The early signs of worse things to come began to be manifested in every aspect of the civil society, beginning only a few months after January 1, 1959. Some important members of the government, the rebel army, the 26th of July Movement, the non-Communist labor movement leaders, the University Student Directory and other revolutionary groups began to be purged. Some resigned their positions and took refuge in foreign embassies or left the country by whatever means they could find. Others were arrested and imprisoned or summarily executed.

By the beginning of 1961 the Communization was practically completed. The events were so bizarre that for many of the main participants it became difficult to accept that they had been betrayed. They were devastated. Some were so distraught that they opted to commit suicide. Many rebel army units and commanders went back to the mountains to fight again, this time against Castro. The overwhelming forces the government had thrown against them made it very difficult to succeed. They were slowly annihilated; Castro's army took no prisoners. These valiant heroes became victims of a fraudulent revolution they had helped to succeed.

From the very early stages of the revolutionary government, important civilian and military members of the regime began to feel uneasy about the pronouncements of Castro and his overly antagonistic attitude against the United States, as well as his alliance with the leaders of the old Communist Party. They were afraid to talk to each other about their skepticism and disagreement with the gradual turn of events for fear that they may be accused of conspiring against Castro. The entire system was permeated with spies and snitches. An incrimination of such magnitude would be considered treason and, in the absence of a legal structure, it would bring incarceration or death by a firing squad. The revolutionary tribunals were only a fake. The government was the prosecutor, the defense and the witness.

The reign of terror established in the nation overruled all vestiges of justice. That is why there was no possibility of any concerted action against Castro's excesses and abuse of power. He was the omnipotent ruler and, as he repeatedly proved, a very inhumane one. The natural instinct for survival was in the mind of many who, under the circumstances, decided to accept the status quo and convert or adapt themselves to the prevailing winds. They became the chameleons of the revolution. However, there were some who decided to buy time waiting for the proper opportunity to exit and find a way to get out of the country. Only a few left-leaning members of the initial Cabinet, and a handful of others holding important positions, decided to go along for a while longer. They sold their souls to the tyrant. Some made the total conversion and joined the Communist bandwagon.

Castro began dismantling the 26th of July Movement and rearranging the rebel army to suit his already-designated priorities. He purged all of the pro-democracy leaders of the revolution and displaced the recently-elected labor leaders, practically all from the 26th of July Movement, and replaced them with old Communist Party trade union activists. The old Communists took control of the Confederation of Cuban Workers (CTC). The free press was annihilated. By the end of 1960 all of the newspaper, radio and television enterprises had been either dismantled or taken over forcibly by organized gangs with the support of troops under the command of his brother Raúl, or the equally infamous "Che" Guevara. They were his hatchet men. Concurrently the anti-Communists were persecuted and muffled. To raise the banner of anti-Communism became equivalent to opposing the revolution. Those who did were labeled as traitors and arrested. The sad truth is that many who opposed Communism were initially followers of Castro and later regretted their mistake.

The Liquidation of Free Enterprise

Once Castro and his Communist cohorts had achieved complete control over the entire country and suffocated the opposition to the conversion through a reign of terror, they accelerated the confiscation and expropriation of all private property, beginning with the U.S.-owned companies and following with the Cuban-owned businesses, including the world-famous Bacardi rum firm. The Bacardi family had contributed large sums of money to Castro's insurgency. They were a patriotic family who had a compassionate feeling and were very generous in support of charitable institutions. Through their entrepreneurial efforts they provided employment to thousands of Cubans.

José M. Bosch was president and general manager of the company. As a result of his support of the Castro movement against Batista, he had to go into exile in Mexico. After Castro took over, he rapidly returned to Cuba to help in restoring the economy of the country. He had been a Minister of Finance during the Prío presidency and was known as a respected, dedicated, honest and extremely competent businessman. Bosch and the Bacardi family exited Cuba shortly after the company was confiscated. They became part of a long list of hard-working, decent people duped by Castro's promises.

Not only large enterprises were affected by the reckless expropriation policy. The takeover extended to medium and small businesses, including shoe repair shops, barber shops and ambulant vendors. In other words, every venture that implied a profit-making activity by private individuals was confiscated. By the beginning of 1961 the entire conventional free economy had been disintegrated. The state became the omnipotent power controlling all aspects of the economy, the society and the lives of its citizens. Free enterprise, freedom of expression and any vestiges of democracy were severely suppressed and replaced by a totalitarian domination of all means of production, distribution of goods and services, and the will and intellect of the people. This was only the prelude of worse things to come. The system failed miserably and resulted in poverty, corruption, persecution and despair for the Cuban people. The nation had been desecrated.

Operation Peter Pan: A Heartbreaking Saga

Beginning in 1961 until the Missile Crisis of October 1962, 14,000 children under sixteen years of age were sneaked out of Cuba by an underground Catholic Church organization under what was called Operation Peter Pan. The Castro regime did not seem to detect the exodus. It had not been out of the ordinary for upper- and middle-class young children to travel to the United States where for years they had been sent to civilian and military schools, or, for a short vacation, to join friends from American families who had visited Cuba or Cubans who had visited the United States.

The Peter Pan children, as they were called, were given entry visas negotiated by officials of the Catholic charities in the United States. The operation was well coordinated. Children were placed in Catholic summer camps, foster homes, private boarding schools and other religious institutions. Most of them stayed in the South Florida area, mainly in Miami. A few were sent to other states. What made the parents accept this painful separation from their children? When it became clear that Castro was converting Cuba into a Communist state, there was panic all over the island. Day by day additional steps were being taken by the regime to suffocate freedom in all of its forms. Drastic changes were taking place in the way of life previously existing in Cuba. It was alarming to observe the rapid advance of Communism. Every single day a new measure or decree was announced by the oppressive regime toward the dismantling of the free enterprise system and the elimination of individual rights. All private schools, religious and secular, were confiscated, followed by the expulsion of nuns, priests and principals from the country.

An indoctrination campaign began to take place in the schools and in newly created "infant circles." An intensive brainwashing was instituted not only at educational institutions, but also at all places of work. Children's minds were filled with distortions and hate for America. They institutionalized the teaching of Marxism-Leninism at all levels of the population and attempted to destroy all religious principles and faith. Children were taught not to trust the authority of their parents, but rather that of the state. Evidently the Communists, beginning with Castro, were afraid of the influence of parents on the spiritual and cultural formation of the next generation. This was tantamount to rejecting the beliefs and moral principles of the elders. The Communists wanted to create a "new society" based on the Marxist-Leninist materialism credo and servitude to the state. They were denying the existence of God. These were palpable circumstances which were intended to permeate the home environment and destroy the family unit. All of these teachings were totally opposite to the historically profound family ties of the Cuban society.

Under these difficult and unexpected circumstances, many parents opted to take whatever steps were necessary to save their children from such a horrific fate. Against their inner feelings of love and in desperation, they contacted Operation Peter Pan to arrange for the escape of their children from what was perceived to be a dark future. They thought that at a later, but not too distant, day they would be reunited again, either by the fall of Castro or by their own exit from Cuba.

Heartbroken parents in desperation reluctantly acquiesced to extricate their children, hopefully only temporarily. They saw them depart from their loving care to the safe haven offered by America. Rivers of tears flowed from their eyes – both parents and children – at the time of departure, and continued for many months after their torturous separation. The suffering at both ends of the ocean had no parallel with terrible moments experienced by other human beings in history. I know because I have relatives who had to go through this excruciating experience. Fortunately, many Peter Pan children had the profound and moving experience of joining their parents again in the United States. However, the months and sometimes years of separation left indelible scars on their bodies and in their minds. Many of those scars were healed by love and faith. Unfortunately, some of the children and their parents were not so lucky. Nevertheless, practically all of these children grew to become productive citizens of this great country. Many excelled as students, and later as professionals, making outstanding contributions to their communities.

Not only were the families of Operation Peter Pan separated from their loved ones, but also those who have left the island over the years have been detached from their relatives and endured the consequent suffering, longing for what in most cases has been only a vanishing hope. Another sad reality is that the overwhelming majority of families who participated in Operation Peter Pan were initially supporters of Castro. Their dream for a better Cuba was shattered in a very dramatic and painful way.

Empty Promises

When Castro descended from the mountains on January 1, 1959, and gave a six-hour speech before a welcoming multitude at the Cespedes Central Park in Santiago de Cuba, the provincial capital of Oriente, he textually said:

> Personally I have to say that I have no interest in the assumption of power nor I think of occupying it. I will only be attentive to prevent that the sacrifices of so many compatriots not be frustrated no matter what my future destiny may be.

His entire speech that day was published in the *Información* newspaper, Havana, January 5, 1959. The speech in Santiago, the first one he gave after coming down from the mountains, demonstrated the consummate liar he was. No wonder the popular joke was: "It was easy to tell when Castro was telling a lie. All he had to do was move his lips."

After he named Urrutia as provisional President and then selected the cabinet members, he was initially designated by Urrutia as Delegate to the President before the Armed Forces. At that time Urrutia had taken seriously his role as President. It was obvious from Day One that Castro vested himself with all the power of a dictator. Who was he kidding? The President and the entire cabinet were used conveniently for the purpose of giving him time to carry out his design for the conversion of Cuba into a Communist society. After he took the Prime Minister spot, he overtly began to reshape the government and later on maneuvered to occupy the Presidency, although this was simply a matter of changing titles. He was the "Supreme Leader," as he likes to be called by his subjects.

The Resignation of the Prime Minister

It is significant to note that the most dedicated supporters of the revolution were those that, at the risk of their own lives and well-being, conspired and fought against the Batista regime for ideals which were completely unrelated to the Communist conspiracy concocted by Castro. The first prominent defector was Prime Minister Dr. José Miró Cardona, a distinguished lawyer, university professor and civic leader. He promptly realized that he was occupying that position only on paper. He noticed that his tenure was only window dressing and that his good name was being used as a front. His voice, opinions and proposals based on democratic principles were being ignored. Castro was acting not only as Prime Minister but also as President. He was, in fact, directing all of the government functions from a temporary office he established at the plush Havana Hilton Hotel in the heart of metropolitan Havana. Dr. Miró Cardona resigned on January 17, 1959. Eventually he went into exile fearing for his life. It didn't take Castro too long to fill the position himself. On February 16th, a month after Miró Cardona resigned, he was installed as Prime Minister by Provisional President Urrutia, who was also a reluctant puppet of Castro, although he did not want to admit it. Urrutia honestly thought that he was going to prevail in his views for a democratic Cuba.

The Defection of the Chief of the Air Force

The next prominent defector was Commander Pedro Luis Díaz Lanz, Chief of the Air Force, who had served as Castro's personal pilot. Díaz Lanz was a popular hero of the revolution. He had, on several occasions, transported arms in small planes to Cuba from Central American countries at great risk and fought bravely with the rebel army. He had personally corroborated that Communists were indoctrinating the troops and officers in training schools. "Che" Guevara and Raúl Castro were behind the widespread indoctrination campaign within the military, including all new recruits. Díaz Lanz was enraged to see such a thing happening and he found out that Castro knew what was going on. He had mentioned it to President Urrutia and other non-Communist members of the government; however, they couldn't do anything about it. When he became suspicious that he was being followed closely, he resigned from his post and defected on June 30, 1959, to avoid his imminent detection. He left Cuba with his wife in a small boat and miraculously arrived at the South Florida coast. He was blasted by Castro as a traitor and accused of being a spy for the CIA – another victim of the Castro betrayal who happened to save his life in the nick of time.

The Resignation of President Urrutia and Its Repercussions

On July 16, 1959, provisional President Dr. Manuel Urrutia Lleó, a man of proven integrity, a conservative judge and a respected member of the opposition to Batista, resigned and promptly took refuge in the Argentina Embassy, and later, under diplomatic protection, escaped to the United States. Urrutia had shown his valor as a member of the judiciary during the trial of the Granma expedition insurgents who, under the direction of Castro, were captured after landing on the southeastern coast of Oriente Province on December 2, 1956. Castro managed to escape to the mountains along with his brother Raúl, "Che" Guevara and nine other survivors. Urrutia was one of the three-member tribunal who tried the prisoners. He was the only judge who voted in favor of absolution, supporting the defense arguments. After that he resigned from the judiciary. Concerned with the uncertain political climate and the risk of his decision at the trial, he left the country with his family and came to the United States.

Urrutia returned to Cuba following the triumph of the revolution against Batista. His vote in the Granma case was a major factor in his selection as provisional President. His resignation was prompted by his sharp criticism of the Communist influence permeating the labor unions, the military and all other government institutions. He was also concerned with the lack of action on the part of Castro to stop the infiltration, as well as the harassment of free enterprise and the press. Urrutia had made a public appeal to Castro to stop the infringement of the principles of justice, freedom and democracy, which were the bases for the revolution.

Immediately after Urrutia valiantly decried the Communist penetration, Castro took to the airwaves and crudely denounced Urrutia as a traitor of the revolution. Urrutia had presented his resignation several times before, knowing quite well that he was being used as a cover while Castro was eroding the establishment of a democratic system. The elections promised for 1961 were no longer a topic of discussion. All of the political parties had vanished except the old Communist Party. The provisional President, following protocol, presented his resignation to the Cabinet Council, which of course accepted it because it was the will of Castro. Street mobs organized by Castro and his brother Raúl immediately gathered outside the office of the President, uttering insults and accusations of treason. These were called the "acts of repudiation" which became common every time someone opposed or became critical of Castro and his policies. The mobs were organized by committees which were precursors of the later officially created "Committees for the Defense of the Revolution" (CDRs) used as a weapon of intimidation to subdue any sign of opposition to Castro. The tactics of the CDRs became standard procedure: to harass, abuse and beat dissidents of the regime.

The conservatives and moderates within the government, including those in the cabinet, did not dare to offer any defense of Urrutia. They were concerned with their own safety and future plans to exit the government services, as many of them did in the months to follow. The resignation of Urrutia was a hard blow to Castro. Afraid of negative repercussions, he immediately addressed the people with a long list of promises, including lowering house rents, the cost of electricity, gas and telephone services, an advanced economic plan to provide employment and improve the Agrarian Reform Law, expanding the recreational centers and the school system, adding new free healthcare facilities and many more government services. He was attempting to appease the concerns and uneasiness felt after Urrutia's resignation and to placate the accusations of Communist infiltration. It was his way to excite the Cuban people and gain support for his Socialist agenda. The people were beginning to see the reality of the revolution aggravated by observing the disillusionment and frustration of the top respectable revolutionary leaders. There was uncertainty in the air and Castro began to lose some of his spell over the masses. Those were critical times. Too many true revolutionaries were defecting.

Repression began to accelerate to instill fear among those in government who were discontent with the situation and ready to jump ship. It was regrettable that because of fear of retribution, including death, the revolutionaries opposed to Communism could not get together on a plan to oust Castro and take over the government. Under the circumstances there was lack of trust among them. It was uncertain who was in favor or against the existing pro-Communist trend. The same doubt prevailed among the military. Those who were openly defying the Communist infiltration were executed, others fled the country, some were imprisoned and hundreds went back to the mountains to regroup and begin to fight all over again.

After Urrutia's resignation, Castro designated a Communist, Osvaldo Dorticós Torrado, as President. His new appointee, a lawyer, had previously been a minister without portfolio, one of the planning architects of the Socialist economy and an unconditional puppet of Castro. Dorticós held the ceremonial position from 1959 to 1976. After he was dismissed, Castro vested himself with the titles of President of the State Council and of the Cabinet Council, and as such assumed the Presidency of Cuba. He was anxious to hold that title although, for all practical purposes, he had been, as dictator, the head of the state since he came into power. To keep Dorticós happy he gave him the post of President of the Central Planification Council. Later on he was named Minister of Justice. Dorticós committed suicide on June 23, 1983. He had served his master obediently. It is said that he took his life out of deception and remorse for the sorrowful role he played as a docile pet of Castro.

The execution of disgruntled rebel army officers, who at one time trusted Castro and fought bravely during the insurgency against Batista, continued without any sign of compassion or remorse on the part of the dictator.

Justice Denied

Early in 1959 forty-three Air Force pilots and mechanics of the deposed regime were accused and judged before a revolutionary tribunal for crimes they did not commit. Castro personally, in a previous meeting he had with the detainees, assured them that they would have no problem. But, as usual, he was hiding his true intentions. In the absence of evidence about their criminality, they were found not guilty by the court. This was a surprising, yet honest, verdict. People with lesser accusations had been sent to the firing squads. Commander Felix Pena had presided over the trial. Pena had been a leader of the Catholic Youth organization in Santiago de Cuba and a dedicated rebel army member with a reputation for fairness. Castro was enraged with the outcome of the trial, publicly denounced the verdict and immediately ordered that they be retried.

Castro, as we can see, had total control over the justice system. The national lawyers association and the local lawyers association of Santiago de Cuba, seat of the trial, protested the arbitrary retrial. Early in 1959 the professional associations were still acting independently of the government. In spite of the "not guilty" decision, the accused were kept incarcerated by the will of Castro. A new trial was immediately set up. This time the prosecutor and the judges were handpicked by Castro. As anticipated, the accused were found guilty and sentenced to long prison terms. The jury had paid its obedience to the master. This case represented an outrageous injustice and abuse of power. Incidentally, Commander Pena, who presided over the first trial and previously had had differences with Raúl Castro about the presence of Communists in the rebel army operating in the Sierra Maestra Mountains, was assassinated outside of the Air Force building in Havana. His death, as usual, was officially attributed to "suicide."

The Resignation and Torture of Commander Huber Matos

One particular defection which caused a lot of turmoil among the troops and the population was that of Commander Huber Matos, Chief of the Armed Forces in the cattle-rich province of Camagüey. On October 20, 1959, Commander Matos, a very popular, patriotic and brave rebel force leader, fell in disgrace. As a civilian prior to joining Castro's insurgency, he was a school teacher and chaplain of a Masonic Lodge in Santiago City, Oriente Province. Matos was leading the tranquil life of a middle-class educator in the midst of a happy family home when he altered and sacrificed his peaceful, placid environment to join the 26th of July Movement, and later the rebel army to fight for a cause he thought proper and just. He was an idealist who dreamed, like many others, of reestablishing a rightful and democratic government in Cuba. He fought courageously against the Batista forces and reached the rank of commander, the highest grade granted in the rebel forces.

Matos resigned from his post and wrote a letter to Castro regarding his concern about the turn toward Communism that the revolution was taking. He was preoccupied with the arbitrary abuse toward ranchers and farmers in the Camagüey Province on the part of some officers of the National Agrarian Reform Institute (INRA). Matos observed an increasing action against the free enterprise system and disagreed with the events taking place. He had, on previous occasions, talked to Castro about the uncomfortable situation developing in the whole nation. He made it clear that he didn't fight Batista for the purpose of eliminating freedom and private enterprise. Matos had thought that Castro wasn't totally aware of the Communist influence taking place in the name of the revolution. He reiterated that the intentions of the revolution were to establish a democratic and free society.

After reading Matos' letter of resignation, Castro became enraged and accused him of treason and conspiracy against the revolution. Castro immediately ordered Commander Camilo Cienfuegos, Chief of the Army, to arrest Matos and 34 officers of his staff who unanimously supported Matos' position. They were given a short military trial in which Castro acted as the main witness for the prosecution. He delivered a long harangue lasting several hours that was broadcast over radio and television. He called Matos a coward and a failed revolutionary, and accused him of sedition and being a traitor of the revolution. Castro defended the Communists in the rebel army and admitted that he would not oppose them or remove them from the military forces. Matos defended himself, denouncing the Communist infiltration and the destruction of the principles for which the revolution had been fought. Matos was sentenced to 20 years in prison and the other officers were given lesser prison sentences. This was a totally arbitrary and unjust act, a miscarriage of justice. All Matos did was to resign from his post in an honorable and decent way.

Throughout his prison term Matos was tortured, beaten, given meager nourishment, stripped naked at times, kept incommunicado, humiliated, denied medical treatment, put in a small cell ("stinking hole") and submitted to other abuses. He endured long hunger strikes in protest of the condition of his cell. During one hunger strike he was on the verge of dying until he was fed intravenously. Matos did it all to gain an improvement in the type of cell in which he was being kept. International human rights organizations interceded in his favor through the efforts and petitions of family members. Finally after completing his 20 years of imprisonment, he was released on October 21, 1979, into the custody of Costa Rican diplomats and flown to the United States. His survival was a miracle.

To further demonstrate Commander Huber Matos' courageous stance, I have translated into English a second letter he wrote to Castro on October 17, 1991. This letter was published by the press in several countries. I read it in a December 1991 publication of the CID (Cuban Independent and Democratic) organization, of which Matos was the Secretary General. The letter contains some of the points he expressed in the initial letter of resignation to Castro. It is a testament to the plans Castro had to convert Cuba to Communism. The inner thoughts of Castro are revealed by a heroic figure, one who fought bravely for the true ideals of the revolution. Castro's treason is documented beyond any reasonable doubt. The letter reads as follows:

Miami, October 17, 1991

Señor Fidel Castro:

Thirty-one years ago, October 19, 1959, I wrote a letter to communicate to you my resignation to the post of Chief of the military district of Camagüey Province and my total disconnection from the government presided over by you. I could not accept the treason I was seeing developing against our people and the democratic and humanistic revolution we had promised to carry forward once in power.

On previous occasions I had repeatedly expressed to you, based on evidence, my preoccupation and disagreement with steps being taken behind the back of the people toward the establishment of a Communist dictatorship. I was convinced that denaturing the Cuban revolution to entrap it in the straitjacket of the Marxist totalitarianism was immoral and catastrophic. This is why I indicated in my letter of resignation the following thoughts, among other things:

I only conceive the triumph of the revolution counting with a united people, ready to withstand the most difficult sacrifices in spite of the many foreseen economic and political adversities; that unification and combativeness of the people cannot be achieved or sustained if it is not based on a program which will equally satisfy their interests and feelings under a leadership that can capture the Cuban complexity in all of its dimensions.

I committed the error of assuming you capable of assimilating my resignation and its ethical foundation with the rational criterion which corresponds to a political leader with the valiant attitude that we, your subordinates and fellow fighters, had credited you.

Your answer to my letter was a despicable and cowardly one. You immediately ordered my arrest and isolation. You uttered upon me a mountain of insults and calumnious accusations. You did not dare to execute me because you were afraid to pay a high cost regarding the opinion of the international community. At that time your image outside of Cuba had some value. You had to be resigned to sentence me to twenty years in prison under a farcical court in which you not only selected the jury but also acted as the prosecutor and accusing witness.

I served the prison term until the last day of the 20 years of isolation. While in prison I was the subject of abuses, systematic mistreatment, beatings and torture. Only by the grace of God, the solidarity of the international community and the denunciations and appeals of my family before various human rights organizations permitted me to exit Cuba and return to liberty while still alive.

Today I write to you again, Mr. Castro. The tragedy I wanted to prevent became a heartbreaking reality that has accumulated through three decades of suffering of our people and exhibits a landscape of ruin and bad presages for the nation. You have made Cuba a totalitarian and militaristic feudal system where terror, deceit, frustration, family breakdown, hunger, false pretenses and contained rebellious sentiments prevail in the population.

After thirty-two years of your arbitrary exercise of power, your promotion of subversion and terrorism to different latitudes and the belligerent neo-colonialistic campaigns under the servitude of the Kremlin, you are a complete failure. Communism is finished in the world and eventually it will be in Cuba. It has been defeated by the people and condemned by history. Ignoring these realities, you continue to resist a transition to a civilized solution. You had your last chance during the IV Congress of the Communist Party of Cuba, but you persisted in your Stalinist continuousness. You are in fact forcing our country to find a solution through the road of violence and a blood bath. But that is not sufficient. You are predicating the sinking of Cuba into the depth of the sea, giving the impression of provoking a war with the United States, as if you were pretending to hide your failure and defeat by bringing about an apocalyptical end that only your sick egotism would desire.

Cuba belongs to the Cubans. No one has delivered to you the ownership of the island or its people, or those born there who were forced by you to go into exile. Your obstination to impose your will on the Cuban people will only result in adding to the treason and crimes you already have in your record. No matter what, sooner or later the Cuban people will sweep you away. The cards you are holding for your final act are repulsive: genocidal terror against the Cubans and the war against the United States. Enough is enough, Mr. Castro! Don't inflict any further damage on Cuba.

Commander Huber Matos B.

The Death of Commander Camilio Cienfuegos

Commander Camilo Cienfuegos, upon complying with Castro's order to arrest Matos and his followers, was courteous and friendly to Matos and treated him with respect. He even regretted that he had no choice but to carry out the mission. Cienfuegos was as popular as Castro among the rebel forces. He was a charismatic and moderate leader who was acclaimed as a hero by the population. Because of his popularity and warm personality, Castro, and particularly his brother Raúl, were somewhat envious of Camilo. Raúl considered him as a potential rival for the second spot in the hierarchy of the revolution. Castro's resentment grew as Camilo's charismatic attraction, simplicity and popular following became almost mythical. At times he exceeded Castro in the applause and admiration of the audiences, and that was difficult for Castro to swallow. Additionally, they (Castro and Raúl) had not been too happy with the way Camilo behaved when he arrested Matos. Camilo had expressed misgivings about the kangaroo court held during Matos' trial. Castro began to suspect Camilo as a possible defector. He could not afford to have a defection of that magnitude following the Matos' episode. It could have been tantamount to an explosive chain reaction in the army and the Cuban population, which in turn could have resulted in the toppling of his government. Plans started to develop very rapidly. The plot got thicker. A sequence of bizarre events, briefly summarized below, began to occur.

On October 28th, only a week after the Matos' crisis, Commander Camilo Cienfuegos mysteriously disappeared. He was seen for the last time boarding a small Cessna plane piloted by an experienced rebel air force pilot, Lieutenant Fariñas, with another companion as a passenger. On orders of Castro, Camilo was returning to Havana. No trace of the plane or its occupants was found, in spite of an intensive search by the rebel air force. Coincidentally, an armed Sea Fury English fighter plane commanded by an air force officer was seen departing from the same airport shortly after the Cessna took off. According to witnesses, an explosion of an airplane on the south coast of Cuba occurred shortly after the departure of the two planes. A series of murders, "suicides" and executions of rebel army officers, interlaced with the Camilo disappearance, occurred under puzzling circumstances. The chief of the control tower at Camagüey Airport, a witness to the departure of the two planes, was found dead a few days later, his death attributed to "suicide."

Commander Cristino Naranjo, a close friend of Camilo who was investigating his death and suspected that he was the victim of an assassination, was "accidentally" shot to death by Captain Beatón of the rebel army as he was entering the army camp Liberty City (formerly Camp Colombia) in Havana. Beatón was detained and kept at the Cabaña Fortress, also in Havana, where he had some privileges. He had been useful to Castro; nevertheless, he was considered dangerous because he knew too much. Beatón was a time bomb just waiting to go off. The Castro brothers were concerned that he could spill the beans. Fearing for his life, he escaped and took refuge in the Sierra Maestra Mountains where he joined an insurgency group. A commander of the rebel army, Pancho Tamayo, was sent to the mountains undercover to find Beatón and convince him to surrender. Beatón killed Tamayo during the course of the negotiations. Surrounded by army forces, he was captured and taken to prison in Santiago de Cuba. There he was visited by Lieutenant Agustin Onidio Rumbaut, who obtained compromising information about the death of the officers associated with Camilo's elimination. Captain Beatón was given a quick trial by a military tribunal, sentenced to death and executed before a firing squad. Lt. Rumbaut, who had extracted substantial incriminating information from Beatón about the disappearance of Camilo, was subsequently killed in what was described as a "military accident" by the Communist press.

The sequence of events occurring around the death of Commander Cienfuegos are based on several reliable sources of information, particularly the testimony given to the press by a credible witness, an ex-close associate of Castro and one of the founders of the 26th of July Movement, Dr. Juan Orta Cordova (in the Spanish language publication *Libre,* November 9, 2001, Miami, Florida). Dr. Orta was a professor, holding a doctorate degree in Education. In 1956 he served as a liaison between Castro and ex-President Dr. Carlos Prío Socarrás when the latter, after meeting with Castro in a border town between Mexico and the United States, agreed to finance the 83-man Granma boat expedition from Mexico to Cuba. That incursion signaled the beginning of the armed struggle which resulted in the toppling of the Batista regime two years later. After Castro took over the post of Prime Minister in February 1959, he designated Dr. Orta as his Chief Secretary. In that position – as a confidant of Castro – he was privy to Castro's contacts and maneuvers. Dr. Orta became displeased with the authoritarian style of Castro and the progression of Communism. He resigned in April 1961, taking asylum in the Venezuelan and Mexican Embassies, respectively, for over three years until he finally left the island in 1964.

The Rebel Insurgency Against Castro

While the execution of civilians and disaffected rebel army military personnel was taking place, the conversion to Communism was accelerating at a rapid pace. At the beginning of 1960 many ex-rebel combatants saw the treason of Castro against the democratic principles of the revolution and his support and encouragement of the Communists, who began to occupy important positions in the various government departments. They decided to return to the mountains to renew the fight once again, this time against Castro. By the mid-1960s the rebel force opposing Castro was significant and it had expanded to practically all of the provinces. The insurgency in the Escambray Mountains of the central province of Las Villas was the most numerous and effective, and they found a lot of support from the peasants and farmers of the region. However, a massive assault against the rebels was unleashed by the overwhelming military forces of the regime, well equipped with advanced weapons that Castro had acquired from the Communist bloc. The sweep was completed with success, including the displacement and relocalization of thousands of farming families whose members were accused or suspected of aiding the insurgents.

The rebels were practically annihilated. Some were captured and executed on the spot. Among the rebel leaders who were victims of the executions were ex-officers of Casto's rebel army, Commander Plinio Prieto; Captains Sinesio Walsh, Clodomiro Miranda and Porfirio Ramirez (President of the Santa Clara University Student Federation); and the labor union leader Gerado Fundora. The Castro military operation which wiped out the insurgents and affected the civilian population living in the zone was dubbed "the Cleaning of the Escambray." In spite of this episode, insurgents continued to offer resistance to the Communist repression in both rural and urban areas. The resilience of these heroic Cubans had no parallel, even knowing that their efforts were against enormous odds.

The Cruel End of del Pino, Boitel and Cubelas

Thousands of other supporters of the revolution fell victim to Castro's rage throughout his cleaning campaign to rid those who did not acquiesce with the course of events. Rafael del Pino was one of the companions of Castro during the "Bogotazo," the violent Communist-inspired rebellion in Bogota, Colombia, in 1948. He turned against Castro, and was wounded and arrested while attempting to leave Cuba in a small plane in 1959. Then he was imprisoned and tortured. While in prison del Pino fell very ill and had colostomy surgery. He was not given proper medical attention and did not fully recover. Del Pino appealed for his freedom based on his deteriorating health condition. After his request was denied, he committed suicide by hanging himself in his cell. Because del Pino knew a lot about Castro's early connection to Communism, Castro was afraid and had to eliminate him. He could not afford to let del Pino go free.

Pedro Luis Boitel was a student leader at the University of Havana and a prominent member of Castro's 26th of July Movement. He was not a docile follower of Castro, but a fervent revolutionary with democratic ideas who participated in the civil resistance against Batista. After Castro took over, Boitel aspired to be president of the University Student Federation. He was opposed by another young revolutionary who had fiercely fought in the Escambray Mountains against the Batista army, Commander Rolando Cubelas. Castro favored Cubelas as the "unity candidate." Castro put his resources behind Cubelas, who won the election in a close contest. It was important to Castro to have one of his close followers in that politically sensitive position. He wanted to have control over the important student movement.

Boitel saw the light and began to oppose the Communist infiltration. He was ordered detained by Castro and was imprisoned for activities against the revolution. After years of incarceration and several hunger strikes to protest the inhumane conditions that prevailed in jail, Boitel died. He had survived for 53 days without food and medical attention during his last strike.

Cubelas also had a disagreement with Castro and was jailed and tortured for many years. News about Cubelas' fate in prison was silenced. It was later reported that he died while in prison as a result of the harsh treatment he received. Such was the fate of two young, idealistic revolutionaries who had good intentions and hope for a democratic republic. The cruelty of Castro cannot be measured by any human standard. It transcends the limits of comprehension.

Virgilio and Tapita: A Barbaric Crime

A truly sad case of barbarism was the execution of two young University of Havana students on April 18, 1961, Virgilio Campanería and Alberto (Tapita) Tapia Ruano. The later was a nephew of a good friend of mine, Dr. Carlos Tapia Ruano, a distinguished lawyer and diplomat who left Cuba fleeing from the Castro regime. Later he and his wife America became devoted pastors of the

United Methodist Church in Chicago, while continuing to maintain their activism against Castro until their deaths. Virgilio was studying law and Tapita, Architecture. They were both good students and devoted Catholics who had put a lot of faith in the revolution against Batista.

Soon after witnessing the betrayal of the revolution by Castro and his gang, Virgilio and Tapita became disillusioned. They, like the majority of the Cuban people, had supported the revolution thinking that its purpose was the restoration of the Constitution of 1940, to establish a system of justice and protection of human rights, a democratic government and the return of the electoral process. Instead, what they were experiencing was the negation of all the promises made by Castro and the imposition of an even more tyrannical system than that of Batista.

Virgilio and Tapita were members of the Revolutionary Student Directory and began with an idealistic vision and valor to rebel against the Communist dictatorship being imposed on the population through terror and fear. They felt their obligation was to resist the negation of the values that the government was systematically destroying. They became activists and began conspiring with many other students.

One day in March 1961 they and another friend, Tomasito Fernandez Travieso, were detained by the police while in the house of a friendly neighbor, Mrs. Manola Alvarez Borbón. Tomasito was 18 years old, Tapita, 22 and Virgilio, 23. They, along with Mrs. Alvarez, were taken to the secret police headquarters in Havana. All four were accused and formally charged with having explosive devices. Then they were transferred to the infamous La Cabaña military prison and kept jailed until the day of their trial on April 17th.

The judicial process was a farce; the accusing police officer was not even present. Tapita and Virgilio were sentenced to death. Manola, the owner of the house, and the younger boy, Tomasito, were given 20 years in prison. The pleas from their families for a fair trial and to spare the lives of the two young students fell on deaf ears. The day they were sentenced coincided with the Bay of Pigs Invasion. Evidently the regime wanted to set an example to instill fear in the population.

Other executions took place that day and the days following the invasion. The young men walked to the execution wall (paredón) crying out loud, "Long live God, long live Cuba, long live the Student Directory, long live Christ the Lord!" Then the shots of the firing squad were heard. That was the brutal end of the young, heroic Cubans who died for the redemption of their beloved country. And more innocent blood stained the hands of Castro and his henchmen.

The Torture of Valladares

Another innocent victim of Castro was Armando Valladares. His horrendous ordeal is worth mentioning because, like Valladares, thousands of other Cuban political prisoners have been given similar treatment in the filthy Cuban jails. He was apprehended by Castro's dreaded secret police one night in 1960. Valladares was not a political activist, but simply a quiet, young man working as a clerk in a postal savings bank, a branch of the Ministry of Communications, and attending to his university studies. His only political sin consisted of not being a Communist. He honestly objected to accepting Marxism as his ideological model. Valladares never expected to be jailed for expressing his views in a peaceable way at a time when the regime had not made it officially known that the revolution was going to be converted into a Communist order. Little did he know that he was going to be kept in prison for a long time. In fact, soon after he was arrested at his home, Valladares told his relatives that he would be back in a short time because he had done nothing wrong. No incriminating evidence was found after they searched his residence. He was given a quick mockery of a trial and sentenced to 22 years in prison.

The incarceration of Valladares was not only a lengthy one, but it also turned out to be an extremely tormenting experience. He was brutally beaten with cables and on one occasion a guard jumped on his legs, breaking one and injuring the other. He was starved, burned, kept in a tiny cell and exposed alternately to darkness or excessive light from fluorescent bulbs. At times he was subjected to extreme cold and wetness, and other times to heat and dehydration. Rats and roaches were roaming around his cell. When he fell asleep, rats would bite him. Defecation was done through an unsanitary hole in the floor. The smell of excrement was suffocating and the repeated beatings were excruciating. He was deprived for days of essential foods and given little to eat. His captors expected that he would not endure the extreme environments to which he was exposed and the torturing techniques employed to break his will. He did not ask for mercy and he would not be conquered. That made his tormentors very angry and perturbed. Only Valladeres' sustaining faith in God, his strength of mind and his determination to endure and survive kept him alive. Even under the intense abuse he had to bear, Valladares wrote poetry during his confinement. How he did it is a testimony to his courage. He managed to have his poetry smuggled out of the prison by his wife. His poems reached Europe where intellectuals read them and fell in love with his works and style.

Valladares was elevated, and rightfully so, to a cause célèbre. Along with his poems, his undertakings and long suffering were made known among the literary and political circles in Europe. The revelations about his harrowing experience in jail caused an uproar which moved many important personalities to intercede in his favor. There was a worldwide effort to promote his release, aided by the participation of The Cuban-American National Foundation, Amnesty International and many other prestigious international organizations. French President Francois Mitterand was approached to request his release since he had learned of Valladares' poetry from the French literati. Mitterand made a personal appeal to the Cuban dictator and Valladares' release was finally consummated in 1982 after 22 years of enduring an unbelievable racking event he had miraculously outlived. It should be noted that after 22 years, Valladares had already served his term. However, as often happens, prisoners in Castro's jails can be kept captive for as long as the dictator wishes. The justice system in Cuba does not exist. Valladares was flown to the United States on a flight arranged by an international effort of his supporters. He wrote a book, *Against All Hope*, where he detailed the wrenching saga of his prolonged internment in Castro's dungeons. I wonder why there are still left-wingers and radical scholars portraying Castro as a charming, charismatic and romantic reformer, when he really is – as has been proven by history – a common, sadistic criminal and despot.

6

THE DEVELOPMENT AND EXECUTION OF CASTRO'S GAME PLAN

"From the beginning of his government he had the purpose of creating hostility toward the U.S. and embracing Communism, but we Cubans were blinded and did not realize what we had in front of us until it was too late and the damage had been done."
— DR. LÓPEZ FRESQUET

The Secret Castro-Soviet Entente and its Execution

EVERY MOVE CASTRO made toward his alliances with the Soviet Union and the plan to Communize Cuba was kept in secrecy until effective control was exerted – politically, militarily and economically – over the island. There was a reasonable "safe time" before the consortium with the Kremlin would be revealed openly. Logistically, the Soviet Union had to be prepared diplomatically and militarily for any type of anti-Castro maneuver or belligerence on the part of the United States. They would prefer to prevent any serious confrontation at an early stage. The Cuban-Soviet deliberations contemplated the readiness of the Soviets to provide crude oil to Cuba the moment the U.S. refineries in Cuba were confiscated. This was of utmost important to keep the country running without a major and disastrous disruption. The sale of sugar to the Soviets was undoubtedly discussed to fill the void of the U.S. purchases that would be discontinued after an anticipated and provoked break in relations.

It was not by a miracle that these detailed transactions and many others began to fall into place at the proper moment. During the first few months of the revolutionary government Castro tried to maintain a façade of moderation while undermining the Cuban institutions and the civil society, although he wasn't totally capable of restraining his impulses and intense hatred for the United States. He took advantage of the majority of the population which had been mesmerized by his steadfast campaign of disinformation and false patriotism. Castro had in a sense brainwashed the people and most of his close advisors.

He had intentionally lied and distorted the facts. He proved to be a well-trained demagogue and a deceptive specimen never seen in Cuban politics before. That explains why so many trusted him blindly, only to repent later when the damage to the country had been perpetrated.

While Castro was visibly turning the country to Communism, the resignations, replacements and defections, both among the civilian hierarchy and the military ranks, accelerated through the end of 1959 and beyond. It was evident that the revolution was being systematically radicalized and it was departing from its true objectives. The dissatisfaction among the moderate members of the cabinet could not be repressed. Castro was not heeding their advice to tune down the rhetoric against the United States, to maintain a free enterprise system, to encourage the establishment of a democratic government elected by the people under a multi-party system and to restore the Constitution of 1940. There was no longer talk of elections for 1961. Before the end of 1959 the following moderate cabinet members were either dismissed or resigned: Elena Mederos, Social Welfare; Commander Humberto Sorí Marín, Agriculture; Roberto Agramonte, State; Commander Luis Orlando Rodríguez, Interior; Manolo Fernández, Labor; Manuel Ray, Public Works; Faustino Pérez, Recovery of Stolen Property; Angel Fernández, Justice; Felipe Pazos, President of the National Bank; Justo Carrillo, Director of the Bank of Agricultural and Industrial Development (BANFAIC). They were all replaced by pro-Communist, unconditional supporters of Castro and/or his brother Raúl. A significant change, among others, was the appointment of Commander "Che" Guevara, a Communist, as President of the National Bank. This appointment brings to mind the classical anecdote of letting a bull loose in a china shop.

It cannot be said, like some liberals suggested, that Castro reacted against private business because they were adopting an antagonistic position against the revolution. That allegation was a totally unacceptable excuse for his actions. On the contrary, the cooperative attitude of the business and social leaders at the onset of the revolutionary government was admirable. There was a genuine desire to help the revolution in what was generally perceived as the restoration of a democratic and just society. A sincere enthusiasm and generosity prevailed as shown by the exemplary stance of the business community. They deposited a lot of confidence in the moderate provisional president and the first cabinet designated to reorganize the government functions. They were mostly persons of impeccable reputation, proven capacity and democratic ideals. Many large and medium-size enterprises paid their taxes in advance and contributed generously with large sums of money to prop up the economy. Castro, knowingly and cynically, took advantage of the largesse and goodwill of the business sector while he was developing his hidden agenda.

Not many suspected the tragic outcome that was in store for the nation. It did not take too long before the honeymoon was over. His intentions began to show only a few months after he consolidated his grip on the nation.

The defections and dissentions that followed caused Castro great concern. He started to wield his power with no restraint. By the end of 1959 there was evidence that the Socialist roadmap was in the works. It became obvious that the Castro-Soviet strategy had an early beginning, long before January 1, 1959. Castro's initial contacts with the Soviets took place through the Russian Embassy in Mexico, where the preliminary charting for the conversion of Cuba to Communism was drafted. In 1960 he promptly established relations with Moscow to conveniently expedite the specifics of the plan on Cuban soil. It all seems like a truculent scheme, but it happened.

The Implementation of the Game Plan

During the transformation phase to Communism there were several developments distinctly marking the pathway being followed to execute the game plan. Let's follow the trail.

In October 1959 the militias were officially created, beginning with the enrollment of the workers now totally controlled by the takeover of the Confederation of Cuban Workers (CTC) by the old Communist Party trade union leaders with the help of Castro. Students were also recruited into the militias at the various educational centers. The National Directory of Revolutionary Militias became an official paramilitary organization submitted to an intensive political indoctrination by the veterans of the old Communist Party and to military training by pro-Communist army officers. The main task of the militias was to instill fear in the population and principally to those opposing the regime or showing discontent with the path of the revolution. They were trained for civilian warfare, mass intimidation and as a backup for the regular army in case of emergency.

In February 1960, Anastas Mikoyan, Deputy Premier of Foreign and Domestic Commerce of the Soviet Union, arrived in Cuba and, after meetings with Castro and other officers of the government, a five-year commercial agreement between the Soviet Union and Cuba was signed. In the agreement the USSR granted Cuba $100 million of credit to purchase Soviet industrial equipment. During Mikoyan's stay in Cuba, a large demonstration was held at the Havana Central Park against his presence in Cuba. The police brutally dispersed and chased the crowds. Spearheading the demonstrations were anti-Communist students, ex-labor leaders of the 26th of July Movement forcibly displaced by old Communist unionists, and members of revolutionary, religious and civic organizations opposed to the Castro betrayal. Many were detained and beaten by the authorities. Needless to say, in his speech in Havana, Mikoyan blasted the United States, uttering, among other propaganda pretenses, that "capitalism was a failure and could not compete with the Communist system of state-planned production as evidenced in the Soviet Union." It goes without saying that history has negated his claim.

On April 26, 1960, Castro appeared before the General Assembly of the United Nations and for over four hours ferociously attacked the United States and defended the position of the Soviet Union in international affairs. He met with Khrushchev during the meeting, and they embraced and praised each other. Castro began to use his relations with the Soviets as a deterrent against any move against Cuba. Moscow began to send military and personnel to Cuba to train the Cuban armed forces.

On May 7, 1960, Cuba resumed diplomatic relations with the Soviet Union. The relations with Moscow had been broken off in April 1952 after Batista took power. The official return of Moscow's emissaries to Havana facilitated the Cuban-Soviet strategy to be followed and accelerated the Communization of Cuba. The blueprints were now discussed on an everyday basis without any communication barriers. The mechanisms and steps for transforming the free market economy into a state-controlled order were eased with the daily advice and direction of theoreticians and technocrats right on the scene. The Soviet establishment of a military base of operation and surveillance in close proximity to the U.S. had been accomplished. Shortly thereafter crude oil began to arrive in Cuba. Up until then Cuba was consuming gasoline from the three U.S. refineries in Cuba; namely, Esso, Shell and Texaco.

The United States was tolerant and unbelievably restrained to the fast unfolding of the Castro grab of U.S. investments in Cuba. The United States abstained from playing the bully in dealing with Castro and was careful to avoid criticism from the liberal news media in the U.S. and abroad. The left-wingers in the State Department were very influential in the adoption of an appeasement and non-aggressive policy toward Cuba. Meanwhile Castro was unrestricted in his attacks and vilification of the United States. He and his Communist associates were being rude and discourteous to the U.S. Ambassador.

In June 1960 the United States, seeing that there was no end to Castro's verbal and economic offensive against its interests, decided (and rightfully so) to suspend the purchase of the Cuban sugar quota. However, as already pre-arranged, the Soviets began to purchase the sugar allotted to the U.S.

On June 19, 1960, "Che" Guevara, who was President of the National Bank at the time, ordered the American refineries to process the Russian oil. The refineries refused for technical reasons connected with the quality of the oil. As a result, they were immediately seized on orders of Castro, who also cancelled a 60 million dollar debt to the companies. After that Castro, in a fiery speech, made it clear that he would confiscate *all* American property, down to the last nail in their shoes. In the same month Cuban and American-owned hotels were confiscated, including the two most luxurious hotels, the Havana Hilton and the National. The excuse given for the takeover of the hotels was that they were not doing enough to attract tourists to Cuba. Castro alleged that the "American aggression" was preventing tourists to visit the island when, in fact, his anti-American posture and the uncertain environment he had created were the reasons why people had stopped coming to Cuba. Castro did not wait to reduce the workers salaries and to fire many hotel employees to cut costs. Before the revolution this type of offense against the workers was not permitted by the labor laws.

On September 28, 1960, Castro created another group to strengthen the persecution of people discontented with his steering of the revolution called the Committees for the Defense of the Revolution (CDRs). The main task of this organization was to harass those labeled as counter-revolutionaries and dissidents and to keep track of their activities. Concurrently, the regime toughened the laws against those accused of being against the revolution. Anyone found conspiring or committing acts against the power of the state could be sentenced to death or given stiff penalties. In practice these sentences were already in place when Castro took over.

In addition to the CDRs, other similar organizations were created. For instance, the Vigilante Committees spied on neighbors suspected of anti-government persuasion on a block-to-block basis. The Rapid Response Brigades consisted of organized groups of goons who would get together at a given location within a short time to demonstrate against persons accused of treason, people attempting to leave the country because of contempt with the government line, or simply participants in non-violent acts protesting the abusive treatment given to political prisoners or relatives incarcerated in the horrible jails of Castro. These organized groups oftentimes ruthlessly beat innocent, defenseless people – men, women and children – with sticks, billy clubs, baseball bats and other artifacts. They were protected and supported by the political police during such cowardly attacks. The abused dissidents were sometimes detained and thrown into crowded, filthy jails occupied by common criminals. In addition, they were occasionally accused of counter-revolutionary activities and given prison terms. That is what is called "revolutionary justice." Human rights abuses were rampant and vicious. There was no respect for human dignity.

Between August and October of 1960 the Cuban government had promulgated five edicts confiscating all remaining privately-owned property, both Cuban and American. The appropriation without compensation included public utility services, telecommunication enterprises, banks and bank accounts, real estate, farms, livestock ranches, sugar mills, industrial plants and commercial businesses of all kinds. Private enterprise at all levels came to an end. The Socialist-Communist process was totally completed in 1961 by the confiscation of any remnant small businesses and private schools that might have been overlooked previously. The destruction of the rural and urban bourgeoisie had been accomplished.

On January 31, 1961, the United States was forced to break off relations with Cuba after Castro defiantly demanded that the U.S. reduce the diplomatic personnel at the American Embassy to eight. He charged that there were 300 officials in the Embassy and he considered that excessive. The truth was that the United States had only 75 officials, along with 200 Cuban employees. Castro also accused the U.S. of using the Embassy for counter-revolutionary activities.

His rude provocation was a retaliatory gesture for the legal claims of the United States requesting a fair compensation for the confiscation of American properties in Cuba. Needless to say, Castro never made good for the expropriation of both the American and Cuban assets. He had intentionally provoked the breaking off of relations with the United States as part of his already sworn allegiance to the USSR. It was palpable from the very early stages of the revolutionary regime that Castro avoided an amicable and mutually beneficial relationship with the United States. As a result, the U.S. was compelled to take drastic action against the attacks and intolerance of the Communist regime.

Castro's Sinister Plan Revealed

The positioning of Cuba as a satellite of the Soviet Union through the strategy concocted by Castro was so evident that you didn't even have to connect the dots before coming to that conclusion. The potent proof of this assertion is exposed by the revelations of Dr. Rufo López Fresquet, Castro's economic advisor and Minister of Finance during the first year of the revolutionary government, and in exile since 1960. Dr. López Fresquet was a well-respected name in Cuba. Before he joined the revolutionary movement he had been a writer, university professor of economics, ex-Director of the Bank of Agricultural and Industrial Development of Cuba (BANFAIC) during the government of President Carlos Prío Socarrás, and assessor to the National Association of Industrialists. He publicly declared, after going into exile, that

> it was not true that Castro had been forced to accept the Soviet Union cooperation in lieu of aid from the United States. From the beginning of his government he had the purpose of creating hostility toward the U.S. and embracing Communism, but we Cubans were blinded and did not realize what we had in front of us until it was too late and the damage had been done.

Dr. López Fresquet knew exactly what he was saying. He, jointly with Dr. Felipe Pazos (who had been designated by Castro as President of the National Bank and then fled in 1961) and then-Minister of Economy Dr. Regino Boti, accompanied Castro on his trip to the United States as economic advisors in April 1959. During that trip it became quite clear that Castro had never been planning to ally himself with the U.S. in attempting to obtain the needed financial aid to help strengthen the Cuban economy and improve the infrastructure after years of turmoil. Dr. López Fresquet held an interview in New York with the distinguished exiled Cuban journalist Dr. Guillermo Martínez Márquez and shared revealing information about Castro's intentions. Dr. Martínez Márquez was the Director of *El Pais*, one of the most widely-circulated newspapers in Cuba before it was taken over and closed by Castro. He was also President and Founder of the prestigious Inter-American Press Society (SIP).

The dialogue between these two respected personalities was published in an article by Dr. Martínez Márquez which appeared in the Spanish language newspaper *Diario de las Americas*, Miami, Florida, on June 2, 1985. Dr. López Fresquet reiterated that it was false that Castro was forced to solicit economic assistance from the Soviet Union because of the intransigence of the United States. He further said that it was also false that the U.S. had negated help to Castro's government from the very beginning. The truth is totally different. He said, "I was a witness and can testify to the facts which are completely opposite to what has been generally accepted." He added:

> When I accompanied Castro on the trip to the United States in 1959, he warned me, as we left Havana, that I should avoid discussing Cuban economic issues with the U.S. authorities, the bankers or potential investors. That is why, when I held conversations with the then-Secretary of the Treasury, Mr. Anderson, I sort of intentionally side-tracked the suggestions Mr. Anderson advanced regarding the favorable view of the United States toward economic collabora- tion with our country. In my visit with the Under-Secretary of State for Latin American Affairs, Mr. Rubottom, I also had to pretend that I did not give much attention to his specific request about how and in what form the U.S. govern- ment could assist Cuba in the solution of pressing economic issues.

The ex-Minister López Fresquet admitted that the Cubans, including himself, were blind. Otherwise, he said to Martínez Márquez, "We would have been able to see, a long time before, some of the perceptible signs of Castro's travesty." These affirmations made by a prominent ex-member of Castro's cabinet are tes- timony of the true intention of Castro in converting Cuba into a Communist state under the aegis of the Soviet Union. It also demonstrates the fabrication of the liberals and assorted Castro defenders accusing the United States of pushing Castro into the orbit of Moscow by denying aid to the revolutionary govern- ment because of its "nationalistic and reformist" platform.

Dr. López Fresquet was the brains behind the Tax Reform Law approved by the Council of Ministers in the early months of the Castro government. He ex- plained to Martínez Márquez that he had worked on this project for many years before the revolution. It was the fruit of his personal efforts finally converted into reality. Castro signed the document and Dr. López Fresquet was elated to see his pet project become law. He said he embraced Castro at that moment. He told Castro: "I can now die in peace because I think I have accomplished some- thing important on behalf of Cuba." Castro showed a light smile and replied: "Be careful because maybe by the time you finalize the reorganization of the Tax Code you may not have any taxpayers." Fresquet went on to say:

> I was so emotionally overtaken by the occasion that I didn't understand the intention behind the remarks. The Ministers laughed but I doubt they knew the real meaning of Castro's phrase. Either he was being facetious or he was insinuating what was to come in the future. Later I surmised that he was think- ing of his plan to nationalize the industry, commerce and all private property.

In a country where the state owns all the businesses and means of production, a direct tax over the capital becomes irrelevant. The law I wrote would become useless and inapplicable under a system of state ownership of all the economic resources of the country.

The hoodwinking of brilliant people like López Fresquet, who admitted that he trusted Castro blindly, is a typical case of what happened to many other Cuban intellectuals, top professionals and heroic rebel leaders who were cynically used by Castro until they woke up to the crude perception of what the hypocritical liar was concocting for the country.

The defection of important revolutionary leaders continued as Castro removed his veil of deception. In early 1960, Commander Dr. Raúl Chibás, General Director of the Cuban Railway system and brother of the populist deceased leader Eduardo Chibás, resigned and fled Cuba in an outboard motor boat, reaching the coast of Florida. Chibás had been a prominent and well-known member of the 26th of July Movement and one of the three signatories of the Manifesto of the Sierra Maestra, issued on July 12, 1957, along with Fidel Castro and the prestigious democratic leader Dr. Felipe Pazos. In the Manifesto, issued as a declaration of principles of the revolution, it was made known that, among other things, the revolution was going to restore the Constitution of 1940, call for elections within a year after victory, establish absolute freedom of information and reestablish a truly democratic government. The document was issued to gain general support from all segments of the population and to counter any doubts about the Communist trend cast upon the rebels by the Batista regime. The Manifesto was published in its entirety in the popular *Bohemia* magazine, an anti-Batista publication which survived in spite of its editorial opposition stand. The Manifesto was not suppressed by Batista.

Tribulations of Commander Artime and Other Prisoners of the Bay of Pigs Invasion

Another distinguished popular rebel leader, Commander Manuel Artime, who occupied a high post in the Bank of Agriculture and Industrial Development (BANFAIC), resigned and fled Cuba in November 1959. He became an active participant in the anti-Castro movement and was one of the leaders of the heroic Brigade 2506 during the Bay of Pigs Invasion in April 1961. I happened to meet Artime on one of my business trips to Nicaragua in the 1970s. He related to me passages of the revolution before and after Castro took power. Airtime was a dedicated patriot and an anti-Communist fighter. He was a prisoner in Castro's jails for 18 months after he was captured at the end of the failed invasion. He was brutally tortured and given perhaps the harshest treatment among all of the hundreds of captive fighters.

To visualize the abuses that Airtime suffered, let me describe the methods used by Castro's subordinates during the interrogation of prisoners. The higher the rank of the prisoner, the more brutal was the abuse. They were severely beaten, kicked while laying on the floor, kept without sleep for days by means of noise, menaced with getting shot by a pistol muzzle held against the temple or in the mouth, deprived of food, subjected to bright lights aimed at their faces, submitted to degrading and abusive insults not worthy of being printed in this book, strapped to chairs and doused with cold water as they were about to lose consciousness, and other sub-human tactics. The tormentors were to get a signed confession from their victims, including a denunciation of the United States. They were labeled as cowards and mercenaries. These brave men decided to die with honor rather than bend to the desecrating treatment received from their captors.

The Shameful Extortion

In March 1962, after about a year in confinement, the Bay of Pigs prisoners were tried as war criminals by a spurious tribunal arranged by Castro. They rejected a defense counsel appointed by the fake court. When the farce was over, they were all condemned to death. Meanwhile, Castro, knowing that the United States was planning to negotiate an exchange through intermediaries, began to devise an extortion of major proportions. He had decided that it would not be to his advantage to execute the prisoners. Internationally such mass killing would provoke a scandal that could seriously hurt his already-discredited regime. On the other hand, he surmised that he could get a substantial ransom for their freedom. Castro decided to commute the death sentences and gave them each a 30-year prison term instead. Immediately he began to transact a settlement for the exchange of the prisoners. Emissaries from the United States, backed by the Kennedy Administration and acting as representatives of the Cuban Families Committee organized by Cuban exiles, began contacts with Castro's representatives to officially negotiate the transaction.

After many months of intense discussions and proposals at both ends, a final agreement was reached on December 19, 1962. The 1,000 prisoners began to arrive in Florida on December 23rd and by Christmas Eve they had all landed, Commander Manuel Artime included. The Red Cross was designated to act as a liaison for the operation. The total value of the prisoners exchange amounted to over $60 million worth of medical supplies, food and cash. Castro made out like a bandit. Indeed, he showed the world what he really is and the United States had to swallow a bitter pill for an invasion that was ill-prepared and not given the backup support it needed for success.

The members of Brigade 2506 were the true, valiant heroes of the whole episode. God bless them! Pathetically, my friend Commander Artime died in exile at a relatively young age, his health affected by the beatings and miserable conditions under which he was kept while a captive of the callous despot.

More Victims of Castro's Reprisals

In March 1961 Commander Humberto Sorí Marín, ex-Minister of Agriculture in the first revolutionary cabinet who had resigned and escaped from Cuba in 1959, returned to Cuba on a conspiracy mission. He had been the architect of the first Agrarian Reform Law, which was promptly replaced with a far more radical law drafted by Communist militants under Castro's directives. The new law resulted in the truncation of private ownership of all farmland, regardless of size. In the years to follow the prosperous Cuban agriculture was mismanaged and ruined. The end result was poverty and slavery for the farm workers.

Sorí Marín was opposed to the Communist course of Castro and his cohorts. He was one of the courageous revolutionaries who, at the risk of his life, began to conspire while still within the government. After he disembarked on the Cuban coast, he went to a house in the Miramar suburb of Havana and met secretly with a group of other underground plotters. A whistleblower had called the secret police to give the location of the meeting place. Castro's intelligence unit raided the house, shots were fired and Sorí Marín was wounded and captured, along with a group of other leaders of the underground on March 18th.

Among the conspirators caught during the raid was Rogelio Rodríguez Corzo, a young agronomical engineer, ex-supporter of the revolution and a key underground activist. I had known Rodríguez Corzo when he was a freshman at the University of Havana. He was a model student with a promising professional future. Sorí Marín, Rodríguez Corzo and the other co-conspirators were summarily executed in April 1961. Castro had promised the mother of Sorí Marín that the life of her son was going to be spared. It was nothing but an empty promise. Castro had never learned the meaning of the word "mercy." Also executed in 1961, shortly before the Bay of Pigs Invasion, were Commanders William Morgan – an American – and José Cabrera. Both had defected from the revolutionary army and joined the insurgency against Castro.

In March 1961 Castro publicly announced to the world that he was a Marxist-Leninist and would continue to be one until the day he died. He admitted that, while he was in the mountains, he had concealed his true ideology to keep the support of his non-Communist followers. In March 1962 Herbert L. Matthews, the *New York Times* journalist who made Castro famous and defended him at every opportunity and before many forums, finally repented of his blind defense of Castro and criticized the role of Castro on the side of the Sino-Soviet block and his rabid anti-American stand. It was a pity that Matthew's liberalism had negated Castro's cynical and destructive role in the dismantling of a beautiful country and its rich culture.

Mass Detentions, Inhumane Treatment and a Bloody End to the Insurgency

Adding to the misery of the aborted Bay of Pigs Invasion was the massive roundup of over one hundred thousand people, which took place prior to and during the disembarkment of the Cuban patriots on April 17, 1961, at Cochinos Bay (the Bay of Pigs) and Girón Beach on the coast of Zapata Swamps. Castro had an inkling that the invasion was forthcoming, which was reinforced by the sporadic and incomplete bombardment of his air force planes by anti-Castro Cuban pilots on April 15th. The attack did not attain the expected result of impairing the bulk of his fighter planes. The Castro police coordinated a blitz, rounding up and detaining thousands of people across the island suspected of being opposed to the regime. The names of the victims were supplied by the Vigilante Committees who were deployed by the government at the neighborhood level. Among the detainees were many leaders of the underground movement, as well as innocent people from all walks of life: professionals, workers, farmers, students, businessmen, journalists and teachers – the whole spectrum of Cuban society. Because most of the jails were already too crowded, they were hoarded into baseball stadiums, gymnasiums, schools, theaters and other public locations. These places were converted into jails and concentration camps.

Abuses, physical and mental, of the detainees were indescribable. They were treated like beasts. A good number of the most suspicious and well-known dissidents were executed without trial. The places of internment were so cramped that they became inhospitable and unhygienic. Many sick people were incarcerated without access to their medications for diabetes, heart conditions and other infirmities. Others got sick while imprisoned and lacked the necessary medical care. Excrement flooded the toilets available at the detention places. The stench was unbearable as the containment was prolonged for several days. They slept on hard floors or the ground, depending on the site. Water, barely available in the stadiums, was provided through a single hose. All prisoners had to stand in line to get access to the water. Food was scarce or not dispensed at all. Many, particularly the elderly, died of starvation or disease. It was hell. Panic and consternation gripped the island once more. Castro's sadistic purpose was accomplished: to instill fear against any attempt to derail his brutal dictatorship.

The spectacle created by the mass detention was deplorable and totally inhumane. There are no words to describe the scenes of misery and despair that people suffered during the days they were confined. The anti-Castro movement inside of Cuba had been dealt a mortal blow. It was the beginning of the end of any serious conspiracy against the Communist regime. From that point on there was discouragement about joining any organized activity to fight Communism. Nevertheless, brave ex-rebel revolutionary leaders continued to fight during the mid-1960s, mostly from the Escambray mountain range of central southern

Cuba and other mountainous regions of the country until they were practically exterminated by the well-armed and well-equipped military forces of Castro.

By 1966 the active armed struggle of insurgents was non-existent. Over 4,000 guerilla fighters died in the valorous effort. Many farmers had joined the insurgency after they lost their lands as a result of the so-called "Agrarian Reform Law." The anti-Castro forces were depleted of weapons and ammunition and found that it was extremely difficult to obtain support from outside of the island. Thousands were caught and executed on the spot. In some cases their bodies were grotesquely exhibited in public places in the small towns near the foot of the mountains to deter people from joining the rebels. The decimation of the anti-Communist insurgency brought a bloody end and a bitter disappointment to the cause of freedom. Nonetheless, the yearning for liberty and justice has remained lurking in the animus of the Cuban people, as evidenced by the stalwart activity of the opposition movement.

I would be remiss to not mention the thousands of courageous women who have also been detained and convicted for political activities against the Communist regime. They have been subjected to the same nefarious treatment as the men in Castro's jails. The prisons for women are as infamous and the methods utilized are no different than those applied to the men; namely, solitary confinement, unsanitary conditions, lack of food, deficient medical and dental attention, physical and mental torture, extreme noise and loud broadcasts of Communist hymns and slogans, beatings, passing through a gauntlet while being verbally abused and stripped of their clothing. It is appalling to hear the accounts of their tribulation. In Communist Cuba there are no exceptions when it comes to punish the patriotic anti-Communist dissidents whose only crime is clamoring for freedom and the right to a decent living.

(Top photo) A typical daily execution squad firing their rifles at individuals who were accused of being anti-Castro and sentenced to death by kangaroo courts. January 1959. (Bottom photo) A prisoner is given his last rites by a priest before his execution. Note the corpses of other prisoners already executed en masse. January 1959.

(Top photo) Castro during a long harangue, his face full of ire, frenetically gesturing in a manner similar to Hitler and spewing hatred toward the United States. January 1959. (Bottom photo) The Prime Minister of the Revolutionary Cabinet, Dr. Miró Cardona, accepting his designation. He is surrounded by Monsignor Alfredo Muller and functionaries of the department. January 1959.

(Top photo) Designated President Dr. Urrutia at the Presidential Palace speaking before a group of Cabinet members, rebel army officers and other invited guests. January 1959. (Bottom photo) President Urrutia embracing the President of the University of Havana, Dr. Clemente Inclán, at a University event to welcome the new regime. January 1959.

(Top photo) The first meeting of the Revolutionary Cabinet presided by President Urrutia, in January 1959. By the end of the year the President and most of the ministers shown in this photo had resigned and left the country to save their lives. (Bottom photo) In a gesture of support for the revolution, Cuban and American industrialists are shown paying their taxes in advance, with the Minister of Finance receiving checks for nearly $1 million. All of those in the picture left Cuba during the early stages of the conversion to Communism, their enthusiasm dampened by the treason of Castro.

(Top photo) The Minister of Finance, Dr. Rufo López Fresquet, at his inauguration ceremony, flanked by a Catholic priest and sugar industrialist Julio Lobo. Other friends and revolutionary leaders are also shown in the picture. They were all victims of the Castro Communist regime. January 1959. (Bottom photo) Commander Huber Matos (right), a hero of the revolution, and Castro as the latter entered the Camagüey Province en route to Havana on January 1, 1959. It didn't take very long for Matos to resign after discovering the treason of Castro. Matos served 20 years in prison under constant torture and abuse.

(Top photo) Castro visiting with Vice President Richard Nixon during his trip to Washington, D.C., while still disguising his dislike for the United States. April 1959. (Bottom photo) Castro pretending to be friendly at the time of his U.S. visit, meeting with New Jersey Governor Robert Mayner and ex-Secretary of State Dean Acheson. Castro ignored all offers of economic assistance from the United States.

(Top photo) Castro greeting the Ambassador of the Soviet Union, Mikhail Menshikov, during a reception he hosted at the Cuban Embassy in Washington, D.C. At the center is Dr. Ernesto Dihigo, the Cuban Ambassador. Long before this photo was taken, the secret agreement between Castro and the Soviet Union had been hatched. April 1959. (Bottom photo) Castro talking to famous Cuban big league pitcher Camilo Pascual during his visit to Washington, D.C. Castro banned professional baseball in Cuba. Camilo never returned to the island. April 1959.

7

CASTRO'S EXPORT OF TERRORISM. DEBUNKING THE MYTH OF YANKEE IMPERIALISM.

"Contrary to Castro's litany of accusations and allegations of imperialism against the United States, the relations between the U.S. and Cuba before the revolution were always conducted in an atmosphere of mutual respect and were equally beneficial to both countries."

Castro's Terrorist Activities as a Soviet Puppet

MY EXPERIENCE WITH the early phases of the Castro scheme to convert Cuba into a Soviet satellite was very disturbing. It became apparent that the Cuban people were going to pay dearly for the trust they had placed in him. He also represented a threat to the United States as it was proven later, particularly during the Missile Crisis of 1962, which brought us close to Armageddon. Castro proved during the course of this crisis, which provoked a dramatic U.S. confrontation with the Soviet Union, that he had no compunction about using nuclear weapons against the United States. His hatred for America was beyond any comprehension. The crisis ended with the retreat of the Soviet Union and the removal of the missiles they had installed in Cuba. However, the settlement reached by President John F. Kennedy and Nikita Khrushchev proved in the long run to be tragic for Cuba, as will be explained later in this chapter.

Not content with the subjugation of Cuba, Castro began exporting revolution to other countries, acting as a pawn for the Soviet Union. His perverse hand was extended to the Central American and Caribbean countries of Nicaragua, Salvador, Guatemala, Panama, Honduras, the Dominican Republic and Grenada, and the South American countries of Colombia, Peru and Bolivia. In all of these countries he promoted and backed Communist movements and insurgencies. His aggression and participation in international terrorism not only affected the Americas, but also went as far as Africa and Asia. During the mid-1960s through the 1980s he sent expeditionary forces, acting as Soviet proxies, to fight in the African countries of Angola, Somalia, Ethiopia, Sudan, Congo, Zaire and Mozambique. In the Asian continent Castro's military units not only trained, but also participated in combat jointly with, South Yemenite Communist guerrilla groups in the fight against the neighboring country of Oman in the southwest corner of the Arabian Peninsula bordering on the north with Saudi Arabia. The Cuban military contingent in South Yemen organized the militias under the command of Cuban officers, which also structured the "Committees for the Defense of the Revolution," mimicking the equivalent Cuban committees.

These bizarre, belligerent incursions gave Castro an opportunity to grandstand his bravado and satisfy his limitless ego. He eagerly wanted to project his image as a world-renowned figure. Moreover, he was showing his servile gratitude for the financial aid – to the tune of six billion dollars annually – he was receiving from Moscow to keep the island afloat. Over 40,000 young Cuban troops were deployed to the various African and Asian countries to support the territorial ambitions of the Soviets. Thousands of Cuban soldiers lost their lives during the African campaign alone in a vain struggle that had nothing to do whatsoever with the well-being of the Cuban people, let alone the promised purpose of the revolution.

These warring actions in obedience to the Kremlin masters contrast starkly with the fact that in the entire history of the Cuban republic era from 1902 to 1958 not a single Cuban soldier had been sent to fight on foreign soil. In retrospect, it is important to remember that, in spite of Cuba's historical, close, friendly relations and strong economic ties with the United States before Castro's advent to power, the American government never asked, or even suggested, that Cuban military personnel join with their American counterparts in the wars against the enemies of democracy, such as Nazists, Fascists and Communists. Nevertheless, many Cubans fought in those wars as part of the U.S. forces, either as volunteers or to fulfill their patriotic obligation as residents of this nation. What a difference between a democratic nation like the United States and a Communist dictatorship like the now-extinct USSR. The United States always respected the sovereignty of Cuba.

Castro allied himself with other terrorist groups around the world, such as the militant separatist Basque terrorist organization ETA (an acronym for Basqueland Freedom), which for nearly four decades has been attempting to convert the autonomous Bascay region of Spain into an independent country. This organization has committed horrible acts of terrorism in which innocent people have died or been seriously wounded. Castro has steadfastly supported the radical and fanatical pro-independence movement in the Commonwealth of Puerto Rico, with the purpose of inflaming anti-American disturbances in that country as well as in the United States.

It is pertinent to mention that Puerto Rico, through free elections, has decided to maintain the status of the country as a Free Associated State of the United States. People born in Puerto Rico are considered U.S. citizens with all privileges and rights granted by the laws. I have seen with great concern how Cuba under Castro has become a military and ideological training ground, as well as a supplier of weapons and personnel to pro-Communist movements and terrorists all over the world. This in itself speaks volumes about the perversity of this delusional tyrant.

In summary, over the years Castro has maintained in excess of 50,000 troops in 16 different countries spread over four continents. While he spent human resources, war materials and money on foreign struggles, the Cuban people suffered misery and deprivation. During the course of his regime he has continued to display his psychopathic syndrome in many ways and forms. Castro militarized the Cuban society and converted the country into a bellicose bully at the disposal of the Soviet Union. It is estimated – as of the writing of this book – that he maintains a military and paramilitary apparatus of about 300,000 members, by far the largest in Latin America. The cost of such gargantuan forces reaches over two billion dollars annually. The militarism in Cuba was not only used outside of the island boundaries, but also internally as a formidable repressive force to maintain a grip on the enslaved citizenry. To my amazement I have been asked by some, "If things are so bad in Cuba, why has Castro been in power for so long?" People asking that question had to be one of three things: living on the moon for the last 48 years, politically illiterates, or blithering leftist idiots. The question that may come to the mind of many is: "Why did the Soviet Union spend such an enormous amount of money and military resources to maintain a puppet government in a small country like Cuba?" The answer is easy if we analyze the ambitions the Kremlin had to expand Communism and dominate the world.

Soviet Military Base in Cuba and the Missile Crisis

For years the Soviet Union had been dreaming to have a center of surveillance and aggression in close proximity to the United States, the most powerful country in the Western Hemisphere. Cuba was prized real estate for that purpose. Through planning and plotting they finally found a sanctuary in the Caribbean. Cuba was the ideal logistical location. They used it as a base of espionage and as a military base of operations.

After the aborted Bay of Pigs Invasion of April 1961, the Soviets were emboldened by the perceived weakness of Kennedy in not backing the invasion by a contingent of brave Cuban exiles, as was originally planned. They accelerated the build-up of their military capability in Cuba to discourage future operations of that nature by anti-Communist fighters and did not waste any time in installing advanced electronic surveillance equipment in several locations on the island to spy on the U.S. military installations and their maneuvers. To compliment that aim they also used long-range naval reconnaissance aircraft from their bases in Cuba. They delivered 240 MiG fighter planes which could be used as bombers with a nuclear capability. They built a base for nuclear submarines at the city of Cienfuegos on the central-southern coast of Cuba, where they kept and repaired nuclear submarines. The Soviets had delivered to Cuba 42 intermediate range ballistic missiles with nuclear warheads. These offensive weapons were detected and photographed by U.S. reconnaissance planes on the western part of Cuba. The Soviets had gone too far in using their bastion in Cuba as an offensive base to intimidate the United States.

As a result of the U.S. findings, the Missile Crisis erupted in October 1962. A serious confrontation occurred between the United States and the Kremlin. The whole world was shaken about a possible nuclear conflict between the two countries. Eventually, the missiles were removed during the U.S. naval blockade of Cuba after the Kennedy-Khrushchev accord. Under this agreement the United States committed to prevent Cuban patriots from preparing and conducting another military attack against the Soviet bastion established on the island.

During the U.S. and Soviet deliberations, Castro, as a puppet, was totally ignored, although he was encouraging a nuclear attack against the United States. The Kennedy-Khrushchev accord delivered a severe blow to the anti-Castro forces inside and outside of Cuba. The "no invasion" pledge given to Khrushchev was viewed as a Kennedy weakness and not as the victory that the liberal media claimed. At that time the United States had an immense military and logistical superiority over the Soviets. Kennedy made other concessions to Khrushchev in return for the removal of the missiles. It was considered unnecessary to betray the Cuban aspirations to liberate the country from the scourge of Communism. The liberals on the Kennedy advisory team overwhelmed the few conservatives in the group who were in favor of stronger action to remove the offensive missiles. They were frightened by the boasting, bragging and nuclear blackmailing tactics used by Khrushchev, which was very typical, of course, of the Communist modus operandi. Cuba had been abandoned to Communism and its fate had been sealed. As he did after the failure of the Bay of Pigs Invasion, Castro took advantage of the momentum created by the circumstances to conduct a brutal and bloody follow-up military action against any suspected civilian or military opposition to his government.

In spite of the agreements which ended the Missile Crisis, thousands of tons of Soviet military equipment kept arriving to the island. Underground locations were used to store sensitive materials. The Soviets significantly increased the troops and logistic personnel stationed in Cuba. The peak of the buildup occurred during the 1970s and 1980s. Soviet personnel in Cuba reached over 7,000 civilian advisors, a combat unit of 8,000 soldiers, 2,000 military advisors and about 2,100 technicians. Cuban exiles I have spoken with told me that the Soviets were arrogant and despotic, acting as if they owned Cuba, which in fact they did. According to the "Brezhnev Doctrine," the military aid to Cuba was guided by the necessity to prevent a menace to the Socialist system and a reversal to a capitalistic society, and was applicable to all countries allied to the Soviet Union. The "Brezhnev Doctrine" was clearly an instrument created by the Soviets to apply the Communist neo-colonialism in Europe, Asia, Africa and Latin America.

The blatant intervention of the Soviets in Cuba was a violation of the Organization of American States Charter, the Rio Treaty, the Monroe Doctrine and the Tlatelolco Treaty (the Treaty for the Prohibition of Nuclear Weapons in Latin America), all of which were in force within the Inter-American system. The Kremlin made a mockery of all of these treaties. Of course, they have been known for their total disregard to abide by international treaties, particularly those signed by capitalistic nations.

Cuba-United States Relations Before Castro

Contrary to Castro's litany of accusations and allegations of imperialism against the United States, the relations between the U.S. and Cuba before the revolution were always conducted in an atmosphere of mutual respect and were equally beneficial to both countries. The U.S. acted with much tact when internal political crises flared up in Cuba. On one occasion in 1906 – at the request of the Cuban President – the United States intervened to restore order and reestablish the constitutional process. This intervention was of short duration, and the United States did not have any intention of taking over the island. The political parties in contention agreed to return to the electoral process and a new president was elected.

In 1933, after the Machado dictatorship was toppled by a combined effort of the opposition parties, the students and the military, the U.S. Ambassador acted as a mediator to find an amicable solution to the crisis. The young republic eventually solved its political entanglement after a short span of disputes and entente. The republic was saved without U.S. intervention. During this crisis a rising army sergeant, Fulgencio Batista y Zaldivar, who led the revolt within the army, surged ahead as an influential leader. He was later promoted to Colonel, then Chief of the Army, and years later to General. He emerged as Cuba's strongman and held a decisive function in the island's affairs for many years.

With the passage of time there appeared to be a gradual change in the political temperament of the Cubans as maturity, education and tolerance began to take hold during the course of democratic growth from 1934 to 1952. It is important to mention that in 1940 a model and advanced Constitution was enacted by a Constitutional Assembly, consisting of popularly elected delegates from all political parties. Constitutional elections were held in November 1939 with the full support of General Batista, who was then the Chief of the Armed Forces and had wielded tremendous power and influence over the political life in Cuba since 1933. In July 1940 Batista was elected president by popular vote and the

Constitution was subsequently approved and ratified by the Constitutional Assembly. It should be noted that the two successive presiding delegates of the Assembly, Dr. Ramón Grau San Martín and Dr. Carlos Márquez Sterling, were political opponents of Batista. The Constitution of 1940, as it was called from then on, was born out of a truly democratic process.

A setback to the normal political course occurred when Batista forcibly took the reigns of government in 1952, disrupting the constitutional succession of power. Batista had undone what he had so enthusiastically supported. Some of the provisions of the Constitution were temporarily suspended. Political instability returned to Cuba after years of significant progress.

A subsequent and more fatal setback befell the country at the beginning of 1959 when the Communist conspiracy betrayed a revolution initially supported by moderates, conservatives and well-intentioned members of the Cuban society at large. The aftereffect of this revolution was an unanticipated turn of events which catapulted the country into a tyrannical Communist dictatorship and drastically ended the republican era. Castro had betrayed the Cuban people. The rape of a nation had begun. Physical and mental slavery replaced the civic society.

The role the United States played in attempting to safeguard the republic of Cuba has been grossly distorted by Communists and leftists, and maliciously labeled as acts of interventionism and imperialism. The truth is that the U.S. was magnanimous and invested heavily in developing the resources that made Cuba a very prosperous and advanced country. The unrest that erupted in Cuba a few times during its maturation and growth was, for the most part, the result of its idiosyncrasy and political temperament. The United States on various occasions acted somewhat as a referee to assure the republic of Cuba kept its course within the framework of a civilized and democratic society.

Great strides were made in spite of the internal squabbles manifested throughout the republican era. Our Cuban political heritage was perhaps inherited from our European-Spanish roots. We should have no one to blame for our own vices and shortcomings. It was purely an ingrained characteristic of our political DNA and even perhaps, to bypass the metaphor, of our biological DNA which had strands of intolerance. Our political behavior was not the fault of our more balanced and mature cousins to the North. Although they also had their own difficult moments during their formative years, progressively they found the solutions to their queries without interrupting the solid foundation of their political system. On the contrary, after every obstacle they came back stronger and more determined.

Cuba had the blessing of its proximity to the United States, a nation always ready to lend a helping hand, no matter what the circumstances. The close ties which existed between the U.S. and Cuba and the benefits of it can be exemplified by the events leading up to World War II. To understand the total picture of today's Cuban tragedy I have to include, out of necessity, interrelated subjects depicting historical events considered important to the analysis and rationalization of the facts. My objective is to debunk the fallacies of Castro, including the deceptive accusations and diatribes he has repeatedly uttered against the United States. Many of Castro's close associates, who broke with him when they discovered his true intentions, have also been victims of the same technique. Castro was so bent on discrediting the U.S. that he played his role as a pawn of the USSR to the hilt. He had been preparing for this task from his prior training by Communist mentors. Castro knew how to skillfully apply the Stalinist-Leninist style of attack and spread disinformation about his adversaries.

Mutual Cooperation of the United States and Cuba

On December 7, 1941, Japanese planes launched a surprise attack against the United States Naval Base at Pearl Harbor, Hawaii, home of the U.S. Pacific fleet. This prompted the U.S. to immediately enter into the war against the Germany-Italy-Japan Axis. The Japanese bombardment destroyed or severely damaged the bulk of the aircraft, ships and structures on the base, thus crippling the U.S. naval power in the Pacific. The American casualties included 3,400 dead or missing and over 1,300 wounded. The attack caused a sweeping U.S. public opinion condemnation of the Japanese behavior. President Franklin Delano Roosevelt summarized his speech to the nation on December 7th as "a day which will live in infamy." At the end of the war the United States proved one more time, with the reconstruction of Japan, how forgiving and noble this nation is.

Cuba, in a gesture of solidarity, decisively supported the United States and cooperated in many ways to aid the war effort. Batista was the duly elected President of Cuba and at his request, two days after the attack on Pearl Harbor, the Cuban Congress voted unanimously to join the U.S. in the conflict against the Axis nations. The mutually beneficial relationship between Cuba and the U.S. was patently demonstrated throughout the course of history. Cuba helped the war endeavors through various specific actions. For instance, immediately after the declaration of war, Cuba sold the sugar stockpile to the United States at a lower price than the prevailing open world market value. In later years the U.S. would pay higher-than-world prices for the Cuban sugar. Cuban officials rounded up hundreds of Germans, Italians and Japanese that were suspected of using the island for spying or sabotage activities and confined them to secured detention centers.

Furthermore, Cuba helped during those trying times by facilitating the construction of the large San Antonio de los Baños Air Base near Havana from which the United States would conduct training exercises to prepare for operations in the Pacific and other regions. Existing military airports were expanded and new ones were constructed so that U.S. bombers could use them for their tactical maneuvers. They also served as a base of attack against German submarines which were operating near the coast of Cuba and sinking merchant vessels in those maritime areas.

A plant to extract nickel was also built in a remote jungle of Eastern Cuba by the United States. Cuba granted tax exemptions to the U.S. government and lifted labor law restrictions to facilitate the development of war-related projects. Workers and the general population welcomed the opportunity for the thousands of jobs created by these significant undertakings. These moves proved to be of benefit to Cuba. The economy improved beyond what was expected, in spite of the initial loss of tax revenues due to the exemptions provided to the United States. The transactions became a win-win situation. In addition, it helped to advance the country industrially and technologically. Many small businesses were created by Cuban entrepreneurs in the villages around the facilities built as a result of the combined agreements between the U.S. and Cuba. For instance, restaurants, theaters, clothing and appliance shops, pharmacies, shoe repair shops, barbershops, grocery stores (bodegas) and many other types of establishments emerged.

Cubans were hard-working people, never missing an opportunity to apply their creativity and innate entrepreneurial drive. This was amply demonstrated when they arrived in South Florida after fleeing from Communism. They transformed Miami from a slow-growth city into what it is today, a dynamic and fast-growing international business hub. It has been amazing to observe the Cuban exiles rapidly ascend from humble beginnings, working initially in menial jobs to sustain themselves, to promptly getting to engage in their careers, professions and other endeavors. This opened the door to other Cuban immigrants who continued coming to our shores. Some opened shops, restaurants, construction companies and gas stations. Others became real estate tycoons, financiers and bankers. Still others got involved in the communications industry: radio, TV, cable and the printed press. Many became administrators and executives of large corporations. They participated actively in politics, getting elected to municipal, county, state and congressional posts. By their activities and integration into the American life, they gave South Florida the impetus necessary for investments, tourism and growth, creating opportunities for all. In their search for success, many Cubans moved to other states where they settled and expanded their professions and trades.

The U.S. Contribution to the Economic Growth of Cuba

While there are many more illustrations of the significant contributions the United States made to the economic development of Cuba, allow me to mention two others. The United Fruit Company helped enormously in the industrialization and agricultural progress of Cuba. Its principal office was in Boston, Massachusetts. The company established a passenger and freight steamship service connecting New York, New Orleans and Havana. It had a vision for the nascent republic and, conversely, Cuba needed assistance for growth and investment to develop its untapped resources, create jobs, originate income and advance the agricultural and industrial potential of the island.

From the early stages of the republic the company initiated a development program establishing two large sugar mills on Nipe Bay in the Oriente Province. The land bought by the company was in the wilderness. It proceeded to pump water resources from the springs and wells at the base of the adjacent mountains and piped the water to the mills and the small towns or villages (bateyes) formed around the sugar mills populated by the mill employees (workers and administrative personnel). Nearly 300,000 acres were cleared of tall grass and wild shrubbery and transformed into productive cane sugar lands and fields for cattle breeding. By 1935 the company had grown to a value of close to $40 million. Approximately 40,000 people were living out of the income derived from the two mills and related activities. It was reported that the annual payroll amounted to $10 million and kept growing.

The company developed many facilities within the two cities in proximity to the two mills, Preston and Banes, including water and electrical services, housing, schools, dairies, and two top-rated hospitals with competent medical and nursing staffs. Many stores sprouted in the area which brought thousands of workers to the mills. The company established an educational program to stimulate the planting of vegetable gardens. It even distributed seeds, helped with plowing and provided technical advice at no charge. To improve safety, health and nutrition, pasteurized milk from their own dairy plant was made available at low cost to their workers. Employees were treated with respect and management complied with the demands of the labor laws existing at that time. The company reinvested heavily in agricultural research, cultivation techniques and other productive activities. By 1934 the Preston mill sugar production was the highest of all sugar mills in the world. Thousands of Cuban employees were hired by the United Fruit Company, including technical and administrative personnel, while the American employees were only a handful.

Information describing the benefits brought to Cuba by the investments of the United Fruit Company was based partly on my trip to the Oriente Province in the early 1950s and, to a larger extent, on the narrative given by Dr. Mario Lazo in his brilliant book *Dagger in the Heart: American Policy Failures in Cuba*. Dr. Lazo, an eminent corporate lawyer, was the founder of a prestigious law firm in Havana, Lazo and Cubas. He had law degrees from Cornell University and the University of Havana, and he served as a captain in the U.S. Army during World War II. Among his clients were major U.S. corporations, the U.S. Government and an extensive number of Cuban companies. At the time of the Bay of Pigs Invasion by Cuban Freedom Fighters, he was imprisoned and kept in two different jails and in an improvised concentration camp at a baseball park, along with about thirty-five hundred detainees rounded up by the Castro secret police. He suffered misery, hunger, cruelty and denigration at the hands of Castro militias and security agents. Sick and debilitated, Dr. Lazo was finally released from prison and escaped to the United States with the help of his wife. His book gives one of the best accounts of the Cuban misfortune. He was an innocent victim of an unconscionable despot. He died in exile after a long and illustrious career.

Another case worthy of mention was that of the Hershey Corporation. The Hershey family of Pennsylvania, the world-famous chocolate makers, built a model sugar mill and refinery in the 1920s in what later was known as Hershey City in the province of Havana. The mill had a beautiful batey (a village surrounding the sugar mill). The company built a school for children, a hospital, a theater, a sports club and rows of neat wood-and-concrete houses. It built a henequen (hemp) plant to produce textiles (yarn, rope and cloth) and a refined peanut oil plant, which also produced peanut meal and other by-products. Within the area of the mill it erected a hotel with comfortable rooms, excellent food and a large swimming pool. The golf course built next to the hotel was one of the best in Cuba with lockers, showers and complete accommodations. Easy transportation from Havana to Hershey was provided by the Hershey Cuban Electric Railway. Thousands of workers were employed by the Hershey enterprises in Cuba. The Hershey Center became a tourist attraction for Americans and Cubans. It was another example of the contribution of American entrepreneurs to the economy of Cuba during the republican era.

After Castro took over following his anti-American campaign, the name of the mill was changed to Camilo Cienfuegos. And under Communism, what happened to the mill, the town and the other industries developed by the Hershey Corporation's altruistic investments? Today the place is in shambles, the mill is shut down, the town has deteriorated and is practically abandoned, the once bustling center is now desolate and in ruins. This shrinking of the sugar industry is all part of the failure of the state central planning and restructuring of the Cuban economy. Over 70 out of 161 mills existing at the end of 1958 have been closed. The specific factors behind the deterioration were poor cultivation techniques, lack of fertilizers, deficient research for new and improved varieties of sugar cane, poor sugar yields, lack of spare parts for the mills and agricultural equipment, and absence of incentives for the workers.

Things got worse after the collapse of the Soviet Union when the huge subsidies to Cuba abruptly ended, compounded by the weakness of the international markets, low prices and, very importantly, the non-competitiveness of the sugar mills mismanaged by the state administrators. All of the above can be summarized as the aftermath of a Socialist system which doesn't work for lack of human motivation, unlike those existing in a free society. A similar calamity occurred with the expropriated productive investments of the United Fruit Company and other American and Cuban enterprises.

The United States' Sacrifices for Freedom and Democracy

Private enterprise, respect for human rights, freedom of expression and tolerance of political discrepancies within the framework of democracy built this nation and made it the most powerful country in the world. But as if those achievements weren't enough, the United States helped many nations recover from the disasters caused by extreme ideologies which brought war and destruction to their lands. The same thing can be said of the U.S. help extended to many nations devastated by natural disasters. Many specific examples can be given of countries which have benefited from the largesse and humanitarian efforts of the United States.

Consider the reconstruction of Japan, at one time a formidable enemy, and today a peaceful, advanced and powerful democratic nation. Many European nations have been liberated by the sacrifice and endurance of the United States, and today they stand free and prosperous. They received massive assistance from the U.S. for their reconstruction and recovery through the Marshall Plan, also known as the European Recovery Plan, and named after Secretary of State General George C. Marshall, the proponent of the program. For this achievement he was awarded the Nobel Peace Prize in 1953. The plan was funded by the United States and began to take effect in 1947 under President Truman's administration. It provided economic and technical assistance for the reconstruction of Western Europe and its return to political stability after World War II. In a speech General Marshall delivered in a commencement address at Harvard University in 1947 he defined the U.S. position in world affairs as follows: "Our policy is directed not against any country or doctrine, but against hunger, poverty, desperation and chaos." These thoughtful words beautifully project the greatness and magnanimity of America.

The United States participated as the leading force, along with troops from other United Nation's countries, in containing and reversing the Communist North Korea and China invasion of South Korea. The Korean War (1950–1953) ended in a stalemate. The North Koreans failed to conquer South Korea. Thousands of American soldiers lost their lives in this war to preserve freedom in South Korea. Once again, after the war was over, the U.S. gave massive financial assistance to South Korea to repair the damage inflicted by the ravages of the conflict. South Korea recovered and today is a very prosperous nation as compared to militarily strong, but economically very poor, North Korea. History repeats itself insofar as Communist countries are concerned: the failure of the system to solve the human aspects of life while emphasizing the menacing military strength. Today North Korea, instead of feeding its poor and advancing the non-military aspects of its society, spends billions of dollars in building up a nuclear and missile capability to intimidate and blackmail the free world. Do you see any similarity with other defunct Communist or current terrorist tyrannies? The irony of all of this is that the despotic enemies of America, including some in our own hemisphere like Castro, and recently the new clown in town (and a dangerous one) Chavez of Venezuela, continue to call the United States an imperialist nation.

On August 2, 1990, Saddam Hussein's army invaded and took possession of neighboring Kuwait. The Iraqi tyrant committed a monumental error. The United States, together with the United Nations, demanded his immediate withdrawal from that free country. It was an outrageous adventure. Dictator Hussein defied the U.S. and the U.N. and obstinately rejected the repeated overtures to solve the crisis by peaceful means. After all diplomatic efforts were exhausted, there was no alternative but to remove Hussein's hordes forcibly from Kuwait. Hussein had shown contempt for a last-minute peaceful resolution offered by the U.N. His attitude was arrogant and defiant. He thought he could get away with his transgression by stubbornly stalling and threatening. The U.N. Security Council passed a resolution authorizing the use of force. The U.S. Congress approved military action to dislodge Hussein from Kuwait. Meanwhile, the Hussein army continued the pillaging and plundering while digging in and committing crimes against the population of Kuwait, including its children.

On January 16, 1991, President George H.W. Bush declared war on Iraq. The United States was joined by twenty-eight other nations in an effort to run Hussein's army out of Kuwait. The U.S. and its allies used massive air strikes on military targets. The U.S. forces won a decisive victory in the desert and practically destroyed his army and equipment. Hussein's soldiers gave up fighting in droves and surrendered to the allied forces. The U.S. Operation Desert Storm, under the command of General Lt. Norman Schwarzkopf, had an outstanding success. Within a relatively short time Hussein's hordes retreated from Kuwait, but before leaving they set fire to many of the oil wells. They wanted to cause as much damage as possible before retreating. It took time to control the flames, but Hussein's forces were gone. They suffered many losses on the road back to Baghdad. The road was so clogged with damaged army vehicles that many soldiers could not go through, and they were taken prisoner.

The United States did not intend to occupy Iraq. The war came to an end when Hussein's beaten, bruised and demoralized forces gave up the fight. The U.S. air attacks had destroyed most of Iraq's chemical, biological and nuclear weapons capabilities. Kuwait was grateful to the United States for its liberation from the destructive five months of occupation. Hussein was humiliated after his resounding defeat. As soon as he recovered from this disaster, he would create another crisis that would finally bring his regime of terror to an end.

Terrorism: Enemy of Humanity

The United States has proven its good intentions over and over again. However, terrorist groups continued their path of hate and destruction, aiming their fanatical anger toward the U.S. and other free nations. Let's consider another example of the bravery and determination of this heroic country.

On September 11, 2001, a cowardly and unexpected attack was conducted on the United States. This time two passenger planes were taken over in mid-air by suicidal terrorist hijackers and flown into the Twin Towers of the 110-story World Trade Center in New York City. The towers completely collapsed as a result of the impact, amid panic and disbelief. Moments later another plane manned by terrorists was directed against the Pentagon in a similar manner. A fourth plane overtaken by terrorists was thwarted by passengers from flying into a heavily populated area and crashed in rural Pennsylvania. There was a shock wave of horror and grief in the U.S. and all over the world as the unprecedented ghastly episode of terror unfolded. These attacks caused the deaths of 3,000 innocent people of practically all races, religions and nationalities. We all saw the towers disintegrate before our eyes on television that sorrowful morning. It was a satanic inferno. Then we heard about the attack on the Pentagon and the fate of those on United Flight 93 crashing in Pennsylvania, adding more grief to an already sad and dark day.

Once the air cleared and it was known the source of the instigators of the attacks, the United States had no choice but to retaliate against the culprits. The murderous, cruel and treacherous terrorist attack was planned and conducted under the order of Osama bin Laden, the leader of the terrorist organization Al Qaeda, with its base of training and operation in the rough mountains of Afghanistan. This monster was under the protection of the Taliban, a radical Islamic sect which managed to take power in Afghanistan under a system of terror of incredible proportions. The head of the Taliban regime was a fanatical radical Muslim by the name of Mullah Mohammed Omar. Twenty-six days after the terrorist attacks, on Sunday, October 7, 2001, President George W. Bush, backed by Congress, ordered an intensive air and missile assault against the terrorist training camps and military installations in Afghanistan. The President vowed to defeat the terrorists in a speech from the White House. Announcing the initiation of hostilities, he said, "We will not waver. We will not tire. We will not falter. We will not fail." The U.S. and British forces launched the assaults with great precision and success. The U.S. military campaign was given the name "Operation Enduring Freedom" and it was spearheaded by General Tommy Franks. Many other nations joined and gave support to the United States.

The air strikes were followed by a ground invasion which promptly eliminated the abusive regime of the Taliban and sent the terrorists on the run. Osama bin Laden and his followers retreated to the mountain range on the border with Pakistan and took refuge in the caves where they had stored supplies and weapons for survival and further fighting. It should be mentioned that these cowards manage to survive by sending fanatics to their death while they escape to safe ground. Any similarity with Castro in this respect is purely coincidental. Or is it?

Afghanistan became a country free of slavery imposed by the Taliban and backed by Al Qaeda forces. Al Qaeda was routed out of Afghanistan training camps and now is confined to sporadic acts of terrorism to frighten the population and disturb the normal rhythm of civil recovery. In a short time, with the assistance of the United States, Afghanistan held parliamentary elections, approved a Constitution with the accord of various political parties which emerged after the collapse of the Taliban regime, and elected a president with the enthusiastic participation of a huge voter turnout, in spite of the threat of terrorists still lingering in the country. The armed forces were organized by the fledgling democratic regime with the help of the U.S. military and other allied forces. The country is moving in the right direction in many phases of reconstruction and organization. It is not an easy task to bring a country such as Afghanistan back to normalcy – a country whose infrastructure, political organization, economy, civil society and educational system had been severely damaged by a radical and fanatical system for so many years. There are still pockets of terrorist activities, but the government's military, with the aid of the coalition and NATO forces, is pursuing the remnants of these fanatical criminals. The search mission to find bin Laden and bring him to justice is still very much in effect. Aid to Afghanistan to recover from the miseries of the past has been ample on the part of the United States.

Based on the above, is the United States an imperialist nation or a liberator? The facts speak for themselves. President Hamid Karzai, a true patriot of Afghanistan, has the last word on this matter. He has thanked the U.S. repeatedly for the sacrifices and efforts to establish a democratic nation out of the ashes of a ruined and ancient civilization. Karzai himself has been an important factor in the unification, democratization and resurgence of his nation.

In the soul searching of the true grit of America, let's return to Iraq. The infamous dictator of Iraq, Saddam Hussein, was not content with having been defeated by the United States and its allies once in 1991, nor was he thankful that he was not ousted after such a humiliating experience. His reconstruction program of chemical, biological and nuclear weapons of mass destruction (WMDs) and his defiance of U.N. resolutions attempting to stop his threats to world peace, brought about a second war that resulted in his downfall.

Hussein placed all kinds of obstacles in the way of inspections being conducted by the U.N. experts to verify the absence or presence of nuclear capabilities and other WMDs. It was known that, after the 1991 war was over, he used poisonous gas bombs against his own people and murdered hundreds of thousands of Iraqis, mostly Kurds and Shiites, subsequently burying them in mass graves in the desert sands. Some of these graves were found by the U.S. and allied forces after he was toppled. According to defectors of his own government, many of the WMDs were shipped to Syria to hide them from the U.N. inspectors. Most of the weapons were transferred just before the military invasion took place. Hussein undoubtedly posed a serious risk to the U.S. and other countries, according to the intelligence agencies of Great Britain and the U.S. He also had harbored known terrorists from other countries in Iraq. The world could not afford to have a terrorist nation of that magnitude in the midst of the Middle East, headed by a ruthless and bloody dictator.

The United States, Great Britain and supporting allies from 35 other nations saw justification for military action against the Iraq regime. It was additionally based on several U.N. Security Council resolutions breached by Hussein, and specifically Resolution 1441 which urged Hussein to disarm or face serious consequences. The U.S. Congress gave President Bush the authority to take the necessary measures to eliminate the threat posed by the mad tyrant.

The military campaign began on March 19, 2003, when President Bush ordered the beginning of surgical air strikes on military targets, followed by a ground invasion by primarily U.S. and British forces. The duration of the war was not as long as expected. Thousands of Hussein's troops abandoned the fight and evaporated from the scene when they realized the power and determination possessed by the allied contingents in all phases of the conflict. Hussein, his two sons and his closest surviving associates in crime fled Baghdad and went into hiding. It is interesting to observe how these tyrants flee the scene of their crimes when in imminent danger. In spite of their vociferous braggadocio, they run and hide like the cowards they are. Later many of them, including Saddam, were found and brought to justice. In 2003 Saddam was captured while hiding in a spider hole on the outskirts of Baghdad. He was given a fair trial by his peers, found guilty for his crimes against humanity and executed at the gallows on December 28, 2006. The end of a criminal, inhumane murderer had finally arrived. Justice was served in the name of the Iraqi people. Let the critics and scholars comment and critique the outcome of the case. After all, they didn't have to suffer the pain, torture and death of hundreds of thousands of innocent victims – men, women and children – who fell to the rage and hate of this despicable tyrant.

In the case of Iraq, the United States and coalition forces eliminated a mad tyrant who posed a threat to humanity. Elections were held in Iraq with approximately 70% voter turnout, a new Constitution was approved by popular vote, a parliament was elected and a provisional head of state was selected by the parliament. Later, in another successful popular election, a new parliament was elected and a president, prime minister and parliament speaker were approved by the parliament after intensive discussions were held by the various political parties representing Shiites, Sunnis and Kurds. Democracy had been born in Iraq.

Meanwhile, terrorists led by Al Qaeda and other insurgent groups were committing many acts of violence and terror to sabotage the democratic process. Thousands of Iraqis, civilian and military, have been killed by suicidal terrorists, factional fights, roadside explosive devices, kidnappings followed by executions, beheadings and other means of human destruction. To make the situation more complex, the terror activities are also being fueled by Iraq's rogue neighboring countries of Iran and Syria, who have a vested interest in the region. The U.S. troop fatalities since the beginning of the conflict amount, as of this writing, to over 3,700. While regrettable, it is unfortunately part of the sacrifice we have to sustain in an extremely difficult battle to eliminate or diminish the impending danger of terrorism on our own soil. The men and women serving in the U.S. military are true heroes who deserve our deepest respect, appreciation and support. If we run away from terrorism, our enemies will be encouraged and become more aggressive, knowing that they will not have a deterrent to their criminal and fanatical behavior.

In spite of all the setbacks, the resiliency of the majority of the Iraqi people has not diminished. After the death of over 100,000 civilians to sectarian violence, the Iraqi-elected government, shortcomings aside, is determined to continue on the path of democracy amid a near civil war provoked by extremist groups. The American, British and other allies have steadfastly continued the training and preparation of a professional Iraqi army. The number of Iraqi troops and officers has increased at a steady pace. The United States is committed, in spite of all the adversities, to continue helping in security operations until the Iraqi forces are ready to take full command and control of all facets of the military and police operations. The Bush administration and the U.S. armed forces are dedicated to completing the task until the moment the Iraqi regime can handle the security situation. Many high-ranking Al Qaeda terrorists have been killed or captured. The Iraqi troops have been taking the lead in many anti-terrorist incursions with bravery and success. Also bear in mind that much of the Iraqi territory – about four-fifths of it – is relatively peaceful and prospering. Only in Baghdad and the surrounding areas do terrorist activities abound. Iraq cannot be abandoned and left to the mercy of the terrorists. This would cause a disaster of major proportions, with gargantuan repercussions to our nation and the entire world.

Radical Islamic organizations, in an attempt to spread hate and destruction, have unfortunately made an effort to hijack the Muslim religion. It is hoped that the true Muslims will not allow the desecration of their faith by the extremist factions. The fratricidal terrorist acts are aggravated by the fierce antagonistic attitude among many Muslims themselves, that is, Shiite versus Sunnis. They are polarizing segments of the Iraqi population creating, as a result, instability and resentment. Sunnis, the minority that was dominant during Hussein's tyranny, claim they don't have a fair share of the political and economic spoils of Iraq under the democratically-elected regime. The bitter adversity between these two groups is being ignited by the Al Qaeda insurgency to create consternation and exacerbate the splintering of the Iraqi society. The ultimate aim of Al Qaeda is to create chaos, to bring about the fall of democracy, and to take over the government to establish a fundamentalist Islamic nation as a deterrent to the democratization of the Middle East.

The fight against terrorism inside the United States and abroad has to continue as a part of our lives and for the sake and safety of future generations. This is a war the likes of which we have never seen before. The tactics needed to defeat the enemy have to be radically different than what was applied in the conventional wars of the past. The terrorist armies and secret cells are not dressed in battlefield attire. Instead they are dressed like you and me and are intermingled with the entire population. The war fronts are no longer delineated. We now have to consider that the development and potential use of nuclear and biological weapons by terrorist nations or fanatical terrorist groups looms large in the future of humanity. The eruption of armed conflicts to eliminate the destructive menace to civilization by the hands of lunatic radicals remains a distinct possibility.

Terrorism, as the result of a doctrine of intolerance, hate and destruction, may last for many years, but at the end, like we have seen in many other difficult times, democracy, peace and understanding among people will emerge victorious. We cannot falter and let our guard down. Every citizen has to participate in one way or another to help defeat our common enemy. And while all of this is going on, we are dismayed to see the likes of Castro, Chavez and other U.S. haters in our own backyard planting the seeds of discord and antagonism in an effort to undermine democracy and freedom. They court and embrace the enemies of humanity, siding, cheering and making deals – mostly for weapons – with the intent of defying and weakening America's position in the world.

The United States: Beacon to the World

It should be noted that, after the U.S. actions and sacrifices to liberate many countries from the ravages of Nazism, Fascism, Communism and terrorism have accomplished their noble and heroic task, not a single square inch of foreign territory has been retained by this great country. Furthermore, the nations liberated received generous humanitarian and economic assistance from the United States to recover from the destructive path of the exploiters, tyrants and oppressors. Only the rabid, fanatical and hateful enemies of this admirable nation refer to America by the grievous epithet of "Imperialist." It is no coincidence that these enemies of freedom gang up together in today's world to discredit the U.S. and obstruct the efforts to advance the cause of human dignity and democracy. Moreover, we should never forget that whenever there has been a serious natural disaster anywhere in the world, the U.S. has been willing and ready to lend a helping hand and deliver needed economic and humanitarian assistance to relieve the misery and despair caused by such human tragedies, whether an earthquake, a tsunami, a flood, a hurricane, an epidemic disease or other calamitous event.

Presently the United States continues to pour billions of dollars from government, corporations, religious organizations and charity foundations to combat the ravages of AIDS, particularly in African countries affected by the malady. Furthermore, the U.S., without much fanfare, implements donation programs of food and medical supplies to the needy in the international community, and provides agricultural, educational and public health assistance to many developing countries. The goodwill and generosity of America have no limits or boundaries.

I would like to pay tribute to the United States of America with the following poem I wrote. It synthesizes my sentiments for this great country, vilified by enemies within and without our borders.

To America

Never shaken, never soft
A country that does not give up
A monument to courage
Forging ahead with indomitable thrust
Nothing stops the giant
No sleep under adversity
No rest, no tears, no fears.

Stoically supports the blows
Heroically fights its crises
No enemy attack, no flood, no disaster
Will slow America down
A country made of granite
Of endless energy and resources
Of steel, of iron and will.

No matter what lurks around
America always rebounds
Stronger, determined, undaunted
Looking to the future
With deep faith in its destiny
Model of endurance and bravery
Of character and temper.

An example to the world
A democracy that holds the torch
Of liberty, human rights and justice
Full of caring and loving people
United by its roots
Strengthened by diversity
America, you are the greatest!

The maligning of the United States by tyrants and terrorists that are now appearing on the international scene as leaders of certain nations is a sad spectacle that sooner or later will come to an end, as it has in the past, because of their lack of moral fortitude. Human dignity can be temporarily repressed, but it cannot be erased. By the force of nature and the will of God it will return so that the values and legitimate rights of the human person can be restored in Cuba and other enslaved nations of the world.

8

AN ANALYSIS OF CASTRO'S EARLY TURBULENT CHARACTER AND COWARDICE

"It is said by many of his former rebel army commanders, who defected after he took power, that Castro never participated in a single battle during the time they were fighting the Batista army. He always stayed behind giving orders to others to carry out the fight while he hid in a protected ensconce."

Castro's Behavior Explored

When we look at Castro's behavior as a ruler, it could be said in retrospect that his morphing should have been anticipated. But, regrettably, many opted to ignore his erratic past in the fervent attempt to dislodge the Batista regime. To build upon this assertion and to set the record straight, let's digress for a moment and go back to the earlier days of Castro as a pro-Communist troublemaker.

To better understand Castro's behavioral pattern it is fitting to analyze his turbulent trail and the deep-rooted fallacy of "Yankee Imperialism" he uses as his favorite sing-song to paint the United States as the bogeyman. This tactic is now mimicked by Hugo Chavez of Venezuela and other despotic apple-knockers of this world when, in fact, they should be searching their own souls and considering their own dismal failures before daring to attack this great country. It would be proper to group Castro with other tyrants like Hitler, Mussolini, Ceausescu and Hussein who, when confronted with perilous circumstances, promptly fled and hid to save their skin rather than face the risk with dignity and courage.

Castro was notoriously known for his cowardice and survival instincts. Let me relate several cowardly acts he committed when his life or well-being was in jeopardy. On every occasion Castro had the self-preserving ability to ride out the storm without even a scratch. It's time to unmask his much-exalted "bravery" and "heroic aura" trumpeted by his leftist defenders so the world can judge him based on proven facts instead of myth.

The Infamous "Bogotazo"

In 1948 Castro survived the "Bogotazo," as the bloody uprising incited by Communist provocateurs in Bogota, Colombia, was commonly known. The disturbances in Colombia, in which he actively participated, began on April 9th and lasted for about three days. The revolt was flamed by an organized group of international Marxist students who converged on Bogota with the objective of sabotaging the Ninth International Conference of the American States. The student organization had called for the anti-imperialist meeting to coincide with the Conference. The President of Colombia at that time was Dr. Mariano Ospina Pérez of the Conservative Party. The leader of the opposition leftist Liberal Party was Eliecer Gaitán, a defiant and staunch enemy of the President. He had been involved in an ongoing, nasty dispute over undocumented accusations he had made against the President. Political tension was building up over the arguments between conservatives and leftists. All of the ingredients for a confrontation existed at that moment for what seemed to be a concentrated effort to embarrass the President, interfere with the American States Conference, create chaos and ultimately bring down the government of Ospina Pérez. Followers of the leftist leader Gaitán called for street demonstrations. The Communist students fueled the fire to incite riots and destructive action.

It was no coincidence that Castro and three other leftist Cuban students – Enrique Ovares, Rafael del Pino and Alfredo Guevara (Castro's Communist mentor) – were there to attend the anti-imperialist meeting. Ovares was a founder in 1946 of the Anti-Imperialist Student Union, organized in Prague, Czechoslovakia. I had known all four of them from my days at the University of Havana and can attest to their pro-Communist persuasion. They all joined the anti-government disturbances. Castro was seen delivering leaflets to incite a revolution a few days before the uprising. The demonstrators began to gather in downtown Bogota to march on the Presidential Palace. Suddenly word spread that Gaitán had been shot to death. Communists began to broadcast over the radio that the United States was responsible for his death. They would do anything to incite the mobs. In fact, it was discovered that a mentally disturbed drifter, later identified as an ex-inmate of an institution for the insane, was the assassin. He was subsequently dragged and beaten to death by the crowd.

The multitude became increasingly violent, riots erupted, fires were set in over one hundred buildings and looting was rampant. Shootings were heard everywhere. The mobs were in a state of frenzy and kept marching toward the Presidential Palace. There was chaos and confusion. Castro was a participant in the march and was armed with a rifle. Wild rumors were spreading as fast as the fires, including that the President had fled. The police and the military responded with heavy equipment and powerful weapons, trying to contain the furious and destructive insurgents. When the riots subsided, over one thousand people were dead and many more were injured. Downtown Bogota was in shambles and many buildings were totally destroyed by fire or damaged by the looting and the rampage.

Finally order was restored. The Communists and left-wingers failed to bring down the democratic government of Colombia. Meanwhile, Castro and his companions, closely followed by the police, took refuge in the Cuban Embassy, leaving the mess behind. The Cuban delegate to the American States Conference, Dr. Guillermo Belt, facilitated the exit of Castro and his three friends on a cargo plane destined for Cuba. Once more he had conveniently left the scene of an ugly event he had helped to create and secured his safety. As a result of the uprising, the government of Colombia, convinced that Moscow had its hands on this affair, broke off relations with the Soviet Union. With the passing of time the Cuban people forgot that Castro had been an instigator of this sad page in the history of Colombia. He would continue to hide and deny his tie to the international Communist conspiracy until the time was right for him to disclose his Communist identity after the Cuban revolution of 1959.

A University Leftist Gangster

During Castro's years at the University of Havana he was a member of UIR (Revolutionary Insurrectional Union), a terrorist organization which had been involved in shootings against members of other similar competing organizations. He was a gun-toting leftist hoodlum. On June 22, 1948, he participated in the killing of his nemesis at the university, Manolo Castro Campos, a respected student leader and ex-President of the University Student Federation (FEU). Campos was gunned down along with another student, Carlos Pucho Samper, as they left the Cinecito Theater on San Rafael Street in downtown Havana. A few days later Castro was arrested by the police, but then was released under unexplained circumstances.

On July 4, 1948, he was identified as one of the killers in the murder of Sergeant Oscar Fernandez Carál of the University of Havana police unit. Sgt. Carál had known of Castro's participation in several shootings and was determined to put him in jail. Castro had told some of his friends that he had to eliminate Carál. The following day he was detained for this assassination, but again was set free and the case never came to trial. Castro had the protection of politicians in cahoots with the UIR group with which he was associated at the time.

Earlier in 1947 while he was a member of a rival gang called the MSR (Socialist Revolutionary Movement), and an aspirant to the presidency of the FEU, Castro was involved in an attempt on the life of Lionel Gómez. Gómez was the President of the student body of Havana High School No. 1 and was affiliated with the UIR. Castro perceived him to be a potential enemy once Gómez enrolled at the University of Havana, following his upcoming graduation from high school. Gómez was ambushed by Castro on Ronda Street, just outside of the university stadium where he had been watching a varsity football game. Gómez was wounded in the lung, but survived. Castro went into hiding for a few weeks and sent emissaries to make peace with the UIR. He even transferred his allegiance from the MSR to the UIR. Rolando Masferrer, the leader of the MSR, was pleased to see Castro leave his group, according to friends, because he was an uncontrollable, erratic and overly-ambitious person. In my opinion, Masferrer sized up Castro exactly right.

A Failed Expedition to the Dominican Republic

In 1948, when a failed armed expedition of adventurers was being prepared in Cayo Confites, a tiny island in the proximity of eastern Cuba, with the purpose of landing in the Dominican Republic to oust Dictator Leonidas Trujillo, Castro joined in the flagrant venture. The leader of the expedition was none other than Rolando Masferrer, who was well known for his rebellious actions in Cuba. The Cuban government, then under the presidency of Dr. Ramón Grau San Martín, facing an international scandal for tacitly abetting this daring adventure, decided to thwart the invasion and sent army and naval forces to the site. They confiscated the ships, weapons, ammunition and planes and proceeded to root out nearly 990 members of the expeditionary force. Castro managed to escape by hiding and swimming to the Cuban shore. He proved to be a scoundrel, an opportunist, an adventurer and a troublemaker.

The Skunk

There are other violent events in the past history of this skunk to review. This description fits the mold because Castro was a smelly, unclean and filthy individual. He was known at the University of Havana by the nickname of "bola de churre," which translates into "ball of dirty grease" or "ball of filth." This contrasted with the scrupulous personal cleanliness of the Cuban people at that time. Suffice it to say that, in the decades before the revolution, Cuba was one of the leading countries in the per capita consumption of soap. And this was reported when the statistics were not manipulated by the government, as they are today.

The Assault on the Moncada Army Post

On July 26, 1953, Castro took a group of youthful followers for the assault on the Moncada Army Post at Santiago, Oriente Province. His revolutionary 26th of July Movement took its name from the day of this attack. About a hundred combatants were killed on both sides. The cowardly Castro brothers, Fidel and Raúl, did not enter the fort and did not participate in the fight. In fact, they both fled from the scene when they realized that the daring action had failed. They, and a small group of survivors, ran and hid in the nearby mountains and later surrendered under the protection of the Archbishop of Santiago, Enrique Pérez Serantes. The Catholic priest negotiated the surrender with the understanding that Castro, his brother Raúl and the handful of remaining rebels were not going to be mistreated and would be given a fair trial. At the civil trial they had an adequate defense and were sentenced to fifteen years of imprisonment. Less than two years later they were given a pardon by Bastista as part of an amnesty for all political prisoners. At least Batista showed mercy, a quality that has been missing from Castro's abominable record.

An Expedition From Mexico to Cuba

In 1956 Castro again fled to safety unscathed after an armed expedition from Mexico landed on the southeastern coast of Cuba. Most of the participants were killed upon arrival by Batista's troops. But he and his brother Raúl, along with a small band of survivors, found a way to avoid confrontation with the army and hid in the nearby mountains of the Sierra Maestra range, where they endured and began the revolt against the Batista regime.

It is said by many of his former rebel army commanders, who defected after he took power, that Castro never participated in a single battle during the time they were fighting the Batista army. He always stayed behind giving orders to others to carry out the fight while he hid in a protected ensconce. This is the type of coward and scoundrel who has been glorified by the leftist journalists reporting events in Cuba during the revolutionary process.

A Confirmed Coward and Scoundrel

During the Bay of Pigs Invasion in April 1961, the courageous Cuban patriots of Brigade 2506 were left stranded on the beach and in the swamps fighting Castro's troops and exposed to the strafing from attack planes – without the air power and logistic backup support promised and expected from the Kennedy Administration. Finally they surrendered after suffering many casualties and running out of supplies and ammunition. It was then, when everything was under control and it was safe to make a public appearance, Castro showed up at the scene surrounded by a large group of heavily-armed bodyguards and troops, as if he had been a victorious combatant of this outrageous battle. He wanted to display before the world his "bravery" and "heroism." He also made sure that the cameras and photographers were there to show proof of his "courage."

The Terrorist Gangs Perpetuated by Castro's Regime

For the benefit of the readers not familiar with the socio-political environment of the Cuban culture, let me expand on the nature of the terrorist gangs such as UIR and MSR with which Castro had been affiliated at one time or another during his student days. They were similar to "brotherhoods" acting on the fringe of the legal system and taking advantage of the freedom which existed in Cuba under the right of association. They fought each other for positions in the government or simply for personal animosity. They loved guns and the reputation of being daring. They relished living on the periphery of danger, oftentimes getting involved in shooting battles against each other to gain fame and leverage for prominence. It was in a sense a machismo syndrome difficult to comprehend, a phenomenon which originated from the civil resistance of radical left opposition groups to the dictatorship of President Gerardo Machado.

Machado had been elected by popular vote in 1925 to a four-year term. He then, taking advantage of his enormous popularity and the adulation of his political supporters, extended his term in office by manipulating the Congress and the Constitution. In doing so he became a de facto dictator, a situation similar to what exists today in Venezuela under Chavez. The only difference is that Machado was not a Socialist. He was a populist and did not interfere with the free enterprise system. However, he did impose a very repressive political tyranny and was later overthrown by a coalition of students, militaries and intellectuals.

The radical organizations degenerated into hoodlum gangs, becoming stronger during the democratic governments of Dr. Ramón Grau San Martín (1944-48) and Dr. Carlos Prío Socarrás (1948-52). They obtained political positions and even infiltrated the police bodies. Their circle of action and influence was practically limited to Havana, the capital of Cuba and the seat of the national government and congress. They were all called "revolutionary" organizations with limited membership and, although in theory they were left-leaning, they had no known connection to the Communist Party. In fact, members of these gangs could belong to any party as long as they were loyal to the organization and ready for a call to duty when necessary.

A few students would voluntarily join to obtain support in their aspirations to control the student bodies. I was very familiar with their mode of operation because I knew members of one group or another. However, as a conservative I stayed away from participating in such groups. They just didn't fit my personal style and character. These groups never interfered with the strict rules of academic affairs or the educational process. The political gangs were not involved in drug dealing or robberies. They distanced themselves from common felonies. The law was severe when it came down to mete out stiff penalties for such offenses.

Illegal drugs were not a significant factor in the Cuban society. In fact, as an example, marijuana users were despised and considered as trash. As far as students were concerned, drugs were completely foreign to the social environment of our era. The venal acts of the gangs were confined to guns and sporadic shootings. There was a fierce rivalry among factions which, from time to time, exploded into shootings with fratricidal consequences. Many of the culprits were detained if caught and sentences were applied accordingly by a court of law. Castro, in spite of his many violent interventions, always found a way to escape without a criminal sentence.

It is curious to observe that the leaders of the gangs were mature men (not necessarily mentally mature) of a fair educational level, and some had the baggage of military experience, either from World War II, as in the case of Emilio Tró, leader of UIR, or the Spanish Civil War, in the instance of Rolando Masferrer, leader of MSR. The gangs did not actively recruit; however, oftentimes they had their eyes on the University of Havana, knowing quite well the intense adversarial relationship often existing between student factions trying to dominate the politically powerful University Student Federation. Among members of such groups were ambitious, daring young men – some students – with a desire to achieve a tough and feared reputation. A typical example of the latter was Castro, a bully and psychopath with unlimited ambitions for notoriety. He was intrinsically and subconsciously a coward with an instinct for survival. He would lie, betray and kill to overcome his complexes and demonstrate his pseudo-heroism to achieve recognition, indeed a dangerous specimen since early youth. He deceived many to reach power and fame. Communism was a fitting ideology for a man without a conscience and scruples.

Today, under Castro's dictatorship, the gangs of the 1940s and 1950s pale by comparison. They have been replaced, based on his past experience, by a monolithic repressive state apparatus called Revolutionary Militias or CDRs (Committees for the Defense of the Revolution). These organized groups are everywhere to impose the will of the government and maintain strict adherence to the edicts of the revolution. They are not only present at the universities, but in every educational center as well, to quench any signs of nonconformity with the Communist system.

9

ELECTIONS. NARCO-TRAFFIC AND OTHER VICES. PARADE OF FOOLS.

"The business moguls go to Cuba to negotiate with the dictator, sharing the spotlight with him and his close circle of aids, pleading with their government to mitigate or stop the embargo, while thousands of forgotten prisoners of conscience languish in unsanitary dungeons suffering from deprivation, disease, hunger and humiliation without access to any legal recourse."

The Farce of the Elections

THE ELECTIONS IN Cuba offer no choice of candidates and no voting alternatives. Only one political party participates, the official Communist Party, which is the capital pillar of the state and the only political party allowed in the nation. The voters are given two lists: one for the candidates to the National Assembly of the Popular Power with the names of 609 delegates, and another one for the Provincial Assemblies with 1,192 candidates. The electors are asked to endorse the two official lists. After counting the ballots, a top election official announces that all candidates have been "elected." The election farce is held every five years. People of voting age are forced to go to the polls for fear of reprisals. Voter turnout is always about 98%. Those not voting may be singled out for harassment and isolation, and may even lose their jobs. Abstaining from voting is equated with opposing the regime and considered to be counter-revolutionary. Cuba's ruling Council of State, headed by Castro, proposes the laws and selects the president. The National Assembly rubber stamps the decisions of the Council.

The Communist Constitution of 1976 created the National Assembly and the Provincial and Municipal Assemblies. This structure is called the Popular Power. The Communist Party is the controlling organism which selects the list of candidates from among its members to be elected by the electoral process. Article 5 of the Communist Constitution reads:

The Communist Party of Cuba, the Marxist-Leninist organized vanguard of the working class, is the superior directing force of the society and state that organizes and leads the common efforts toward the high objectives of constructing Socialism and the advance toward a Communist society.

Castro also presides over the Communist Party. In practice he is the law, and he can approve, change or cancel at his will any law or legislative proposal coming before the National Assembly. He is an absolutist that cannot accept any type of formality or limitation. That is why Cuba is a perfect example of a lawless society.

Drug Trafficking and Other Vices

The sins of the Communist tyranny in Cuba have many facets, some of which have made the news in the free world press. The drug connection between Cuba, Panama and Colombia was given attention when the corrupt General Manuel Antonio Noriega was the strongman and virtual ruler of Panama, whose main hobby from 1983 to 1989 was to depose and install presidents. The drug deals between Cuba and Panama during Noriega's rule were uncovered by José Blandón Castillo, a former intelligence aid to Noriega. Blandón provided evidence which served as the basis for the U.S. prosecutors to indict Noriega for drug trafficking activities to the United States.

Castro's direct participation in the management of drugs and arms traffic in Central America and the Andean countries of South America, and between those sources of narcotics and the U.S., was revealed by Blandón when he testified before a grand jury in Miami in January 1988, and then before the U.S. Senate Foreign Relations Subcommittee on Narcotics, Terrorism and International Communications. There was, according to Blandón's testimony, a joint venture of General Noriega, Fidel Castro, the Colombian Marxist insurgent movement M-19 and the Colombian Medallin Drug Cartel to oversee, protect and coordinate the drug shipments from Colombia through Cuba to the United States. The liaison of all the participants was conducted by the Latin American Department of the Communist Party of Cuba, headed by Manuel Piñeiro (also known as "Red Beard"), who was the leader of all subversive movements in Latin America.

The Cuban Ambassador to Colombia at that time, Fernando Ravelo Renedo, also participated as a link between the guerrilla group M-19 and the drug cartel. Blandón indicated that in 1984 the operations were conducted in Panama, Nicaragua and Colombia concurrently, Cuba being the controlling factor in the smuggling activities. Bear in mind that Nicaragua was ruled by the Sandinista Marxists from 1979 to 1990. Nicaraguan leaders were paid in cash for their participation. The money was usually laundered in Panama. Drug shipments regularly went from Colombia to Cuba, and then to the U.S. The operations also made it possible for Castro to provide arms to Communist rebels in Central America and Colombia. According to Blandón, Castro would do anything that he could against the United States.

The above information on drug trafficking was obtained from press releases and other sources, principally from the writings of Dr. Rachel Ehrenfeld contained in a booklet entitled *Narco-Terrorism and the Cuban Connection*, printed and distributed by The Cuban American National Foundation, Publication No. 26, 1988. Reprinted from *Strategic Review*, Vol. XVI, No. 3, Summer 1988, pp. 55-63. Dr. Ehrenfeld has impeccable credentials. She was at the time a Fellow at Freedom House in New York. She has been a Visiting Scholar at the Institute of War and Peace Studies, Colombia University (1986) and a Research Fellow at the Fletcher School of Law and Diplomacy, Tufts University (1984-1985). Dr. Ehrenfeld holds a doctorate degree in criminology from the Hebrew University of Jerusalem (1984).

After the publication of her research on narco-terrorism and the Cuban connection, General Noriega, following his indictment by the U.S. Courts, was deposed and captured by U.S. troops in December 1989 and brought to the United States to stand trial. He was convicted of drug trafficking and racketeering and given a long prison sentence. Originally scheduled for release from a federal prison in Florida in September 2007, he will remain there until an extradition dispute is settled. Noriega has two criminal cases pending, one in Panama to serve a 20-year sentence for murder, and another in France to serve a 10-year sentence for money laundering. He has already been tried in absentia and convicted in both cases, in 1995 for the murder charges, and in 1999 for unlawfully depositing millions in drug money in French banks and laundering the cash. Both countries have requested his extradition. While Noriega's extradition to France has been approved by a federal judge, his attorney has appealed that decision.

Certain aspects of Castro's ties to the cocaine trade with Colombia were reported in February 1978 on the CBS-TV program *60 Minutes*. Correspondent Morley Safer was a commentator on the program. According to the report, funds were provided by Castro to help start the operation in Florida. Federal and local agencies, as well as a federal grand jury, were investigating the connections. Rep. Lester Wolff (D-NY) was interviewed on the program and said that "from several very reliable sources we have been able to confirm the fact that he [Castro] was in the startup of the operation and has had continuing contacts through operatives, who come back and forth to the U.S." Wolff added that various intelligence agencies shared information on the case with the House Committee on Narcotics, which he headed at that time. The AP press release of this report was published in the Monday, February 27, 1978 edition of the *Chicago Tribune* newspaper.

In November 1983 the *Miami Herald* published a report that had previously been kept secret, drafted by the U.S. Drug Enforcement Agency (DEA), concerning the participation of the Cuban government in drug trafficking to the United States. According to the report, the involvement of Cuba in these transactions dates back to 1961, the year that the Communization of Cuba was practically completed.

The news services reported in 1999 press releases that large shipments of cocaine were unloaded by smugglers into South Florida. The *Miami Herald* reported that detained suspects told DEA agents that they brought the drugs through Havana with the personal approval of Castro, and that he had allowed the use of Cuban territory as an intermediate stop for the drug shipments. They off-loaded the narcotics onto speed boats in Cuban waters for shipment to the U.S. The DEA agents searched one of the traffickers' cars and found photos of one of the men posing with Castro. DEA Miami Chief James Milford declared that the arrests proved a direct link between Cuba and Florida.

The DEA and the Justice Department have been investigating the link between Colombia and Cuba in the drug smuggling operations for years. Their suspicions were strengthened after credible witnesses testified at the trial of ousted Panamanian political-military leader General Noriega. News press releases have reported that drug flights have changed course and escaped by sneaking into Cuban territorial airspace every time they have been pursued by U.S. authorities. For years Castro has been lured by the hard American currency to shore up the chronic failure of the Cuban economy brought about by disastrous agricultural and industrial ventures, and worsened even further by the dwindling Soviet subsidies during the 1988-1991 crisis that disintegrated the Soviet Union. Additionally, some of that hard currency has served to enrich the personal pockets of Fidel Castro and his brother Raúl. No wonder his fortune was reported to be $900 million, according to a 2006 report published by the respected *Forbes* business magazine.

The drug connections of Castro have other ramifications touching, as would be expected from the evidence accumulated through the years, his military apparatus. By 1989 the mounting scandal reached such proportions that, at least temporarily, he had to find a way out of the mess that was creating an international uproar. To extricate himself, he found a fall guy. In June 1989 General Arnaldo Ochoa Sanchez, along with Colonel Antonio de la Guardia Font, Major Antonio Padrón and Captain Jorge Martínez, were arrested and accused of smuggling tons of drugs into the United States. General Ochoa was one of the highest-ranking army officers, a decorated hero of the revolution. He had served as Supreme Commander of the Cuban forces in Angola, Ethiopia and Nicaragua. He was revered by the troops and considered a menace to the Castro leadership. Ochoa had close ties with a group of Soviet leaders who were disturbed by the repressive direction of the Soviet Union, desperate to maintain its hold over the Eastern European satellites showing increasing signs of disintegration. These leaders, in concert with Ochoa, were not very keen of Castro's antics. Castro saw Ochoa as a menace to his power and suspected that he was involved with other army officers in planning his demise. Concurrently with that feeling, Castro was afraid that his link with the drug traffic was getting to be too obvious in view of the expanding evidence and reports of his involvement. He had to unload the blame for Cuba's profiteering from such sensitive and illegal business onto the back of someone else. He had the perfect candidate, the man who was now his shadow and the one he suspected was planning a coup to succeed him.

Castro accused Ochoa, and the officers close to Ochoa, of being the culprits for the drug trafficking operation. It was naïve to think that he suddenly discovered that Ochoa was the head of something that had been conducted for years and in massive quantities, using Cuba as the intermediate base without his previous knowledge, in spite of the intensive intelligence and espionage government machinery in place. How could the Cuban officialdom be unaware that military airports and maritime ports were being used to facilitate these extensive and frequent operations? Only a fool would believe Castro's version of the story. Castro forced a public confession and retraction from Ochoa, which was broadcast on the two official television channels. Castro, as usual, made a public spectacle of the trial. General Ochoa and the other three officers were convicted by a summary court martial and sentenced to die before a firing squad. They were promptly executed on July 13, 1989. It is said that Ochoa had been given a sample of the torture he was facing if he didn't confess. Under the circumstances and also for the safety of his family, he agreed to admit that he was culpable. Being close to Castro before he fell in disgrace, he knew what Castro was capable of doing and he also knew that, no matter what, he had no salvation.

Ileana de la Guardia, daughter of Colonel Antonio de la Guardia, one of the four officers executed by Castro, and in exile in France, filed a complaint before a French Court in Paris in January 1999 accusing the Cuban dictator of international drug trafficking. She said that drug traffic in Cuba was a matter of state, organized by the highest echelon of power in the country, and it was impossible that Castro was unaware of what was going on at the state level. She was fighting to clear her father's name. Likewise, the family of General Ochoa and the other victims of Castro's scheme denied that their loved ones had anything to do with the preposterous charges that led to their executions. It is clear that the officers were vilified and falsely accused with the intention of covering Castro's own activities with the drug cartel in Colombia.

Prostitution

In spite of denials by Castro, prostitution – the profession that he promised to eliminate when he came to power – is rampant in Cuba today. Prostitution is practiced by both sexes and includes very young people. Cuba's faltering economy and the meager income of a large segment of the population entice many to enter this degrading occupation in an effort to support themselves and help their families. Prostitutes are seen plaguing foreigners outside of luxury hotels, beach resorts, night clubs, bars and exclusive restaurants. They solicit business not only for money, but for anything else of value they can fetch from the visitors, including perfume, clothing, food, watches and other goods. It is a shameful sight. These places are attended only by tourists, foreign business people and the rich class ruling the country; common people are not allowed to enter. They are part of the popularly dubbed "Cuban apartheid."

On certain occasions Castro has acknowledged that there is prostitution in Cuba. It is so evident that no one can deny it. The state tourist agencies in Cuba have insinuated the beauty and friendly disposition of young women on the island as an attraction in their promotional materials, illustrating the brochures and other marketing materials with suggestive photographs. All Cubans agree that there is more prostitution in Cuba today than before the revolution. Unfortunately, Cuba has become a paradise for the sexual degenerates of the world. It appears that the revolution will do anything to get dollars.

There is a latent danger in the prostitution game; the number of cases of AIDS in Cuba is kept under wraps. The statistics indicating the number of individuals affected with the disease are grossly distorted by the regime to minimize panic and bad publicity. They do not want to scare the tourism industry. People known to be affected by the malignancy are isolated in sanitariums located away from major population centers. The disease was initially spread by soldiers returning to Cuba from the armed expeditions to African countries. People contracting the disease tried to disguise it or deny it for fear of isolation or rejection. Hence the risk of passing this infirmity or other sexually transmitted diseases to eager tourists attracted by the illicit sex industry is great.

Imaginary Invasions

From time to time, as an excuse for his failures and to excite the Cuban population against the "Yankee Imperialists," Castro lashes out at the United States with preposterous accusations of planning a military invasion of Cuba. This is a distracting tactic to divert public attention away from the internal crises that continue to resurface. The trick is well known. It is usually followed by orchestrated street marches and mass gatherings at a designated public plaza. Workers, students from grade school to university, teachers, public workers and other groups are mobilized by the trade unions and other state organizations. They are forcibly recruited to participate in these spectacles whenever the "Maximum Leader" or his brother Raúl appear to speak. On some special occasions, like the anniversary of the 26th of July Movement, May Day or any other commemorative date, peasants and workers are loaded into trucks, trains and buses like sacks of potatoes. Workers are instructed to check with their local delegates at the rally site to verify attendance; otherwise, the may not have a job the next day. Crowds are massive; they are given prior instructions for the slogans of the day and are furnished with banners, posters and flags appropriate to the situation. Intimidation is the weapon used to maximize attendance. Although people are forced to attend, normally they become festive since they don't have to work or attend school. Nothing gives them more pleasure than to be non-productive. They take it philosophically because, after all, they love to find an opportunity to weaken the system. This has been done now for generations as part of a piteous farce.

Parade of Celebrities

For years international celebrities, politicians and misled business executives have traveled to Cuba to visit Castro and have photo-ops with the detestable dictator. They ignore the atrocities and human rights violations he commits against his own people and render submissive tribute to the despot. It has been a pitiful sight to observe. They embrace and shake the blood-stained hands of the murderer in an empty gesture of piety. They promote the goal of reestablishing relations with Cuba and ending the U.S. economic embargo. The United States, and rightfully so, stands firm in its position to maintain the embargo until the Cuban dictator ceases denying political, economic and human rights to the people and brings a peaceful transition to democracy.

Routinely the foreign VIPs, many from the U.S., are taken to well-groomed "showcases" like an experimental beef and dairy operation, a selected school, an elegant residential area occupied by the big wheels of the regime, an exclusive seaside club, a restaurant for tourists or a Castro retreat. They are kept away from slums, shanty towns, dingy places, dilapidated buildings, ruined sugar mills and other ugly sights.

Among well-known Americans who have visited Cuba and ingratiated themselves to Castro and his cohorts are journalist Barbara Walters; Governor of Illinois George Ryan; Governor of Minnesota Jesse Ventura; Illinois Secretary of Agriculture Joe Hampton; former President Jimmy Carter; former U.S. Senator Paul Simon; Democratic Speaker of the Alabama State House Seth Hammett; Chicago Bishop Joseph Perry; Reverend Jesse Jackson; Reverend Lucius Walker, an American pastor and former Executive Director of the New York-based Pastors for Peace; ex-Heavy Weight Champion Muhammad Ali; war protester Cindy Sheehan; actors Danny Glover, Ed Asner, Kevin Costner, Jack Nicholson, Robert Redford and Shirley MacLaine; singer Harry Belafonte; filmmakers Michael Moore, Steven Spielberg, Spike Lee, Oliver Stone and Saul Landau; and a host of other politicians and celebrities.

I remember watching a television broadcast when Barbara Walters was there some years ago. I was nauseated to observe the adulating dialogue she sustained during her interview with Castro. She was very jovial, chatting and joking about the many women in his life.

Carter's visit was a mistake in judgment. He naïvely thought that he was going to convert the dictator into a pussy cat. Instead Castro made a fool out of him. Carter's weak and humble-looking demeanor did not sway the mind of the dictator one iota. I disliked seeing that happening to an American president. Deep in my heart I have a feeling that Carter is a well-intentioned and compassionate soul, and I feel sorry for him.

I critique Jesse Jackson not only for his visits to Cuba, but also for his liberal political ideology, his style and his tactics. However, I give him credit because at least he was instrumental in the release of 26 Cuban political prisoners and 22

Americans from Castro's miserable jails during his visit on June 25, 1984. It was Castro's gift to his admirer. Castro was also doing his best to enhance the political aspirations of Jackson, who at that time was campaigning for President in the forthcoming Democratic primaries. A lot of publicity was given in the U.S. press to the release of the prisoners to Jackson.

Jackson was allowed to take with him a long-suffering political victim of Castro, Dr. Andrés Vargas Gómez, the grandson of General Máximo Gómez, a national hero and legendary figure from the days of the Cuban independence wars against Spain in the mid-1860s and late 1890s. Vargas Gómez was an economist and a diplomat under Castro at the beginning of the revolutionary government. He served as Ambassador of Cuba to the United Nations before a falling-out with Castro in 1959. Like many good revolutionaries, he saw the turning of Castro to Communism and began conspiring against the regime. He helped in the planning of the failed Bay of Pigs Invasion and was captured in 1961, charged with mercenary acts and of being an agent of the CIA. He was sentenced to death by firing squad, but the sentence was later commuted to 30 years in prison. Following appeals from prominent international leaders and private citizens from various countries, he was released in 1982 after serving 21 years. While in prison he was subjected to psychological and physical tortures, abuses and deprivations similar to those suffered by Matos, Valladares, Artime and thousands of other political prisoners as described previously in this book.

Vargas Gómez, a man of dignity, made it clear to Jackson that he would not permit Castro to be called human because he was a dictator that for many years had unjustly kept so many political prisoners in repulsive confinement, and all Cubans at large in a greater jail consisting of the entire island. Vargas Gómez wanted to be heard and he achieved his purpose at every opportunity when he was interviewed by the press. All of the Cuban prisoners released to Jackson had already served their complete terms long before they were freed. This was asserted by Geraldo Martínez Pérez, another of the released prisoners. He added that there was nothing humane in Castro's decision to let prisoners go because, even by revolutionary laws, they had their propriety to be released earlier as a right and not as a favor. Martínez Pérez had completed his 20-year sentence a year before. When prisoners refuse to be indoctrinated, they are punished and kept in prison even after serving their terms. Incidentally, Vargas Gómez died in his home in Coral Gables, Florida, in June 2003. He was a great patriot and a brave human being.

When I read the list of Cuban prisoners released to Jackson and published in the June 24, 1984 edition of the *Chicago Tribune*, I was delighted to see the name of a good, long-time friend from my student days, Gilberto Conde Otero. I hope that he is doing well after over two decades of enjoying his new life in freedom.

Jackson and his entourage went to Cuba again in December 1993 on a visit sponsored by the Cuban Ecumenical Council, a Christian group infiltrated by pro-Castro elements. He doesn't miss an opportunity to return to Cuba inasmuch as he maintains a friendship with Castro and seems to be sympathetic to the Communist regime. He was, as usual, calling for an end to the U.S. embargo.

In October 1994 Illinois Governor George Ryan made a five-day visit to Cuba near the end of his tenure in office in an attempt to add a page to his legacy stained by scandals and fraud, which led to his indictment and conviction after he left office. He suddenly became an advocate for the end of the U.S. embargo. He and his delegation met with Castro and were given the "showcase tour" specifically designed for visiting dignitaries. Ryan insulted the Cuban-Americans in Florida and elsewhere who opposed his trip to Cuba by saying that he did not represent Miami. In my view he represented not only Illinois but the entire United States, although in very poor taste. He was suggesting that an agricultural exchange would be very important for the relationship between the two countries. In doing so he showed, once more, his complete ignorance about the nature and intentions of Castro and his totalitarian regime. Ryan turned out to be an immoral and dishonest public servant. No wonder he had such an attraction for the Cuban monster. He was responsible for the weakening of the Republican Party in Illinois, which has not recovered since his scandalous behavior.

In September 2002 a large contingent of U.S. agribusiness leaders held a U.S. trade fair in Havana to promote trade deals with Cuba. The Chairman of Archer Daniels Midland Company (ADM), a large conglomerate of agricultural commodities and a food ingredients manufacturer, was the chief sponsor of the trade fair, who, along with other U.S. business representatives, organized a lavish Food and Agricultural Exhibition in Havana as part of the trade fair. Minnesota Governor Jesse Ventura participated in the ribbon-cutting ceremony, joined by the dictator, who was all smiles, beguiling the Americans attending the event to gain their favor.

While they were celebrating, drinking, tasting the opulent display of goodies and exchanging niceties, thousands of Cuban dissidents languished in Castro's dungeons suffering from deprivation, and no one dared mention it to Castro. The human aspect of the Cuban misery never came to light. They were blinded by the material benefits and greed. The whole atmosphere was "business as usual." Where was the human feeling? It was lost in the festive atmosphere of the moment. Such is life. Entrance to the fair was restricted to faithful members of the regime. Outside of those halls a population was hustling to survive; but they were powerless, the dispossessed, the forgotten members of society, under slavery, stripped of their rights and a voice to be heard.

What I find basically wrong is that the business moguls go to Cuba to negotiate with the dictator, sharing the spotlight with him and his close circle of aids, pleading with their government to mitigate or stop the embargo, while thousands of forgotten prisoners of conscience languish in unsanitary dungeons suffering from deprivation, disease, hunger and humiliation without access to any legal recourse. The past and present victims of Castro are overlooked. The hatred this man has for the United States is obliterated from the minds of the visitors. The robbery of American and Cuban property during the conversion to Communism is set aside. His alliances with enemies of the United States are not taken into account. The respect for human rights is not even mentioned in the conversations as a prerequisite for establishing trade with Cuba. They are all blinded by short-lived material benefits, bypassing the cruelty of the dictator and his past history as a consummate liar. They ignore the misery he has brought upon this once-prosperous country and its population. No matter what benefits they dispense to Castro, he does not cease to attack and distort the image of America and its way of life. Don't they get it? Castro is a Communist who deep down detests capitalism and the free enterprise system, the very principles upon which the companies dealing with him are founded. This is a contradiction that is difficult to comprehend.

The trade fair was an effort to sell agricultural products to Cuba (rice, corn, beans, chicken, beef, livestock, etc.) and to loosen the sanctions which have existed since Castro converted Cuba into a satellite of the former Soviet Union and confiscated all private property. The embargo to Cuba was eased somewhat in the early 2000s to allow the direct sale of food and agricultural products in exchange for cash, barring U.S. financing.

Notwithstanding the embargo, many American products find their way into Cuba through third-party countries. Some of those products are manufactured in countries where American companies maintain plants; for instance, Panama, Mexico and other Latin American countries, as well as Canada, Europe and Asia. These products, including appliances, are sold at the state-owned special stores called "dollar stores," where only the privileged military and elite civilian class can afford to buy them in dollars. Cubans receiving dollars from relatives in the United States are also given access to the "dollar stores" where they use the hard currency to buy goods. These stores are closed from time to time, depending on the whims of the dictator and as a reaction to the measures taken by the United States to tighten the flow of dollars to Cuba, mostly from Cuban-American relatives. The common "peso stores" are for Cubans who do not have the luxury of owning dollars. At these stores they have to use their "rationing books." In spite of all of the ephemeral contracts signed for cash with U.S. businesses, in reality Cuba is not a great market for the U.S. because it has a mounting foreign debt, an economic system in permanent crisis, and a behavior proven to be untrustworthy and unpredictable.

Among the parade of influential, misguided people visiting Cuba was a ten-member congressional delegation that arrived in Havana in December 2006 with the utopian purpose of ending the hostilities between Cuba and the United States. The delegation consisted of six democrats and four republicans. Evidently democrats don't have a monopoly on ignorance. They were seeking to relax the U.S. economic sanctions against Cuba in exchange for the release of political prisoners. After three days of negotiations, they returned to the U.S. empty-handed and frustrated that they could not get any concessions on the release of political prisoners or the regime's internal policy on anti-narcotics cooperation, immigration, human rights or freedom of expression. They met with Cuban National Assembly President Ricardo Alarcón and Foreign Minister Felipe Pérez Roque. They were unable to meet with Castro, who was still very sick at the time, or with his brother Raúl, the Interim President. The leader of the delegation, Rep. Jeff Flake (R-AZ) said to the press: "It would have been nice to meet with Raúl." Then he added: "It would have been a big signal that a new era had begun. They just weren't ready." This ruefully shows just how far off-base this group of legislators was in their humiliating attempt to seek, as they called it, "a new path." They ought to know that the devil has never found a new path, and he never will.

10

THE PILGRIMAGE OF POPE JOHN PAUL II. CRACKDOWNS ON THE DISSIDENT MOVEMENT.

"Castro closed all religious schools, universities, hospitals and sanitariums and confiscated all properties owned by the churches, expelling hundreds of clergymen and nuns from Cuba. Some priests and nuns were herded into boats and literally pushed out to sea; others were thrown into jails occupied by common criminals."

The Pilgrimage of Pope John Paul II to Cuba

IN A HISTORIC event, Pope John Paul II took his pilgrimage to Cuba in January 1998. It was reminiscent of his trip to Communist Poland in 1979, which began a turning point in the struggle to oust the Communist tyranny in that nation. Unlike other celebrity visits to Cuba, this was a journey of faith and hope. Over a quarter million people jammed the so-called Plaza of the Revolution on Sunday, January 25th for the last of four messages he delivered during his visit. It proved that Cubans still had a spiritual feeling despite the official atheistic policy of the regime and its systematic repression of religion. It was a revival of the faith as evidenced by the microcosm of the Cuban people gathered at the plaza. It revealed that religion was still carried in the hearts of many and passed from generation to generation, albeit in the midst of the persecution and discouragement of the Christian faith, as well as other religious beliefs. People became very emotional at the event, weeping and praying under the short-lived protection afforded by the presence of the Holy Father. The Pope was critical of the Communist system, calling for human liberty, national reconciliation, the reopening of religious schools, an end to all human rights abuses, clemency for political prisoners, religious freedom and the strengthening of moral values. The Pope chided Castro by asking him to let the people be free. The people cheered and the crowd enthusiastically chanted, "Freedom! Freedom!" This could only have happened in the presence of the Pope. Otherwise, the crowd would have been dispersed and beaten by the goons of the secret police.

The gathering at the last mass included Castro and the top officials of his regime. Castro, by protocol, attended the mass, pretending to go along with the event. He thought he was gaining sympathy for allowing the display of faith by the people of Cuba. Bear in mind that we are dealing with a cunning individual who may contradict his instincts if he feels there is a gain in it for him. Let's not forget that churches, both Catholic and Protestant, contribute generous aid to the poor people of the country. One instance is an international Catholic relief agency, Caritas, which disburses millions of dollars every year in food, clothing, medicine and a variety of other goods. Other international and American religious organizations of various denominations also make substantial donations to charitable causes in Cuba, dispensing school supplies, medicines and even computers intended for educational centers and hospitals. It is known by exiled Cubans who held positions in the government that a good portion of that aid stored in government warehouses is loaded into trucks and diverted to military installations for the benefit of the army brass and Castro's civilian partners.

All of the above aid coming from religious groups and the reception that the Pope had is in sharp contrast with the severe blow the churches took in the early 1960s when Communism was imposed on Cuba. Castro closed all religious schools, universities, hospitals and sanitariums and confiscated all properties owned by the churches, expelling hundreds of clergymen and nuns from Cuba. Some priests and nuns were herded into boats and literally pushed out to sea; others were thrown into jails occupied by common criminals. Children were taught to reject God and religion. They grew up without knowing much about Jesus Christ and the basics of Christianity. Not only Christians were persecuted, but many Jews were also expelled, their properties confiscated, their businesses closed and their faith discouraged in what became an atheistic regime. At the end of 1958 Cuba had a substantial Jewish population of nearly 100,000. The Chinese population of Cuba experienced the same type of treatment. Religion was ridiculed by the official radio and television stations and the printing press, all under state control.

It is surprising that people, except for the hardcore Communists, kept their faith through a very cautious family teaching from one generation to the next, hoping that the children would retain some spiritual belief rather than completely falling to the absolutist, materialistic, atheistic, Communistic indoctrination in their educational environment. The faith was maintained in part by the courageous effort of the few priests, pastors and rabbis who were able to survive and keep it going under a very restrictive environment. Castro never dared to totally ban religion, knowing that it was politically risky to stamp it all out. He found some advantage in keeping it functioning, although constrained by harassment and discrimination. Playing games with human tragedy is part of Castro's psychopathic behavior.

Castro, a Catholic during his youth and excommunicated by the Vatican in 1961, began to rethink his position on religion as a consequence of the collapse of the Soviet Union in 1991, when he lost the billions of dollars in annual subsidies provided by the Kremlin to maintain a Soviet satellite in the Western hemisphere. Cuba had not completely recovered from the catastrophe at the time of the pontiff's visit. Castro used manipulation to bring the Pope by pretending that he was opening up the country in an attempt to gain an infusion of economic support from other nations and from the religious organizations providing aid to Cuba. As a calculated gesture before the visit by the Pope, he cleverly opted to "allow" Christmas celebration in Cuba. Christmas festivities in Cuba had been banned by Castro since the early 1960s after he consolidated his reign. As the Pope described it, Christmas was always a part of the religious and cultural patrimony of Cuba. The celebration of Christmas in Cuba before the revolution was a natural happening that preceded the foundation of the republic in 1902. It was an integral part of the culture and exemplified the freedom of religion existing prior to the advent of Castro. No other festivity was celebrated with the intensity and devotion of Christmas. That Castro disallowed and then allowed the Nativity of Christ festivities is an incomprehensible oxymoron, an anomaly in itself impossible to fathom, based on his hate and disrespect for human dignity. It gives us a typical example of the extremes he is capable of committing in his abuse of power and his total lack of humane and spiritual sensibility. That is why he is referred to as a monster.

Reflecting on Castro's conduct, he undoubtedly perceived a general discontent in the population. As an expert of manipulation and deception, he had to reach out and pull off something spectacular from his unending devilish resources. The Pope's visit would break the impasse and bring a lot of the world's attention to Cuba – a publicity stunt of major proportions that had the potential to open up sources of income to prop up the tumbling economic situation of the country. Hoped-for results included increased tourism, more trade with Europe, additional charitable aid from Christian organizations and other side benefits, some of which were mentioned previously. The Pope's visit provided a respite and a hope to the people tired of empty promises for a better life that never seemed to materialize after so many years of tyranny. His presence brought some relief and dreams of a better future. Cubans were reassured that a larger Spiritual Being was present in their lives to guide them on the road to redemption and freedom. That was soothing and inspiring. In my humble opinion, that was good for the suffering people of an enslaved nation. Looking at the electrified audience attending the mass, Castro might have realized that he had miscalculated the candor that the Pope had awakened. Nevertheless, materially he was still reaping some benefits. After all, he had the overwhelming military and repressive power to keep a grip on the nation. Many hardcore Communists in Cuba criticized the Pope's visit, although they had to accept it because it had the approval of the "Maximum Leader" who had a vested interest in the visit.

After returning to the Vatican from his four-day tour of Cuba, the Pope said during his weekly public address to the audience in St. Peter's Square: "I went there [to Cuba] as a pilgrim of peace, to proclaim that Christ is the Redeemer of humanity and that the Gospel is the guarantee of the authentic development of society."

Muffling of the Church

Before the revolution the Cuban population was predominantly Catholic, although Protestant churches were also active throughout the island. Other religions were also present in the mix, all preaching their beliefs with absolute freedom. Under Castro the Church in Cuba has no power. All power resides with the government. To make sure that the Church stays out of political issues, such as human rights abuses, the secret police keep a close surveillance on the leaders of the faith and their ties to dissidents. The Church tries to maintain its survival and safeguard its worshippers. However, if a leader of the Church or a ministry goes too far in criticizing the regime, he may be detained, charged with counter-revolutionary activities and incarcerated to set an example to others so they don't dare cross the line. The Communist system has a disdain for those who preach or practice religion. Its view on religion is softened temporarily at times, only to be toughened again when those practicing their religion deviate from the capricious rules determined to be offensive to the dictatorship. This generates an uncertainty as to how far church officials can go in denouncing political repression and advocating a freer society. Hence, the Church keeps a very tight approach on any political involvement in the rights of dissenters to social justice.

Crackdowns on Dissidents

Immediately after the Pope's visit, the dissident movement forged ahead with renewed vigor. However, the repression on the part of the State Security Police (Seguridad del Estado) was intensified. Ten years have passed since the visit of the Pope to Cuba, and the persecution, harassment and incarceration of those who do not agree with the regime has not ceased. The jails have become a revolving door for the victims of political oppression. The dictator uses the prisoners as instruments of negotiation like objects of trade. Crackdowns on dissenters and independent journalists are the rule rather than the exception. The firing squads continue to be used for those accused and convicted by kangaroo courts of major political crimes. The accused are normally described as mercenaries, spies for the CIA, counter-revolutionaries, seditionists, imperialists, stooges, U.S.-bankrolled traitors and the like. The homes of dissidents are searched, their typewriters smashed, telephone service cancelled, books impounded, and often they are brutally beaten. But amazingly they persist with nothing but guts and a love for freedom and justice. They set an example of endurance for others to follow. Over 200 different independent organizations and illegal political parties acting on the fringe of secrecy are in existence in Cuba, in spite of the uncertain and hazardous political environment. In most cases they meet secretly, knowing that infiltrators could be disguised as dissenters and denounce their activities. They are desperate, daring and patriotic. The dissenting groups are extended to all the provinces and normally work in small cells, liaising only with extreme discretion.

On December 29, 1989, three Cuban exiles who lived in Miami, Eduardo Díaz Betancourt, age 38, Daniel Santovenia, 36, and Pedro de la Caridad Alvarez, 26, landed on the northern coast of Cuba in an inflatable boat. They were captured by Castro's troops and accused of being armed, carrying explosives and planning acts of sabotage and terrorism. A summary trial was conducted. They had no defense, were coerced into a confession, convicted of terrorism, sabotage and enemy propaganda, and sentenced to death by firing squad. The Supreme Court, and the ruling Council of State presided over by Castro, rejected all appeals for mercy. Pleas for clemency were sent to Castro from several Latin American presidents and other world leaders. In spite of the petitions, Díaz Betancourt was executed in January 1990. The death sentences for the other two were commuted to 30 years in prison. There were no witnesses to the charged crimes and no defense counsel to argue the case – the classic kangaroo court of the Communist regime.

In 1991 the AFL-CIO reported that Mario Chanes de Armas, an opponent of Castro, had been imprisoned for 30 years and, at that time, was the longest-held prisoner in the world. The labor organization was trying to obtain his release. He was what is called a "plantado" (planted prisoner), a designation applied to prisoners who refuse to be indoctrinated and whose prison term is oftentimes extended capriciously as further punishment for their stance. As of the writing of this book, the final fate of this brave man is unknown. What is known is that his son died and he was not permitted to attend the funeral unless he wore a prison uniform. He opted to remain in his cell. This is only one example of the type of inhumane cruelties committed by this barbaric system.

The political prisoners are jailed in cells with no windows, only walls, and a hole in the floor for use as a toilet. They are kept in darkness without being able to see the sky for long periods of time. They sleep on a thin mattress in very hot cells, oftentimes developing skin rashes and other diseases for which they receive no medical treatment. They are deprived of visits by their families for months at a time. Many die in jail because of malnutrition or lack of medical care. International human rights organizations have repeatedly been denied access to the Cuban prisons. There are over 300 jails on the island, all of which are overcrowded and filthy. Many times the political prisoners are kept in the same cells that common criminals occupy. Others are maintained in solitary confinement.

In February 1996, a group of Cuban dissidents, organizers of a movement called Concilio Cubano (Cuban Council), were planning to meet in Havana to demand freedom to assemble and respect for human rights. The government denied permission for their meeting and arrested over 50 of the organizers, despite pleas from European leaders to respect the intentions of the coalition of dissidents. The U.S. State Department expressed concern about the crackdown. International pressure was disregarded by the Communist tyranny, even though Cuba had been negotiating an economic package with the European Union, the latter attempting to condition any agreement based on Cuba abiding by respect for human rights. Castro does not seem to care for any obligation that will curtail the human rights abuses prevalent in his regime, nor will he grant the freedom to any dissent from the absolute power of the Communist state. Cuban dissident Gustavo Arcos, one of the Concilio Cubano leaders, was "visited" by the dreaded State Security Police and told in no uncertain terms that his organization was an outlaw group and would not be tolerated. Of the more than 200 groups of dissidents in Cuba mentioned earlier, about 120 of them fall under the umbrella of Concilio Cubano.

On July 16, 1997, four prominent dissidents were arrested and jailed as suspected counter-revolutionaries. Vladimiro Roca Antunes, Marta Beatriz Roque Cabello, Félix Bonné Carcasés and René Gómez Manzano, leaders of a group named "Working Group of Internal Dissidents," were apprehended at their homes. They had the support of a sizable number of smaller dissident organizations. Later that same week the State Security Police detained another dissident journalist, Luiz López Prendes, who was promoting democratic reforms. The trial of the four imprisoned members of the Working Group was held 19 months after their arrests in March 1999. Earlier they had released a paper titled "The Homeland Belongs to All," offering an analysis of Cuba's economy throughout the revolution, proposing reforms to the Cuban Constitution, challenging the one-party system and calling for the respect of human rights. Additional arrests of dissidents occurred after the trial was announced to prevent – in the words of the regime – "the outbreak of disorders outside the court," like those that occurred on August 28, 1998, when dissident Alfredo R. García was brought to trial.

Vladimiro Roca was an economist; a son of the late Blas Roca, one of the founders of the old Communist Party and a long-time trade union leader who was co-founder of the new integrated Communist Party under Castro's design. Vladimiro had been a member of Castro's military force. He became disenchanted with Communism and joined the dissident movement. He was one of the best-known prisoners among the over 1000 political dissidents in Castro's jails. Marta Beatriz Roque was an economist, Félix Bonné was a professor and René Gómez was an attorney. All were graduates of the revolution and sentenced to several years in prison. Their family visits were restricted and their health conditions were not given proper medical attention. Vladimiro and Beatriz had serious medical problems, according to friends and relatives. They were sent to four different penal institutions. Their jail cells, as usual, were unsanitary and cramped. Their sentencing and imprisonment had provoked appeals for clemency from several human rights organizations, foreign governments and intellectuals. After several years of internment, they were conditionally freed.

Beatriz continued her patriotic activities, becoming a leader of a coalition of opposition organizations under the umbrella of a broader conference, the Assembly for the Promotion of a Civil Society. She called for a meeting of the assembly on May 20, 2005, which drew about 200 dissidents from various regions of Cuba, in spite of the obstacles placed by the government to obstruct and sabotage the event. Among other leaders participating in the meeting were Félix Bonné and René Gómez Manzano.

On August 11, 1997, Cuban security officials detained well-known dissident and independent journalist Raúl Rivero and searched his house. Rivero was head of an illegal news agency called *Cuba Press*, which was attempting to provide an alternative to the state-controlled media. Generally the independent journalists in Cuba manage to send their works to other countries because of the tight censorship prevailing in Cuba. Many of the dissident journalists have been persecuted and have gone into exile. Activist foreign journalist organizations, such as the Paris-based journalist rights group Reporters Without Borders and the Committee to Protect Journalists based in New York, have sent appeals to Castro requesting the release of Rivero. The dictator has not budged on his refusal to grant these clemency requests. Rivero was given a 20-year sentence. As of January 2004 he was still in prison. It is said that while serving his time he is writing poetry and reading the works of classic Cuban literary writers. Many other independent journalists are incarcerated in Cuba and suffering from depression and anxiety.

On Friday, August 28, 1998, Alfredo Reynaldo García, age 37, a renowned Cuban dissident and independent journalist who had been arrested months earlier, was brought to a court in Havana and accused of spreading misleading information. Then something unusual occurred. Apparently Cubans had somewhat shaken their fear of the regime after the Pope's visit. A large number of supporters joined the relatives of the accused and staged a demonstration in protest of the trial. They all thought that the charges against Alfredo were going to be dismissed because of the trivial accusations brought against him. They gathered outside the court building chanting "Freedom," "Down with Fidel Castro," "Free the prisoners of conscience," "Justice for opposition leaders" and "Enough of repression." The detainee had been on the Vatican's clemency list. Amnesty International had also requested his release. He was specifically charged at the trial with sending articles critical of the government to the Radio-Marti station in Miami, which broadcasts programs in Spanish to Cuba. The crowds demonstrating their anger were dispersed by the security police and hooligans of the government-sponsored Rapid Response Brigades. Diplomats, foreign journalists and dissident leaders were not allowed in the courtroom.

However, Alfredo's relatives, including his parents and wife, were permitted to be there. He was given a 3-year prison term, a relatively light sentence but, nevertheless, an unjust one because he didn't do anything wrong. It seems that the unexpected attention given to the trial by various nations' leaders, the Vatican and the general public in Cuba served as a deterrent to the tyranny of imposing a longer sentence.

In April 2003 Castro ordered the summary execution of three young black men who had hijacked a ferry boat at Havana harbor in an attempt to flee from Cuba. He declared their executions were necessary as a deterrent to prevent further similar acts. Simultaneously he ordered a crackdown which netted 75 opposition leaders accused of acting as collaborators of the U.S. to weaken the Socialist government. They were summarily judged and condemned to serve up to 28 years in prison. The U.S. and the dissidents denied the accusations. There was an international uproar over the brutal crackdown. The European Union, the United States, Pope John Paul II, Human Rights Watch and other human rights organizations decried the execution of the three young men and the incarceration of the opposition leaders, requesting their immediate freedom. Castro ignored the international protests and continued his defiant attitude of directly blaming the U.S. government and trashing the chief of the U.S. Interest Section in Havana, James Cason, accusing him of flaming the malcontent of the dissidents.

In October 2003 Cuban opposition leader Oswaldo Payá delivered nearly 15,000 signatures to the government demanding democratic reforms, which included civil rights liberties and holding free elections. These signatures were in addition to 11,000 he had previously delivered. The effort to request a referendum by the democratic reform movement, known as the Varela Project, has been going on for several years. Payá, the project leader and a Catholic layman, was unhappy with the Church's hierarchy and with Protestant groups because they had remained silent in this effort. The official Christian organizations had not made any public statements in favor of dissident activities, although they had cautiously criticized the detection and jailing of political opponents of the regime. Payá was the recipient of Europe's highest human rights award and has been considered for the Nobel Peace Prize. Varela Project supporters have been threatened and persecuted by State Security agents, and some have been jailed.

In January 2004 it was reported by the U.S. press that Oscar Biscet has been in solitary confinement since he was sentenced to 25 years in prison at the trial of the 75 dissidents in April 2003. All of the other 74 prisoners have been enduring the same wicked treatment in either solitary confinement or in cells holding hardened criminals. They have suffered the same unsanitary conditions and malnutrition common to the Communist iniquitous treatment of political prisoners.

In that same month Elizardo Sánchez, head of the Cuban Commission on Human Rights and National Reconciliation, a reputable and internationally-respected dissident organization, reported that many political prisoners were seriously ill and that at least ten in grave health conditions should be released immediately on humanitarian grounds. This request was denied.

The long struggle of Marta Beatriz Roque and other dissident leaders for the restoration of democracy to Cuba has opened a new page in the history of the island. On July 22, 2005, she was detained again, along with more than a dozen other dissenters. This time the government's excuse was that the repressive action was triggered by an attempt to smash an anti-government protest that could have caused larger repercussions and the need to defend the revolution against the enemies of Socialism. Marta Beatriz and two other women were released after being held overnight. Others remained in custody, including René Gómez Manzano and Félix Bonné, who, along with Marta Beatriz, continue as leaders of the Assembly for the Promotion of a Civil Society. They were all charged with violating Law #88, the infamous Law for the Protection of the National Independence and Economy of Cuba, called by the Cubans "la ley mordaza" (the gag law).

Under "the gag law," the Criminal Code defines the term "sedition" as a crime which includes non-violent opposition perturbing the Socialist order, the state security, the celebration of elections or referendums, and obstructing any legal disposition established by the state or a military authority. Under the law, citizens must obey the dictates of the government without any recourse. The charge of sedition applies even if no violence or weapons are involved. Other crimes include the distribution of enemy propaganda, rebellion, dissemination of information promoting human rights, expressing views critical of the Socialist policies, and the support of ideologies conflicting with Communism. Those accused of criminal law violations are subject to a sentence of ten to twenty years or more in prison. Executions by firing squad can be applied, depending on the interpretation of violence, sedition or rebellion. It has been stated by Castro and his thugs that the intent of the law is to protect the Socialist state against its enemies. The criminal law is driven to silence any opposition to the dictatorship.

In August 2005 Cuban State Security agents nabbed over 50 opposition activists. This was in addition to the dissidents who were arrested on July 22nd, at least 15 of whom are still in jail. On August 12, 2005, Vladimiro Roca, the well-known dissident leader, was holding a meeting in his home in Havana with a group of his followers, when suddenly over 60 pro-Castro militants appeared outside to intimidate them. They were shouting obscenities and diatribes such as "traitors," "worms," "mercenaries" and "Yankee stooges." The meeting was dispersed and some dissidents were detained. Castro accused the dissident movement of being nothing but a miniscule group of people being paid by the U.S. government. He incited the thugs of his Committees for the Defense of the Revolution to stop the "traitors" through acts of violence. Notwithstanding, the dissidents continue their fight to restore freedom and democracy to Cuba.

In the United States we hear about the abuses of the Cuban criminal law only when there is a large crackdown transmitted by the international news agencies.

However, we seldom hear about the practically-every-day detention of smaller numbers of dissidents and independent journalists throughout the island who are confined for mostly minor violations, either to jail or labor camps. They are often being sentenced by special security tribunals – in closed trials – to punishments varying from one to eight years of confinement.

The frequent crackdowns have been condemned time and time again by the European Union, U.S. human rights organizations, Amnesty International, pro-democracy groups, intellectuals, and many other civic entities and nations.

What I don't understand is that, in many cases, the foreign reporters describing the desperate plight of the prisoners' relatives and witnessing the suffering and deprivation of their loved ones, continue in some sneaky way to refer to the false claims of Cuban authorities about the benefits of the revolution, repeating in their press reports the regime's lies about the country's free healthcare system, universal education and other services. Nothing is free under Communism. The poor people of Cuba are paying dearly for all of those services, which are not as good as they claim to be, with poorly paid labor – through sweat, tears and onerous enslavement – and with the so-called "voluntary" work of young and old, militia duties, and other "revolutionary tasks." Money is taken out of the workers' pay to maintain the much-touted "free benefits." Workers in Cuba are paid in pesos, the equivalent of five to ten dollars a month. It would appear that most news reporters covering Cuba like to balance their act by saying something favorable to the Communist regime. They may not want to be expelled from the country for being too critical, a situation that has happened in several instances. In other cases, their liberalism may influence their favorable comments about the revolution.

Brains as Patrimony of the State: The Case of Dr. Molina

People's bodies and minds are entrapped by a ruthless, inhuman dictator who openly claims that human intellect is the property of the state. To cite one concrete case among many, consider the ordeal to which Dr. Hilda Molina has been subjected for years. Dr. Molina was a loyal Communist Party member, a distinguished physician, and a product of the revolution. She was also a national legislator. As a neurologist she was involved in scientific investigations of fetal tissue transplants to treat certain neurological disorders. She founded the Center for Neurological Restoration. She became a shining star, a favorite of Castro and was given many honors and awards. She was prominently displayed to the world as an example of the scientific achievements of the revolution. In other words, she was used for propaganda purposes. However, in 1994 she had an abrupt falling-out with the dictator over the issue of admitting patients from foreign countries to the neurological health institute. She vehemently opposed converting the institute into an exclusive government clinic for paying patients from overseas. She insisted that the purpose of the institute, as initially conceived, was for Cubans affected with such diseases. As a result of the clash, she resigned as director of the health center, gave up her seat as a delegate to the National Assembly of the Popular Power (the pseudo-legislative body of Cuba), returned all the rewards given to her by the government and denounced the money-making scheme as a betrayal of the revolution.

After the above actions on the part of Dr. Molina, she was constantly harassed and subjected to acts of repudiation by the organized hooligan squads of the so-called Committees for the Defense of the Revolution (CDRs). She was officially declared an enemy of the revolution. Additionally, she has been repeatedly denied a permit to visit with her son, also a neurologist, who lives in exile in Argentina and her infant grandsons whom she has never met. Argentina and Spain have interceded on her behalf to let her travel outside Cuba to no avail. Castro continues to claim that people's brains are the patrimony of the state and that is the reason why she can't leave Cuba.

Dr. Molina has been falsely accused, as have other dissidents, of being paid by the United States government to conduct anti-revolutionary activities. Her situation is very difficult because anti-Communism is the worst sin a person can commit in Cuba. Castro considers that such behavior sets a poor example for the population. The resulting punishment is hellish and intended to send a message to others who may entertain the same idea. The victims of this heresy are vilified, ostracized, and subjected to physical and mental torture. They are removed from society, demonstrating the cruelty of the doctrine and the failure of Socialism. In some instances, the punishment is incarceration and even death. In the case of Dr. Molina, the latter punishments would have created an international uproar because she was well known in the international scientific community through her works and her frequent traveling to attend conferences overseas. Castro was afraid of such scandalous international reaction at a time when he needed to improve his relations with the European community to prop up the declining Cuban economy, still under the effect of the demise of the Soviet Union.

The Ladies in White

For the last few years (2003 – 2007) a large group of women dressed in white have been attending Sunday mass at a designated church, and after services they walk the streets of Havana silently in a demonstration of civil disobedience. The husbands, sons and relatives of most of these women are in jail accused of being dissidents and mercenaries of the U.S. government. The women are called "Las Damas de Blanco" (the Ladies in White). They have become a usual and popular sight in Havana every Sunday. The government wasted no time in discouraging and suppressing this non-violent display of tenacity. They mobilized the state-controlled Neighborhood Vigilante Committees to counter-demonstrate and intimidate the marchers, or to impede those dressed in white from attending the mass and participating in the march. They harass the participants, shouting diatribes and accusations of being traitors to the revolution and stooges of the

U.S. government. Notwithstanding, the Ladies in White ignore the hooligans and continue their march with stoicism, asking for amnesty, which they make known by the imprint on their white blouses or T-shirts generally stenciled with a picture of their jailed relatives. The ladies also carry flowers as a sign of goodwill. In the climate of hate inculcated by Castro in the minds of the fanatical and meagerly-rewarded mobs – the scum of society – it takes a lot of fortitude and determination to do what the Ladies in White are accomplishing. They deserve our kudos!

11

The Aftermath of Communism: Human Rights Violations, Continued Persecutions, Eliminations and a Police State

"Under Fidel, Cuba is not an independent and sovereign nation. It is a colony, a satellite of the Soviet Union. What influenced Fidel above all was his demented ambition for power. That's what brought him to the Communists. They were the only ones who would help sustain him in power for the rest of his life."
— JUANITA CASTRO, SISTER OF FIDEL CASTRO

Human Rights Violations

THE CUBAN ATROCITIES perpetuated by the Castro regime have been repeatedly denounced by the United Nations Human Rights Commission, the Inter-American Commission on Human Rights of the Organization of American States, the European Union Human Rights Commission, the American Division of Human Rights Watch, Amnesty International, the European Parliament and other international organizations.

The European Union legislators in 2003 passed a joint resolution criticizing the "continuing flagrant violation of the civil and political human rights and the fundamental freedoms of members of the Cuban opposition and of independent journalists." They also urged Castro to release all political prisoners. Castro's irate response was that he would no longer accept EU aid and accused it of backing U.S. policies. Castro's regime is undoubtedly the Number One human rights violator in the Western Hemisphere. The blood on the hands of this despicable dictator and his surrounding hooligans is impossible to erase and is not being ignored by the United States and the rest of the civilized world.

Let's continue with the long list of heinous crimes committed by Castro. On July 13, 1994, he personally ordered the sinking of a boat carrying 21 children and 20 adults who were attempting to flee the country. They were all killed. On February 24, 1996, two Cuban Air Force MiGs fired on two un-armed U.S.-registered light planes while still outside of Cuban territorial waters, killing three Americans and a U.S.-Cuban resident while they were on a humanitarian rescue mission. Castro admitted full responsibility for this criminal action. The list of political prisoners who are still in jail after their sentences have expired is in the thousands. Additionally they have been cruelly tortured, both physically and mentally, because they refused to be indoctrinated. Many have been executed or have died in prison as a result of injuries, internal and external, that they have suffered due to beatings, lack of medication or hunger.

The Fate of Castro's Relatives

One of the most relevant testimonies about Castro's debasement is that of his own sister Juanita. She has been in exile in the United States since 1964 where she established a pharmacy in Miami. The terror of Castro touched her in a dramatic way. She had been active in the civic resistance movement against the Batista government and had collected funds for the revolution. Fearing for her safety, she left Cuba in 1957 and arrived in Miami where she was Treasurer of the 26th of July Movement in exile. She returned to Cuba after Batista was overthrown. Propelled by her humanitarian nature, she initially participated with a great deal of enthusiasm in her brother's regime as a social worker in schools, hospitals and other altruistic institutions. She thought the revolution would bring humanitarian and democratic solutions to Cuban problems instead of the tyrannical regime that resulted. Her dreams of justice and democracy began to fade soon after the first few months of the revolution. She could have held a high post in the revolutionary government if she had so desired. However, as a dignified and religious person with high expectations for her country, she refrained from jumping into a role that could come back to haunt her. She was cognizant of the penetration of Communism from the early stages of the revolution.

Castro's father, Angel Castro, was a tough Spaniard who immigrated to Cuba and through hard work and dedication built a fortune, which included a sugar cane plantation, a lumber mill and livestock. Angel and his second wife Alina had seven children: Angela, Ramón, Fidel, Raúl, Juanita, Emma and Agustina. He also had two children from a previous marriage, Pedro Emilio and Lidia. Angel died in 1956. The land that the Castro family inherited was turned over to the state following the radical Agrarian Reform Law dictated by Castro. His mother Alina was left with only a farmhouse and a few acres of land. All the years of hard work and sacrifices of his father were wasted away, with no mercy shown by the cruel dictator. For Fidel Castro, family and love have no meaning. He has proven it many times. The only thing that matters to him is himself and his egotism.

Juanita was a very perceptive individual and was not blinded by her brother's theatrical antics. She knew him well. She was cautiously observing, with apprehension, how he was inflaming passions and broadcasting that the revolution would be protecting the freedom of the press, promoting democracy and political liberties, while in private he was expressing just the opposite. He was planning to make it difficult for the press to survive because it was already critical of some of his revolutionary moves that were negating freedom of expression, political divergence and democracy. As an insider, she noticed that there was deception in the behavior of her brother. From all of the background information we have gathered from other civilian and military leaders of the revolution now in exile, and from my own personal experience at the University of Havana, Castro invariably wanted to impose his will on the world. It was an intrinsic component of his mental attitude since his youth, as confirmed by Juanita. It strengthened the assertion by some that he was a megalomaniac and a psychopath.

Juanita was witnessing as well the persecution, imprisonment and inhumane execution of many good revolutionaries who risked their lives and sacrificed their well-being in the fight against Batista, when all they had done was to oppose the gradual Communist conversion of the revolution. By 1960 Juanita had become totally disillusioned with her brother. She advised him about what she was seeing, but he turned his back on her and denied such things were happening. Furthermore, he insisted that those who fell in disgrace were counter-revolutionaries and traitors.

The Communization process continued, the abuses and intimidation persisted and became worse with each passing day. The press was liquidated; the promises and programs for a democratic system were bitter lies. Juanita joined the anti-Castro movement and helped in the underground conspiracy. Her mother died in 1963 of heart problems. She had suffered over the political course the revolution had taken and was despondent about the human tragedy caused by her son's actions. It was said that she had even denounced him before her death. It was a sad end for such a dedicated mother.

Knowing that her activities and moves were being closely followed by Castro's agents, Juanita defected to Mexico in 1964, and shortly thereafter came to the United States, establishing her residence in Miami. Juanita became an active participant in the anti-Castro circles and traveled to many Latin American countries to expose the Communist takeover of Cuba under the leadership of her brother. In an interview she held with George de Lama, a newspaper writer for the *Chicago Tribune*, published on February 14, 1980, she declared:

> Under Fidel, Cuba is not an independent and sovereign nation. It is a colony, a satellite of the Soviet Union. What influenced Fidel above all was his demented ambition for power. That's what brought him to the Communists. They were the only ones who would help sustain him in power for the rest of his life. They

were the only ones who would help in his quest for world conquest, as we can see today in all those movements in which he has been involved – in Africa, in the Americas... Fidel symbolizes all the worst, let's just make that clear. Any tyrant or dictator symbolizes the worst for a country, the worst of a people, the worst of the human condition.

On December 20, 1993, Alina Fernández Revuelta, daughter of Castro, defected and went to Spain where she was granted political asylum by the U.S. Embassy in Madrid. She sneaked out of Cuba disguised with a wig, using heavy makeup to appear like the woman's picture on the false Spanish passport she was carrying. After reaching Spanish soil, she flew the next day to Columbus, Georgia, and went to the home of Elena Amos, a wealthy Cuban-American who had helped other Cuban defectors. Alina was 37 years old at the time of her escape. She was formerly a model and critical of her father's government. She had been under virtual house arrest and continuous surveillance by the State Security agents. The escape of Alina from Cuba is another indication that all members of the Cuban society, regardless of status, feel unsafe and profoundly disturbed by the Communist regime.

Alina was born out of wedlock to Natalia Revuelta of a wealthy family in Havana. Alina's mother was married at the time to Dr. Orlando Fernández, a notable cardiologist who later left for the United States. Natalia was an early sympathizer of Castro and in the mid-1950s provided protection for him when he was conspiring against the Batista government.

Alina had been an outspoken critic of her father's regime, had called Castro a tyrant and often expressed her bitterness at the lack of freedom in Cuba. She had stated that Cuba's Socialism was a dead-end street and that she associated Socialism with economic collapse and food shortages. Juanita Castro, her aunt, in commenting to the press about Alina's defection, said: "With his [Castro's] own relatives escaping, the signal to the world is clear. The young people of her generation feel defrauded." Alina had left behind her teenage daughter, praying and hoping that her release would be forthcoming. Others throughout the world supported Alina on her humanitarian request. The international press had given a lot of coverage concerning her departure from Cuba. A week later, on December 31st, her 16-year old daughter Alina-Maria Salgado Fernández left Cuba and arrived in Miami, as an intermediate stop on the way to Columbus, Georgia, where she met with her mother, who was anxiously waiting at the airport. Alina-Maria was a happy camper, full of energy and enthusiasm. She had been very unhappy with the dictatorship of her grandfather. At her age she was understandably very excited and exuberant. She said that "she was going to meet a lot of people, learn the language and study a lot, something I could not do in Cuba."

It is no coincidence that at that time Castro was desperate to increase his business ties with Western Europe. Cuba's subsidized economy had been devastated and was still reeling from the effects of the crumbling of the Soviet empire.

Western European countries had been very critical of the human rights abuses systematically perpetuated in Cuba under Castro's despotic rule. The defection of his granddaughter, also a high profile case, was given wide publicity abroad. The whole world was watching the unfolding of this family tragedy closely. He was cornered. It was an opportunity for Castro to make it appear that he was showing leniency. Alina-Maria's departure could not have happened at a better time.

The Quevedo Case: Frustration and Suicide

The betrayal to the revolution by Castro was bitterly denounced by another close friend and one of his most ardent supporters, Miguel Angel Quevedo, the owner and publisher of the weekly magazine *Bohemia*, the most widely-distributed publication of its kind in Cuba and one whose fame transcended to other Latin American countries. Quevedo was a reputable person, his magazine was supportive of the 26th of July Movement and its pages carried many articles defending Castro, in spite of stressful moments during the Batista regime. Quevedo helped to create the legend of Castro and was a factor in his rise to power. *Bohemia's* political influence was significant as Quevedo was looked upon as a credible publisher of unquestionable integrity. After Castro's advent, the magazine continued to exalt Castro and the revolution until Quevedo began to uncover the treason of Castro to the democratic principles which served as the foundation of the struggle against Batista. His deception led him to describe Castro as "a monster far worse than Batista."

Quevedo, who had enthusiastically embraced Castro and proclaimed him a liberator when he descended from the mountains, believed Castro's promises of promoting free expression, reestablishing democracy and holding elections after normalcy was restored. Quevedo's disappointment with Castro was, as he admitted, a heart-breaking blow from which he could never recover. He had put his reputation on the line and felt he had misled the Cuban people by using the *Bohemia* editorial line to edify Castro as a patriotic hero. At the beginning he could not bring himself to admit that Castro was a deceptive individual who was hiding his Marxist ideology to manipulate his faithful followers. Quevedo experienced humiliation, guilt and depression for helping Castro gain power. The magazine maintained an anti-Communist stand which began to bother Castro.

Quevedo harshly criticized Castro's course to Communism. In retaliation, Castro turned his cohorts loose to intimidate the daring publisher. With his life in peril, Quevedo was forced to request asylum in the Venezuelan Embassy on July 18, 1960. From there he fled into exile. The magazine and his properties were immediately confiscated. Practically the entire staff of *Bohemia* journalists followed Quevedo into exile. Their properties were also confiscated by Castro. The Catholic magazine *La Quincana*, which had defended the revolution until the Communization process had significantly advanced, was closed in early 1961, perhaps the last of the free press publications to be confiscated.

Quevedo's feeling of guilt for supporting Castro was a mental burden that he just could not shake off. Dejected and contrite, he committed suicide in August 1969. Before he took his life, he wrote a farewell letter to a journalist friend in Miami, Mr. Ernesto Montaner. A full text of the letter appears in the book *Cuba in Revolution: Escape From a Lost Paradise*, Miguel A. Faria, M.D., Hacienda Publishing, Inc., Macon, GA, 2002. In this missive he asked for forgiveness for his culpability in the rise of Castro. He denounced by name the Latin American leaders of the "Democratic Left" who were his friends until he broke with Castro and joined ranks with the anti-Communist critics of the dictator. He described them as the "titans" who had so little of "democratic" and so much of the "left" – the ones who coldly abandoned him after he had given them moral and economic support. Quevedo hoped that his death would be productive in the sense that it would catch the attention of the liberal press so they would never again become an echo of the uncultured and uninhibited mobs, but instead a lighthouse to guide them. He also castigated the millionaires giving money to left-wing leaders who, once in a position of power, despoil everything.

Quevedo admonished those whose hatred and infamy facilitated the physical and mental destruction of a nation. He conceded that many good things were achieved before the revolution for the benefit of Cuba, no matter who was the president, although intently they were mercilessly attacked by radical and strident leaders. He made reference to the 20,000 deaths attributed to the Batista regime as an invention of a *Bohemia* journalist, Enrique de la Osa, who published the article to inflame public opinion against Batista. Incidentally, reliable sources indicate that the deaths on both sides – the Batista forces and the insurgents – amounted to no more than 900. For propaganda purposes, Castro made a big splash about the grossly exaggerated number of deaths reported.

Furthermore, Quevedo stated that the ruining of Cuba was the fault of many by commission or omission – old and young, rich and poor, white and black, honest and thieves, virtuous and sinners, the politicians, the press, the clergy and the United States – for not doing more to stop the international conspiracy directed by the Communists and the blindness of the people caused by hatred, which overcomes all virtues. He admitted being part of the mistakes and asked for forgiveness for his sins and the bad things he had done, just as he was forgiving all of his compatriots for their participation in the tragedy that destroyed the republic.

Quevedo's farewell was a moving document decrying all of the errors committed leading to the revolution and its subsequent betrayal by Castro. It is a good example to others outside of the fatal Cuban experience to ponder what the radical left can do to trample the legitimate hopes of a nation. Only if you have lived the drama can you fully understand, as Quevedo did, the devastating consequences of blindly and fanatically putting your trust in a maniacal and deceiving demagogue.

The Elimination of Ernesto "Che" Guevara

In Castro's quest for the undisputed domination of the political limelight in Cuba, there was another scheme that he had been contemplating for some time. It was the elimination of Commander Ernesto "Che" Guevara, the Argentine firebrand who was his companion from the days of the preparation of the guerrilla group trained in Mexico in 1956 prior to the landing in Cuba in the Granma boat. Guevara was ex-President of the Central Bank, ex-Minister of Industry and one of Castro's top economic advisors in the revolutionary regime. Castro began to have serious differences with his once-trusted advisor over the planning and execution of various projects. By 1965 the abyss between the two was well known among their close political and military associates. Bitterness and resentment developed over their contrasting styles and the way to carry out the central blueprint for the Cuban economy.

The failure of several ambitious agricultural and industrial projects deepened their oftentimes acrimonious confrontations. Castro began to get rid of Guevara's protégés. Guevara began to fade away. The distance between the two became obvious within their respective inner circles, and even transcended to the public. Guevara was separated from the Central Committee of the emerging United Party of the Socialist Revolution, officially formed in 1965 to consolidate the various revolutionary organizations with the old Communist Party, and which evolved into the new Communist Party under the leadership of Castro in October 1965.

At some point it became apparent that Guevara had disappeared from the scene. His known neurotic condition was exacerbated by the delicate position in which he was cornered. There were rumors about his mental instability. On the other hand, it was public knowledge that Castro's egocentrism would not permit him to be eclipsed by Guevara's popularity among the intellectuals and technocrats. As in the case of Camilo Cienfuegos, Castro commenced to elucidate a plan to remove Guevara, preferably under circumstances that would exonerate him from his elimination. He would rather have Guevara as a symbol, a dead symbol that would not interfere with Castro's ambition to be the only center of the revolution. He opted to get him out of the country in a high-risk mission to Africa, pleasing at the same time the Moscow masters who needed proxies to join the Marxist guerillas in the ex-Belgian Congo (Zaire). Guevara, the eager adventurer, was dispatched to Africa with a group of military officers and one hundred Cuban soldiers. They arrived at the ex-French Congo, then entered into the rebel territory of the ex-Belgian Congo around Kinshasa (Leopoldville) through Lake Tanganyca, where they joined the Marxist insurgents.

They participated in the training of the guerilla fighters and took part in several combat missions without much success. The government of Leopoldville denounced their presence in the civil war and the forces of Moises Tshombe had them in retreat. Guevara went back to Brazzaville, the capital of the ex-French

Congo, where he stayed for several months (July 1965 to April 1966) until he returned quietly to Cuba at the order of Castro. Moscow had a change of mind on the strategy to be followed in that region of Africa.

What was next for Guevara? At this juncture there was no question that Castro wanted him out of Cuba again. He encouraged Guevara to head a guerilla intrusion into Bolivia. Guevara, his ego flying, accepted the task and started to recruit a contingent of his former rebel army combatants, some of whom had participated with him in the Congo fiasco, and others who were Bolivians being trained in Cuba for guerilla warfare. He acquired the necessary weapons, supplies and money for the expedition. Castro was delighted that Guevara had taken on the new venture so enthusiastically. It was the quintessential avenue to finally unload the "guerilla genius" from his back. The Bolivian terrain, the tactics and the logistics of warfare in an inhospitable environment were not fitting for this type of campaign. The odds for success were either slim or practically none.

As expected, Guevara was defeated by the well-trained and well-armed Bolivian army, who was familiar with the jungles and the idiosyncrasies of the indigenous population of the region. He never received any significant backing from the primitive peasants dispersed in the vast wilderness. The sources of food and medication became scarce. He soon found out that this was not comparable to the abundant resources available in the Cuban mountains and its surrounding agricultural lands and small villages with plenty of supplies. In the encounters he had with the Bolivian troops he began to suffer the loss of human lives. Seeing these negative results, Castro decided to terminate any further assistance to Guevara.

After several months of hiding and a few more shooting skirmishes in which he lost additional men, Guevara was surrounded, wounded and captured in the Quebrada del Yuro Mountains. He was interrogated and asked why he had come to liberate Bolivia, a free country, while Cuba was a slave satellite country depending on Soviet aid for survival. He was also reminded of the Bolivian soldiers he had killed, leaving behind grieving widows and fatherless children. During his detention a search was conducted that uncovered assorted items and twenty thousand dollars in cash. He was executed by a Bolivian army officer in the rural village of La Higuera, not far from where he was caught, on October 9, 1967.

Castro had achieved another milestone, the indirect elimination of his last potential rival for the leadership of the Cuban revolution. Thirty years later, in October 1997, the remains of Guevara were located in Bolivia and transferred to Cuba for burial, where Castro built a monument in his honor. A "dead hero" is now only a symbol and no longer a perturbing shadow of the tyrant. Such is the perversity and ambition of Castro. Scholars have written and ruminated about whether Guevara was a better Communist than Castro. It is proper to cite here what Solzhenitsyn said in his article, "Communism at the End of the

Brezhnev Era" in *National Review*, January 2, 1983, about comparing brands of Communism: "It is a dangerous illusion to draw distinction between 'better' and 'worse' Communisms, between more peaceful and more aggressive kinds. They are all inimical to humanity."

An excellent book covering various facets of the turbulent relationship between Castro and Guevara, and the latter's expeditionary adventures, was authored by my illustrious Cuban-exiled friend José Guerra Alemán, and is entitled *Barro y Cenizas, Dialogos con Fidel Castro y el "Che" Guevara* (*Clay and Ashes, Dialogues with Fidel Castro and "Che" Guevara*), printed in Spanish by Fomento Editorial, S.A., Madrid, Spain, 1971. He climbed the Sierra Maestra Mountains as a journalist to report on the insurgency movement and to search for the truth. He knew and analyzed Castro and Guevara while spending time with them in the mountain range. His incisive wit penetrated their intricate mental posture like no other analyst has done. In his book Guerra Alemán emphasized the background of terror and violence which dominated the lives of these two characters. He referred to Castro as a product of the distortion of biology. Without hesitation, I would apply the same description to the no-less-hateful "Che" Guevara.

Guevara was elevated by the liberal press as a heroic and romantic guerilla leader, an icon of the Cuban revolution. Unfortunately, his image became an emblem of restlessness and rebellion for many young people all over the world, when in fact he was a vicious murderer responsible for the death and execution of thousands of victims of the Cuban revolution and his foreign adventures; an intemperate Communist, who helped to break down the Cuban civil society and ruin its economic foundation; a cruel and mentally unstable individual who, along with Castro and his brother Raúl, engineered the conspiracy to deliver Cuba to Communism. The fact that he and Castro had differences was not related to the changeover of Cuba to a Communist state under Soviet influence; on that they fully agreed. Their differences were solely based on taking different paths to arrive at the same point. The best thing that can be said about Castro, his brother Raúl and Guevara is that they have won a deserving place in the rubbish heap of the human race.

The Police State

Another fallacy of the Cuban quagmire brings to mind the commentaries of some who still argue that, if the Cubans had stayed on the island, they would have been a formidable force to oppose Castro. The falsity and naïveté of this assertion is that it could have been feasible only under a government that would allow dissention. However, we must not lose sight that the Castro tyranny introduced something not known in Cuba before; namely, a brutal police state. Gestapo-style fear and terror restrained the population. Long prison terms, torture and abuses suffered by thousands in crowded and filthy jails for simply expressing their views are common practices in a country devoid of a judicial system. Political, military and civic leaders who dissented with the regime they helped to create have been arrested and summarily executed or jailed for many years. Mercy was in short supply, and continues to be after over 48 years of repression. To accomplish this horrendous task, a sophisticated spying system was established that permeated the civil society and the military circles.

Under a system where no one can be trusted and penalties are meted out without any humane consideration, an organized, meaningful and effective opposition is unattainable. Civil rights are trampled. Castro abolished the judiciary when he came to power. He became the judge, the prosecutor and the star witness. As if that wasn't enough, he also appointed the defense counsel. Kangaroo courts have been in effect since January 1, 1959 up to the present time. Today, even under unbearable circumstances, undaunted dissidents, barely surviving in Cuba, are constantly harassed, persecuted, incarcerated and submitted to horrible deprivation in the jails of Castro. Panic has been instilled in the enslaved population. Survival pervades the mind of the Cuban people, always busy, scrapping for something to eat and sustain themselves and their families.

The defections from Cuba have no end. One generation after another continue to attempt to find liberty, freedom of expression, adequate nutrition and other essential needs for a decent living by escaping from the island. It is pathetic to hear what younger generations are saying about the reasons they fled from Cuba and risked their lives and those of their children in makeshift artifacts. You can measure their desperation by the type of improvised vessels they put together to escape. They expose themselves to the hot sun, wind, rain, rough seas, with salt water continuously splashing on their bodies, and lack of fresh water to drink and food to sustain an energy level needed for the trip. The 90-mile trip to the United States in such makeshift vessels could take from eight to thirty days at times. They cannot carry much food and water. Those who survive the long journey to the Florida coast arrive dehydrated with severe sunburn and lacerations, nutrient-depleted and exhausted. In spite of the odds, droves continue to try by putting their faith in God and Mother Nature.

Let me cite one unbelievable case. In the summer of 2003 twelve people, consisting of nine men, two women and a small child, left the coast of Cuba in a 1951 Chevy pickup truck mounted on improvised pontoons, using empty 55-gallon drums as floaters and a propeller connected to the driveshaft of the vehicle to move it through the sea at a very low rate of speed. After about thirty hours at sea they came to within 40 miles of the Florida shore, only to be stopped by the U.S. Coast Guard. They were detained and returned to Cuba. In February 2004, the same two men who invented the Chevy truck boat tried again, this time using a 1950s vintage Buick converted into a sea-going vessel. Once more they had tough luck when their group of eleven, six adults and five children, were intercepted by the U.S. Coast Guard about 90 miles from the Miami coast. They were held and then sent back to their homeland. Their brave and daring stunt failed again. According to immigration accords in effect for several years, Cubans fleeing from the Communist tyranny can only stay in the United States if they reach dry land before being stopped at sea by U.S. authorities. The practice is colloquially known as the "wet-foot, dry-foot" policy. These attempts, and thousands of other frantic and temerarious ones, clearly underscore the hopelessness and frustration experienced by the Cuban people under the Communist regime.

12

THE SELLING OF CUBA TO FOREIGN INTERESTS. THE CHAVEZ-CASTRO ALLIANCE. MISERIES AND LUXURIES OF THE REVOLUTION.

"The arrangement between Castro and Chavez is not unusual, nor does it come as a surprise. Chavez admitted he had been an admirer of Castro, and both share a common hatred for the United States. Castro has again put all of his eggs in one basket - the same error he committed with the fallen Soviet Union."

Failures and Alliances

THE HARDSHIPS THAT the Cuban people have endured throughout the years of the Castro totalitarian regime have been outlandish. A strict food rationing system has been in place since the early years of the revolution. People are issued a rationing card to obtain the allotted essential foods such as rice, beans, meat, chicken, fish, milk, eggs, flour, cooking oil, sugar and other staples when they are available. Shortages of clothing, shoes, underwear, toothpaste, shaving cream, soap, detergents, razor blades and a variety of other household goods are notorious. Nevertheless, the fat cats of the regime have access to special stores where they can obtain everything they want, including luxury items and electrical appliances. For years Castro has been blaming the U.S. economic embargo for the pain he himself has brought upon the poor Cuban population. Let's not forget that Castro has always boasted he did not need the United States for survival. At every opportunity he has castigated America for the miseries caused by the failure of his own Communist economic plan. So why has he been throwing a tantrum and lobbying for the U.S. to lift the embargo? The truth is that he uses the embargo as an excuse to continue his tirades against the United States. From the beginning Castro put all of his eggs in one basket – the Soviet Union – and when the Soviet empire collapsed, the Communist Cuban economy went into a tailspin.

The Soviets were subsidizing and prodding Castro to the tune of over six billion dollars a year in exchange for using Cuba as a military base. The fall of the Soviet Union and its satellites made Cuba an international beggar. In the 1990s Castro reluctantly and out of desperation had to knock on the door of Western European countries – France, Italy, Spain, Germany, Switzerland and others – for economic sustenance. These countries saw an opportunity and extended a lifeline to the rapidly sinking country. Castro hurriedly signed trade agreements that would allow the European capitalist countries to set up industrial and commercial shops in Cuba as joint ventures with Cuban state-owned corporations. Cuban labor was provided by the government under a sinister plan. Among the joint ventures with European countries and Canada are Swiss food conglomerate Nestlé, a Spain hotel chain Sol Melia, Britain's American Tobacco Corporation and Canada's mining conglomerate Sherritt International. Other smaller European businesses entered into agreements with Cuba to set up companies to import a variety of equipment and supplies, from batteries to hospital equipment and other items not readily available in Cuba. Under these arrangements the Western European nations would pay Castro in dollars for every worker employed in their enterprises and, in turn, Castro would pay the laborers the same amount in pesos. Considering that the exchange rate is, at best, about 20 pesos per dollar, this amounted to a flagrant exploitation of the Cuban workers. Additionally, the government would get a percentage of the profits of the companies established in Cuba.

As can be seen, the Socialist structure was modified to accommodate this impious arrangement. Castro was desperate to get needed income to keep the country afloat and did not hesitate to grab this immoral approach to survive and stay in power. The Cuban workers were used as pawns and became victims of another scheme of the Communist maneuvering. Their salaries were miserable and the work was simply a part of the slavery system imposed in Cuba by the Socialist revolution. Labor laws were abolished in Cuba and replaced with the dictates of the Labor Ministry under Castro's directives. The foreign entrepreneurs in Cuba occupied elegant residences, sent their children to special schools and had access to beautiful tourist beach resorts forbidden to the Cuban natives. The apartheid system was successfully instituted in Cuba.

Many of the uncomfortable business ventures with the European countries went sour, particularly those with the small- and medium-sized companies that proliferated in the 1990s. There was an extensive crackdown in 2005 to reduce the clout of too many foreigners in the Cuban ambit. According to Castro, they were becoming too visible and influential in certain communities, giving the native population a perception of their success as entrepreneurs. Their image and way of life were considered counterproductive to the contrasting Socialist mentality being imposed on the Cuban society. In other words, they were perceived by the officialdom as a bad example contributing to the poisoning of the slave environment encroached by Communism.

The very large European enterprises in joint ventures with state-owned corporations were left intact because the income derived from them was still significant to the Cuban economy. Several hundred small and medium companies folded and left Cuba, showing that there is nothing certain about doing business with Cuba under a system which has no laws and no respect for international accords.

There is also the sensitive issue of the flagrant human rights abuses in Cuba which are not very palatable to the European countries, and they have repeatedly made it known to Castro on numerous occasions.

The Chavez – Castro Connection

The connection between Fidel Castro and Hugo Chavez of Venezuela developed into a formal alliance under which Castro received economic assistance from Chavez in the form of cheap oil and low interest loans in exchange for Castro's advice and technical support in the conversion of Venezuela into another Socialist country in Latin America. Castro not only sent political and military advisors to Chavez, but also a horde of physicians to assist in public health programs. Now Cuba is finding that many of the physicians sent to Venezuela are escaping to neighboring Colombia and requesting asylum in the United States. They would like to take advantage of an initiative announced in the summer of 2006 by President Bush to grant humanitarian asylum to Cuban physicians sent to work in foreign countries. Recently over 38 Cuban physicians defected from a mission in Venezuela and are awaiting sanctuary in the United States. As of this writing, nearly 500 Cuban health professionals sent by Castro to 40 countries are waiting to be accepted by the U.S. This is another proof of the miserable conditions under which professionals are treated in Cuba under the Castro "Socialist Paradise." All of these professionals grew up, were educated and indoctrinated under the Communist regime. This speaks very loudly about the "advantages" of a Socialist society.

The arrangement between Castro and Chavez is not unusual, nor does it come as a surprise. Chavez admitted he had been an admirer of Castro, and both share a common hatred for the United States. Castro has again put all of his eggs in one basket - the same error he committed with the fallen Soviet Union. The engagement with Chavez will not be of benefit to Cuba in the long run. Venezuela is overspending in many poorly administered social programs and diverting oil money and discounted oil to other Latin American countries to gain influence beyond its boundaries.

Chavez is squandering a vast amount of oil income by buying weaponry and building an oversized military apparatus, as well as creating a bloated bureaucracy to retain control of the government through a reign of terror and intimidation. He, in fact, has become a de facto dictator. The riches of Venezuela are being wasted, government corruption is widespread, land is being expropriated, private enterprise is in a panic and individual freedoms are being suffocated. Organized mobs are trained and indoctrinated under the banner of the so-called "Bolivarian Revolution" to be mobilized against opposition groups.

The relationship now established between Chavez and Mahmoud Ahmadinejad, President of Iran, should be of great concern to the United States and other democratic countries. These two crackpots are attracted to each other by their hostility toward the United States. It is unpredictable what could come out of it, logistically and militarily, as far as their intentions to cause damage to America are concerned. This diabolical partnership is not to be taken lightly. The surge of Chavez as a menace to our neighboring Latin American countries and the U.S. interests in the region is the consequence of Castro-Communism in Cuba. Chavez felt that if Castro, next door to the United States, got away with successfully defying and insulting the U.S., then he could do the same thing from Venezuela, which to his advantage is farther away. Evidently Castro's bravado emboldened Chavez to challenge the forbearance and the power of the United States. He has uttered ugly and abusive diatribes, unbecoming of a head of state, against President Bush and the United States. This attitude is unexplainable and irrational if we take into account that the U.S. has been the most important trade partner and the biggest oil customer of Venezuela for years.

Chavez Socialism is now being implemented at a faster pace since he assumed the presidency for a second six-year term in January 2007. To make it clear to the world, he declared at his swearing in ceremony: "Fatherland, Socialism or Death." He sounded exactly like Castro, his mentor and idol. He also dared to say that Christ was the greatest Socialist in history. It is obvious that either he doesn't know much about the history of Christianity, or he is blatantly distorting the facts to gain the support of the masses, just as Castro did in Cuba from the beginning of the revolution.

After his second inauguration, Chavez did not wait very long to announce that he was grabbing the public utility companies and the telecommunication industries as another step in establishing a Socialist society. Furthermore, he is positioning himself as a dictator, as if he wasn't already one, by asking the National Assembly (which he controls) to grant him special powers to enact "revolutionary laws" by decree, and to eliminate the presidential term limitation in the Constitution, which had previously been restricted to two terms. Both requests were granted, giving Chavez broad power to accelerate the Communist conversion of the economy and to stay in power indefinitely. He has eliminated all possible obstacles to carry out his plan.

On May 3, 2007, Chavez declared that the nationalization of strategic companies was contemplated in the transition of Venezuela to Socialism. He further threatened the private banks and the Luxembourg-based steel company Sidor with nationalization if they don't abide by his demands regarding the operational procedures established by his regime. He is taking the same course Castro took in Cuba. Eventually we foresee the elimination of all private businesses and the free press, concurrently with the muffling of all opposition parties. As an aftermath of the Communization process, we will see more poverty and despair for Venezuela and an increasing influx of dispossessed people arriving in the United States.

Searching for vainglory, Chavez has evolved into a tyrant in the mold of Castro. He is not content to be the ruler of his country, but he also wants to export his influence to other countries in the region and project himself as an international leader, using the abundant oil resources he now manages as his vehicle for conquest.

There are some developments that should give concern to Chavez and other oil-rich nations' kooks like Ahmadinejad. The fruit of research for renewable alternate sources of fuel to replace petroleum-based fuel is now becoming a reality. Biotechnology fuels produced from corn and sugar cane have been growing at a steady pace. Raw materials like sorghum, cornstalks, grasses, sawdust and a variety of other cellulosic plant substances are being investigated for use in producing biofuel. Brazil and the United States are leading in the production of ethanol fuel from sugar cane and corn, respectively. More and more vehicle engines are now being built to use ethanol fuel, whether mixed with gasoline or on a straight basis. Ethanol has the advantage of being environmentally friendly, burning cleaner than conventional fossil fuels. Ethanol also reduces emissions of carbon monoxide and other harmful particles while having a higher octane. Biofuels will eventually lessen the dependence on petroleum oil fuels.

Advances in biochemistry have made possible the development of technology to transform animal fat, such as beef tallow, pork fat and poultry fat – by-products of the meat industry – into renewable sources of diesel fuel. Presently a cooperative project between a major oil company and a large meat processor in the U.S. is on target to begin limited production before the end of year 2007.

In 2006 the combined production of ethanol fuel by the United States and Brazil was approximately ten billion gallons, and this is only the tip of the iceberg. This amount will multiply several times in the next few years. Other potential ethanol-producing countries will contribute to rapidly augment the volume of biofuels. Meanwhile other technologies are being researched using renewable biological resources to develop energy alternates to fossil fuels.

Sooner or later the price of oil will be depressed for one reason or another and the Venezuelan economy will suffer a heavy blow. The current bountiful income from oil presented the opportune time to expand and diversify the agricultural and industrial resources of the country through a private enterprise climate and a progressive capitalist democracy. This would have created stable jobs instead of government dependency through give-away programs. It is pathetic to watch how this golden opportunity is being wasted by another Socialist megalomaniac, a demagogue with a Napoleonic style. The Venezuelan dictator is not only hurting the present generation in his country, but is ruining the lives of future generations to satisfy his egotistical personal ambitions. I predict dark days for Venezuela before the light shines again.

It seems that Chavez is already preoccupied with the ethanol development as an alternate energy source. At an energy summit he hosted on April 16, 2007, in Porlamar, Venezuela, he proposed a plan based on the vast resources of oil and natural gas in Venezuela to counter the ethanol agreement recently signed between the United States and Brazil to promote ethanol production. He would like nothing more than to derail the U.S.-Brazil accord by attacking its rationale with absurd scare tactics about the monopoly of agricultural lands destined for ethanol-producing crops, alleging that it would result in the starvation of the poor. He already sees a competitive source of energy to his oil empire.

Right now, in spite of the huge oil revenues favored by the high oil prices of recent years, and after six years of Chavez's rule, there isn't much to say about Venezuela's progression. A very large segment of the population is very poor, depending on government give-aways that are wasted and poorly administered. Crime in Venezuela is one of the highest in Latin America, and education leaves a lot to be desired. Prostitution is seen everywhere and drug abuse is epidemic. Government corruption and abuses are notorious. Where is the benefit of Socialism? It is a discredited system that has been proven to be a failure in every country which embraced it or was forced into it. Chavez should have known what Cuba was before Castro and what it is now prior to venturing into his political experiment. He has been inebriated by his grotesque pretension for greatness. In the end, Cuba and Venezuela will suffer the consequences of the unholy partnership of Castro and Chavez.

Miseries of the Revolution and Luxuries at the Top

Adding to the anguish of the Cuban population under Castro's despotic rule are the dismal energy shortages, inadequate transportation, lack of potable water, scarcity of living units and erratic telephone communications. This is in addition to the already mentioned shortage of food and medication, and poor public healthcare facilities for the overwhelming majority of the population. This is true for everyone except the privileged class consisting of the top military personnel and the civilians occupying high positions in the state bureaucracy.

Frequent power failures occur throughout the island. Havana has been paralyzed many times with lengthy blackouts lasting for 10 to 20 hours at a time. Factories have to close. Schools, shops, hotels (except for those having their own generators in case of disruption), banks, movie theaters, government ministries and other offices, as well as many other activities, are affected. The electrical shortages also disrupt the gas and water pipelines, aggravating the headaches of common people who are unable to cook, wash, flush toilets and attend to their daily hygienic and sanitary needs. If they have a refrigerator at home, some of their hard-earned food supplies like chicken, meat and fish, will be lost to spoilage. They know that they will have to wait to replace them until their rationing card will allow them to purchase their meager allotment when it becomes available.

The root of the problem is that the power grid is antiquated, the energy plants are inefficient, the equipment is in a poor state of repair, the transmission lines are faulty and maintenance leaves a lot to be desired. Replacement parts are oftentimes unavailable. When the power is restored, Castro goes on radio and television and gives a long harangue to calm down the restless populace, promising that the problems will be resolved and usually blaming the state energy industry administrators for the shortcomings. What else is new? He also calls for the people to unite and sacrifice for the good and advancement of the revolution, even damning the U.S. imperialists for the embargo that prevents spare parts and new equipment from being imported. Who is he fooling? What about other countries doing business with Cuba? What about him, spending enormous amounts of money to equip and feed the largest military in Latin America? What about his past funding of expeditions to various continents?

Castro takes advantage of every opportunity to excite the Cuban population and twist the facts to vainly gain support for the discredited revolution. People, except for the courageous dissidents, are afraid to speak out against the government for fear of reprisal.

Not only is the energy supply in crisis, but public transportation is in shambles, dilapidated buses are crowded, highways are crumbling and potable water is sometimes in short supply. There is also a crisis in the number of living units available. Families are cramped into miserable housing facilities and telephone communications are poor, to say the least. However, the privileged class has the best and most luxurious houses, many with swimming pools, tennis courts and other amenities. Their houses are equipped with modern electrical appliances, private wells for the times that public water is unavailable, and generators to use when there is a blackout. In many instances they possess more than one house, one for daily living and another as a vacation resort, and enjoy the best European cars. It is known that Castro has many residences along the national territory and a fleet of Mercedes Benz vehicles. The benefits of Communism are shared only by the elite ruling class.

13

THE EFFECT OF THE COMMUNIST REVOLUTION ON THE CIVIC SOCIETY AND ITS VARIOUS ETHNIC COMPONENTS

"...the so-called 'Children of the revolution' who grew up under Castro's pervasive system...
chewed the teachings of Communism, but never swallowed or digested them...In the end
people got fed up with slogans and empty promises. They simply wanted to be free and
enjoy a democratic way of life."

The Exodus

THROUGHOUT THE REPUBLICAN existence of Cuba (1902-1958), the people leaving the country to reside elsewhere were few and far between, even under past political crises. Cubans were not known to be wanderers. Prior to Communism and without any traveling impediments, only a few Cubans opted to voluntarily live in other countries, mostly because they perceived greater opportunities in their careers or professions. During Castro-Communism and in spite of severe restrictions and vigilance imposed by the regime to prevent traveling outside of the country, over two million people have left searching for freedom, human justice and economic opportunities. This phenomenon is unprecedented in Cuban history.

The following two cases, among many that could be mentioned, drastically illustrate the intense degree of desperation and suffering the Cuban population has endured.

The Peruvian Embassy Fiasco

IN APRIL 1980, within a forty-eight hour period, over 10,000 Cubans entered the Peruvian Embassy in Havana in the hope of leaving the country. The rush to enter the embassy grounds began as word spread that the guards around the embassy had been removed by Cuban authorities on direct order of Castro. The guards were withdrawn in retaliation for the Peruvian government's reluctance to abide by an earlier request of Castro to not grant asylum to those attempting to flee the country. Prior to the incident, the embassy had given sanctuary to fifteen Cubans who had requested the protection of the diplomatic cover, and to another group of twelve who had gained entrance to the grounds by crashing a bus through the embassy's iron gates. When the Peruvians would not yield to Castro's request, he was infuriated. Asylum in embassies for political motives had been honored for years in Cuba. A dispute like this had never emerged, even under the most difficult circumstances in the history of the nation.

Immediately after the removal of the guards, the number of people, including families with children, entering the embassy grounds grew at a rapid rate. They were packed into the embassy building and filled the surrounding area. People could be seen in the branches of the trees, on the lawn, and even on the roof. The entire place was cramped. Food was scarce and facilities were inadequate to satisfy the necessities of the immense crowd. The entire place became a messy, smelly and unsanitary environment. Hundreds more were outside the fence desperately struggling to enter the compound. Finally the police had to disperse the crowd and cordon off the embassy. People of all ages and walks of life were there searching for freedom. They were a cross-section of the new Socialist society that Castro was bragging about, educated and indoctrinated in the godless environment of Communism and taught to hate America – the very same country they were now dreaming to reach.

Following several days of negotiations and appeals to various international humanitarian organizations and governments, less than two thousand of the refugees were given entry visas to a handful of countries, like Costa Rica, Peru and Spain. They left Cuba on mercy flights sponsored by the humanitarian efforts of those countries, leaving many thousands behind. After days of confinement in the embassy under tremendous hardship and suffering from malnutrition, dehydration, lack of sleep, gastro-intestinal diseases, trauma and other infirmities with no hope in sight, they left the embassy, were processed by the authorities, declared anti-social and treated as outcasts after they returned to their homes. The whole incredible episode was a sad human tragedy that demonstrated the brutality of the Communist tyranny. It was later admitted by the regime that the purpose of Castro's confrontation with Peru was to create a crisis and set an example for other countries granting asylum to people persecuted by, or unhappy with, the revolution.

The Incredible Mariel Boat Lift

Another bizarre event caused consternation inside and outside of Cuba following the aftermath of the Peruvian Embassy fiasco – the unprecedented mass exodus from the island of 130,000 people in what was dubbed the "Mariel Port Boat Lift." Castro created this outrageous sequel by publicly boasting that Cubans in the United States could send boats to pick up their relatives at the

Mariel Port on the northwest coast of Cuba. This time he was testing President Carter to observe whether he was going to permit such a venture. If he rejected the preposterous offer, Carter would enrage the large Cuban community of South Florida, which already constituted a powerful and influential political enclave in the state. On the other hand, if he opened the door to the would-be refugees, Carter would be exposed to criticism by a considerable segment of the U.S. population for permitting a new flood of immigrants to enter the country under circumstances mandated by an enemy of America. Either way it would cause an embarrassing situation for Carter, exactly what the malicious mind of Castro had intended. Evidently he was determined not only to create a difficult situation for the U.S., but to also gain by letting some of the steam out of the boiling kettle that was Cuba. Discontent was growing fast and loosely-organized dissident groups were getting restless. The populace had had it with empty promises, scarcity of goods, failure of state economic plans, persecution and the brutal repression of dissidents and suspected enemies of the revolution. Additionally, he took advantage of the confusing situation created by unloading hardcore criminals and mentally disturbed inmates from the crowded penitentiaries and dumping them among the people boarding the boats to cause as much damage and turmoil as possible.

Needless to say, after Castro announced the unexpected open rescue policy, thousands of Cuban families in South Florida instantly mobilized their resources and sailed to the Port of Mariel in all kinds of vessels. Some paid owners or operators of fishing boats and other seagoing vessels $1,000 or more per relative loaded into the boats. Some even rented vessels for $10,000 or more to sail to Cuba, while others used their own boats or yachts to bring back family members. It became a frantic run for time before they closed the doors at either end. Key West became a very busy spot as many vessels departed from there. The desperate and unbelievable race for freedom became a spectacle never seen before in the history of the world. Thousands who were not necessarily claimed by relatives cleverly found their way into the vessels. They had come to Mariel Port from all over the Cuban territory by whatever means of transportation they could find. About five months later when the boat lift came to an end, it was estimated that over 130,000 Cubans had left the island while many more were left stranded.

The whole world was looking intensely with awe at this surrealistic exodus. Castro had demonstrated once more the barbaric nature of the Communist tyranny and the lies about benefits he claimed the revolution brought to Cuba. He had not counted on the humanitarian nature of the Cuban émigrés who spent their savings and resources in rescuing their relatives, nor did he imagine the magnitude of the repulsion that the Cuban people had for his persona and his wicked manipulation of human suffering. Castro's tactics backfired because he also received the repudiation of many nations for the pain and suffering he inflicted on so many people.

The exodus had to come to an end because there was no limit to the number of people arriving at Mariel Port to abandon the Communist hell that was Cuba. People spent days and nights at any place where they could find refuge waiting for their turn to board the boats. Streets, parks and grassy lots were full of people. Getting food, water and access to sanitary facilities was gradually becoming critical, particularly for the children and the elderly. Finally, at the end of the nightmare, those left behind dispersed and returned to their homes heartbroken, weakened and sick, their dream of escaping Castro's tyranny shattered.

Over the years the Mariel émigrés were absorbed by the Cuban-American community in the United States and the generous people of this nation. A great majority of the "Marielitos," as they were called, became good U.S. citizens and took advantage of the opportunities they found in America to advance in their professions, trades and businesses. The undesirable people Castro dumped among the boarding vessels constituted a relatively small fraction of the total boat lift population. About 2,500 were detained during the admission process into the United States (evidently they had no identification papers whatsoever) and sent to prison. Castro repeatedly refused to take them back. Some of dubious credentials, sooner or later, found their way back into the cooler, and yet others of the same category straightened out their lives after finding a decent modus operandi in the new country. The sinister plan of Castro had not produced the malevolent results that he expected.

A vast number of those leaving Cuba under Castro's regime have done so under perilous circumstances, fleeing from persecution, deprivation of human rights, poverty and other abuses suffered under the brutal totalitarian regime. It should be noted that the vast majority of those escaping Cuba after the early exodus were raised under Communism and educated under an intense indoctrination campaign. They are the so-called "Children of the revolution" who grew up under Castro's pervasive system. They chewed the teachings of Communism, but never swallowed or digested them. The same paradox occurred in the Eastern European countries and the former Soviet Union under Communism. In the end people got fed up with slogans and empty promises. They simply wanted to be free and enjoy a democratic way of life. The free will of the people is a God-given right and it should never be at the mercy of tyrants. Freedom is a natural desire of the human being; it is the essence of life itself.

Ethnic Groups

The complexity of the Cuban tragedy has multiple facets. It cannot be fully comprehended without an explanation of the many factors affected by the upheaval to which the country has been subjected by the Castro tyranny. It is noteworthy to mention that within the dynamics of the Cuban population there were several lesser-known but well-rooted ethnic components other than Spanish and African. They all equally fell victims to the Communist order foisted upon the nation. Communism does not discriminate when it comes to the application of cruelty and the distribution of misery. The disaster which swept over Cuba like a furious hurricane impacted the entire civil society without distinction.

Among the other ethnic groups of significance at the onset of the Castro holocaust were Americans, Jews, Chinese, and to a lesser extent there were roots of Italians and Irish, who were early arrivals to the island. Italian surnames such as Sanguinetti, Esposito, Dopico, Mancini, Jalandoni, Campanioni, Ferrara, Pinelli, Allegretti, Botti, Maestri, Barletta, Galvani, Baldasarri, Dominici, Facciolo, Onetti, Alliegro, Benemelis, Galletti, Campuzano, Benedi, Benavides, Antonetti and Spirelli, and Irish surnames such as O'Farrill, Walsh, O'Reilly, O'Donnell and Kelly were sprinkled throughout the population. I, myself, had a little bit of Irish from my mother's side of the family. The name O'Douls became Dulzaides (my mother's surname) when her ancestors came to Spain during the Irish potato famine of the 1840s. The potato crops were wiped out several years in a row by a fungus infection. The blight severely affected the nutrition of the peasants as potatoes were their main diet staple. The famine caused 1.5 million deaths and forced an equal number of Irish to emigrate looking for survival. Some emigrated to Spain and, once there, the name O'Douls, in this case, was changed to Dulzaides to make it more acceptable to their adopted country. Later on members of the family emigrated to Cuba. Other Irish names were also converted to Spanish for easier adaptation, while some kept their original names.

The Chinese Contribution

The Chinese in Cuba were numerous. They began to arrive around 1845 to work on the sugar cane plantations and perform other agricultural chores as assigned by the contractors who brought them to the island to replenish the decline in African slaves. Political turmoil in China brought additional Chinese immigrants to Cuba during the early 1900s. It is loosely estimated that, up to the advent of Castro, there were about 100,000 Chinese in Cuba, including their descendants.

The Chinese were known to be hard workers and disciplined people. For some reason, the Chinese dominated the laundry business in Havana and other cities. They also owned restaurants and other small businesses like grocery stores, fruit and vegetable farms and stands. In Havana there was a relatively large Chinatown with many shops, some carrying imports of vases, ceramic figurines, glass articles and a diversity of artistic souvenirs. Other shops sold teas and exotic curative herbs and remedies. They ran their own social clubs, temples, newspaper, theaters, pharmacies and even banks. The subsequent Cuban-born generations were fully absorbed within the general Cuban community.

Many Chinese immigrant descendants inherited their parents' businesses; others became professionals in various fields of endeavor. With the elimination of private enterprise, including small businesses, by Castro-Communism and the suffocation of cultural, religious and entrepreneurial activities, the Chinese population declined rapidly as they fled to more hospitable countries, mainly to the United States. Today the Chinese population of Cuba has been reduced to a few hundred, composed mainly of aging people.

The Jewish Influence

The Jews and their descendants in Cuba were a growing population surpassing 100,000 at the time Communism took over the island. A large number were established in Havana. They were assimilated into the Cuban population with an ease that was notable for its welcome mode. In spite of Cuba being a predominantly Catholic country, there was no anti-Semitism in the hearts of the Cubans. The first Jewish settlers came to Cuba from the United States in the latter stages of the Independence War during 1898 as part of the American troops that landed in Cuba to help liberate the nation from the domination of Spain. Many liked Cuba and decided to stay. Later during World War I, some came from Turkey and Russia fleeing from the turmoil and uncertainty caused by the war. Then during the rise of Hitler and Nazism in Germany, followed by the advent of World War II, they emigrated from Germany, Poland and other Eastern European countries to avoid the cruel persecution and the criminal extermination campaign of the Nazis.

Jewish people made a significant contribution to Cuba's economy. They were laborious, conservative, dedicated and savvy entrepreneurs. Their families were closely knit and they were good citizens. Cubans had a great respect for Jews and never held any animosity against them. After all, they were also considered to be Cubans. There was a harmonious relationship between the Christians and Jews in Cuba. Religion was never an issue or a matter of discussion among Cubans. A sizable segment of the Jewish population lived in a ward of Old Havana where they had shops, an outdoor market, kosher butcher shops, a newspaper printing press and other businesses. However, they were not necessarily restricted to the bustling and colorful ward. They had homes and businesses all over the capital as well as in other towns. They also had their synagogues and private schools. Jews thrived, among other occupations, in the clothing and apparel businesses.

There were several locations in Old Havana where their shops occupied entire streets from one end to the other. They made particularly famous two such streets, Muralla and Acosta. We used to live in Old Havana and I recall my relatives and I frequently shopped in that district. I never forget that the first suit my parents bought for me was tailored by a quiet and humble Jew named Victor and, I should add, at a very modest price.

Jews made sure that their children had a very good education. One of my best friends during my years at Technical College and the University of Havana was a Jew, Alberto (Aaron) Zier Kastner. His parents had fled Germany at the beginning of the Hitler regime. At the university Alberto was a founder with me of the "Committee for the Advancement of Agrarian Affairs." Shortly after Castro took over, he and his family left Cuba and settled in Fort Lauderdale, Florida, to begin a new life under freedom. In the 1940s and 1950s the second and third generation of Cuban Jews were becoming physicians, lawyers, teachers, engineers, land developers, architects, realtors and even politicians. Soon after Castro came to power their accomplishments and dreams were shattered. They lost their businesses and livelihood. Their desire to live in a free society was frustrated by the Communist revolution. To some this was the second or third time they had to emigrate. This was a deceptive and heart-breaking experience for them.

Based on some estimates from Cuban émigrés, fewer than 1,000 Jews are left in Cuba, mostly elderly people. Against the tide of many years under atheistic Communist rule, they are still struggling to keep their identity and hold onto whatever tradition and culture they can retain. Because of the scarcity of all the essentials needed to keep their faith alive, kosher observance is painfully limited. What a sad end to what it was before Castro – a vibrant, successful and productive community, fully integrated into the diverse Cuban culture.

The American Influx

There were several thousand Americans living in Cuba, either temporarily or permanently, before the Castro debacle. The temporary residents (not including tourists) consisted of executives of corporations, contractors transacting businesses, representatives of financial institutions, sales representatives of hospital equipment, pharmaceuticals, foods, textiles, industrial and farming equipment, petroleum and automotive products; consultants, visiting professors and agents of many other products and services. At any given time, Cuba also had many Americans visiting groups engaged in cultural and educational exchanges, religious activities, and experts on many aspects of science and technology.

The permanent residents, including some who opted for Cuban citizenship, were engaged in many businesses throughout the island. Others had entered into partnership with Cuban business people. It is difficult to put a number on the sizable American colony in Cuba as of the end of 1958, although in all likelihood it amounted to over 10,000. They indeed made a significant contribution to the Cuban progress in many segments of their financial, economic, scientific, technological, cultural, humanitarian, commercial and industrial pursuits. All of these beneficial and salutary influxes were denied by Castro from the moment he took the reins of the government. He relentlessly attacked the Americans as exploiters of the Cuban economy, when in fact they had, by their efforts, initiative and investments, created a huge amount of employment, contributed to the vigorous economic growth and helped advance the technical, scientific and health standards of the republic.

Needless to say, very shortly after Castro dominated the scenery, they left the island, forced to leave because of the maniacal animosity of Castro toward anything American. Their businesses were the first to be confiscated without any compensation. Among the American victims of the dictator was a good-natured, hard-working, Cuba-loving American who owned three automobile service stations in Havana. His name was Howard (Andy) Anderson, a reputable businessman. He was a director of the American Chamber of Commerce in Cuba and a member of the only American Legion Post in Cuba.

After the Bay of Pigs Invasion in 1961, Anderson was apprehended and falsely accused of being a CIA agent. He was given a trial by a revolutionary kangaroo court and sentenced to death by firing squad. Castro personally denied the family request to let this innocent man go free and ordered his immediate execution. Many Americans making a contribution to the well-being of Cuba were rounded up and grossly insulted by the goons under Castro's command. Of course, thousands of Cubans were similarly persecuted. The gruesome behavior of Castro, the idol of the far left in the United States and elsewhere, appears to have no boundaries.

To add insult to injury, Anderson, before his death, was submitted to a horrible procedure. His daughter Bonnie Anderson, an American journalist born in Cuba, attested that only hours before his execution they extracted all of her father's blood (as related in the very informative book by Juan Clark, *Cuba: Mito y Realidad (Cuba: Myth and Reality)*, Saeta Ediciones, Miami, Florida, 1990). This procedure was also conducted on many other persons destined to be executed. The blood of the victims was preserved and used in blood transfusions for Castro's wounded soldiers during the early counter-insurgencies of the anti-Castro revolutionary forces that rebelled against the Communist conversion.

Ethnicity and Race Relations Before and After Castro

Before the Castro revolution Cuba was not a racially-divided country, as Castro has tried to portray it in his tergiversation of history. I do not recall a single racial incident during my entire residence in Cuba. The relationship between whites and blacks or any other ethnic groups was cordial and based on mutual respect for each other. During my school, college and university years I was never cognizant of any formal or acrimonious discussion about racial issues. I had black classmates and, as was the case with everybody else, race never entered my mind as a factor in any friendship. It is estimated that as of 1959, Cuba had a population of nearly 6 million people, of which approximately 77% was white, 23% of black or mixed ancestry and less than 2% of other races, primarily Chinese. Of course, the racial makeup of the population has changed over the years. The tyranny makes no distinction in its repressive mode. It continues to equally affect the entire population. Currently the total population of Cuba is about 12 million and many are still trying to exit the island.

It is true that in Havana the luxury hotels, some private clubs and expensive places of entertainment were favored to a great extent by whites, mainly for economic reasons rather than race. On the other hand, there were social clubs exclusively for blacks, such as the now-extinct Buena Vista Social Club and the Antillas Club, just to name two. It was then accepted that this was part of the idiosyncrasy of Cuba based on customs and traditions of the epoch. It was simply a non-issue which was interpreted as part of a sociological phenomenon. Politically blacks, whites and other races had no distinction. They all participated as members, activists or candidates in all of the twelve or so different political parties existing before 1959.

The Roots of Race Relations in Cuba

The harmonious race relations in Cuba began early during the initial conspiratory efforts of the 1810s, and continued to develop through the epic insurgencies against the domination of Spain, which lasted until 1898. Many blacks, slaves and sons of slaves joined the armed conflicts for the freedom of Cuba. A mutual respect between whites and blacks evolved, strengthening the concord between the two races.

Numerous wealthy Cubans of Spanish ancestry liberated the slaves they had working on their plantations and in their sugar mills and households. A good number of slaves who were granted freedom enrolled in the revolt against the rule of Spain, and fought bravely for the independence of Cuba alongside the white Cuban troops.

A hero of the Cuban insurrection, Carlos Manuel de Céspedes, a lawyer educated in Spain, of elevated culture, who traveled through Europe and was from a very wealthy family, can be cited as an example of the devotion the Cubans had for the cause of freedom. He freed his slaves and left behind his fortune, including a sugar mill, after he had completed the preparation for a revolutionary movement throughout the island. Backed by many similar brave Cuban leaders, Céspedes launched a war against the Spanish government on October 10, 1868. He was designated as the President of the Republic in Arms. The struggle was furious and extended from the Province of Oriente to other regions of Cuba. Céspedes lost his life at the hands of the Spaniards in February 1874 and entered the pages of Cuban history as the "Father of the Country."

The conflict lasted ten years and ended when an uneasy peace pact was reached with the Spanish Governor of Cuba in 1878. Other rebellions of short duration occurred until the final war against Spain erupted on February 24, 1895, painstakingly organized and directed by the great patriot José Martí.

A glorious figure of the Cuban revolutionary process during the 1880s and 1890s was Juan Gualberto Gómez, a son of slaves of mixed ancestry. He was educated in France under the sponsorship of his parents, who had obtained freedom from slavery. Their former slave masters were very fond of young Juan Gualberto – as he was known to all. At an early age he had demonstrated a superb intelligence.

It is appropriate to mention for historical and sociological purposes that the generally used term "person of color" originated very early and included people of African origin, as well as the descendants of mixed race (European and African) who had a lighter skin color.

Juan Gualberto Gómez was a lifelong friend and follower of José Martí. He was part of the revolutionary group coordinating the preparation for the new war under the direction of Martí. At the onset of the conflict Gómez was captured, sentenced to 20 years and sent to serve his prison term in Spain. After the war ended in 1898, he obtained a pardon and returned to Cuba, where he actively participated in politics. Gómez was elected a delegate to the Constitutional Assembly in 1901 and contributed to the drafting of the Constitution under which the new republic was created in 1902.

Juan Gualberto was subsequently elected to the House of Representatives, and later to the Senate. He was influential in bringing together a coalition of political parties which resulted in the election of his presidential candidate in 1920.

Juan Gualberto Gómez wrote and lectured extensively and, at one time, founded his own newspaper. He became a powerful voice for understanding, civility and democracy. He was a conciliatory force in matters related to race relations and political maturity. For his merits Gómez received the highest honors and recognition from the Republic. He never thought of race as a polarizing element of society. He advocated comprehension of the goals of the black segment of the population by educating people of different races to accept tolerance and have respect for each other.

Gómez made a substantial contribution to the political and social climate during the formative years of the republic by using love, reasoning and decency as his weapons for the good of all citizens and his beloved country. He was very proud to be a Cuban.

My wife and I have the privilege of being friends of his granddaughter, Dr. Angelina Pedroso, a Cuban émigré and educator who, true to the legacy of her illustrious grandfather, has been a distinguished, long-tenured professor at Northeastern Illinois University in Chicago.

What a difference between those heroic giants of our past and the hateful, criminal and mentally-dwarfed creatures of our present time, like Castro and his equally unworthy bootlickers!

It was not uncommon to see white and black families living in the same neighborhoods. We applauded and admired athletes and performers regardless of the color of their skin, whether they were engaged in baseball, boxing, track and field, or any other sport or artistic activity. There were black teachers, professors, journalists, entrepreneurs, politicians, military personnel, public servants, workers and other professions. They were treated with the same respect as any other citizens. Public hospitals, educational institutions, recreational facilities, ministries and other organizations attended to the needs of the population regardless of color or ethnicity. There was no friction or antagonistic feelings among the racial components of society. Nationality was the main pride of the people; being Cuban was the most important factor. However, I am not claiming that Cuba was a perfect society.

No society in the world can claim perfection; there is always room for improvement. Changes would have been made, if deemed necessary, by the accord and consent of all citizens in a democratic climate. Race was not an issue during the opposition to the Batiste regime. The main cause of the inconformity with the Batista government was political, not sociological or economic. The purpose of the insurgency was to restore a democratic and honest government. After Castro came to power, he made race an issue, although he never mentioned it throughout his campaign against Batista. The so-called racial divide before the revolution was a mirage fabricated by Castro to gain the support of black Cubans, who were somewhat indifferent to the Castro movement.

Blacks and the Castro Revolution

It is significant to observe that among the various revolutionary groups, both civilian and military, blacks were minor participants, but it was not for lack of patriotism. Rather it was a matter of indifference for Castro. It seems that they perceived Castro for what he really was – a troublemaker. The black population of Cuba was rather conservative and not prone to be agitated by his style of leadership. Not too many black leaders were seen among the supporters of Castro's movement and other insurgent groups. This does not imply that blacks were in favor of Batista. On the contrary, they seemed to dislike Batista in the same proportion as the rest of the population.

The Castro regime has shown a hypocritical disdain for blacks in many respects. For instance, blacks are given a tougher time when trying to leave the country. Castro is afraid that black Cuban exiles will diminish the false claims that he has put an end to "racism" and that blacks have found happiness and opportunities within the revolution. The fact is that, proportionately, the black population has never seen so much poverty. Of course, poverty under Communism affects the entire components of the population more than ever before. Another sign of Castro's perfidious attitude and lies is that, since the beginning of his reign, he hardly had any blacks in his cabinet or any other top positions in the government.

Presently black workers and managers are not found very often in the tourist-driven industry. Rarely are they seen working in hotels and resorts, or any other job where they may be very visible or come into contact with foreign visitors. Blacks are normally relegated to inside, menial jobs such as cleaning or work in kitchens, where salaries are also at a very low level of remuneration. The disparity in management positions between whites and blacks is obvious everywhere. As far as housing is concerned, blacks occupy the worst slums in Havana and other cities where poverty is rampant.

I was taken aghast by the ignorance shown by some journalists and scholars covering the Cuban sociological landscape before Castro. One example of this assertion, which was particularly misleading, was authored by the well-known journalist and commentator Clarence Page, whom I perceive to be a moderate liberal. He mentioned in the *Chicago Tribune* on May 29, 2002, that "Castro had outlawed racial discrimination in Cuba five years before the U.S. passed the Civil Rights Act of 1964." Mr. Page was on a tour of Cuba, accompanied by a group of American journalists, at the time he wrote the article. Evidently he had been fed the outrageous claim by the state officials conducting the tour. He clearly demonstrated his lack of knowledge about what Cuba was like before the revolution since he easily swallowed the fabrications of the designated tour propagandists. It is important for Mr. Page and others to know that Castro did not end racial discrimination in Cuba, simply because such a thing did not exist before the Castro tyranny. It is necessary to emphasize at this point that the Cuban Constitution of 1901, under which the republic was created, had established the equality of all races and the illegality of discrimination in all of its forms.

Furthermore, the model Constitution of 1940, which replaced the Constitution of 1901, was drafted by a Constitutional Convention consisting of elected representatives from all political parties and reaffirmed in very clear terms the rights of all citizens, regardless of race, to be free from discrimination. The Constitution of 1940 reads, under Title Second, The Nationality, Article 10(a): "A citizen has the right to reside in his country without being subject to any discrimination or intimidation no matter race, class, political opinion or religious creed." Under Title Fourth, Fundamental Rights, Section First, About Individual Rights, Article 20, it states:

All Cubans are equal under the law. The Republic does not recognize privileges or preferences. All discrimination is declared illegal and is punishable for motives of sex, race, color or class and any other damaging factor to the human dignity. The law will establish the sanctions for the infraction of this precept.

The Cuban Constitution of 1940 has been the subject of study by many expert jurists and parliamentarians all over the world, and it has been acclaimed as one of the most advanced documents of its kind. Even when Batista overthrew the government of elected President Dr. Carlos Prío Socarrás, he kept the precepts of the Constitution in place except for those having to do with the electoral process, which was disrupted by the coup d'état, and other democratic premises. Clarence Page, the previously-mentioned *Chicago Tribune* columnist, to his credit has been critical of Castro's crackdowns on dissidents and other abuses. But he stands corrected, along with several others, on the issue of race relations in Cuba before Castro ascended to power. While I don't blame him for this indiscretion, it is appalling to realize how little was known about Cuba before Castro by many in the U.S. and elsewhere.

The racial discrimination in Cuba today is an insidious internal situation. To the outside world the picture the Communist government presents is totally different. To promote his racial equality theme, Castro tries to maximize the visibility of black athletes in international competitions, using them as instruments of his perverse design. But the regime keeps a wall of silence when it comes to the reason so many talented black athletes have asked for asylum during sports events held outside of Cuba, or have escaped from Cuba under extremely perilous circumstances to reach the shores of the United States. Such is the case with a string of prominent baseball players like pitchers Orlando (El Duque) Hernández and his equally-gifted brother Liván, José Contreras, as well as many others.

Excellent black boxers have also fled the Castro paradise, risking their lives in the process. Black musicians, singers and other black celebrities have been arriving in the U.S. to find the opportunities they are denied in Cuba. Let me cite one example of the many that can be referenced. In 2005 a group of black musicians and singers came to the U.S. to perform in several concerts under a government-sponsored tour. The entire group requested asylum while performing in Las Vegas. They were simply ecstatic. They could not believe the warm reception that they received. It was too good to return to the slavery and misery they had experienced in Cuba. They realized the enormity of Castro's lies about the United States. Justifiably, all they aspired to do was to use their God-given talents to advance their careers, to achieve a better living and to fulfill their dreams in an atmosphere of freedom and opportunity.

The Tragic Death of Singer Beny Moré

Not all attempting to flee the homeland achieve their dream. There was a black singer in Cuba who was not lucky enough to escape from the horrors of the Castro regime. His name was Beny Moré. He was the epitome of popular music in Cuba during the 1950s. He was doing exceedingly well, artistically and financially, in radio, television, night clubs and recordings. His successful career was cut short by the takeover of the free enterprise system. He was robbed not only of his material possessions, but also of his talents, his music, his voice and his right to freely market those personal assets as he desired. The idea of losing what he had cultivated with so much dedication, training and hard work sent chills up his spine. Moré turned against the inequities of the Castro rule and began to express his dissatisfaction in no uncertain terms. When it became known that he was planning to leave the country, he was detained by the Castro police, interrogated, accused of anti-Castro activities and given a brutal beating. He did not recover from the injuries which caused his premature death: a truly sad episode that speaks loudly of the agony of an oppressed nation. There is no distinction between races on the misfortune of the Cuban people. The story of Beny Moré has been repeated many times over, regardless of race. His case is typical of the barbaric absence of the rule of law and human rights under Castro-Communism.

Leonor the Seamstress

This case was related to me by a Cuban immigrant and it reflects the incredible cruelty of the Castro police. I cite it because it portrays the extremes reached by the perversity of the Communist regime. While on a trip to Miami in May 1985 as a delegate to the Convention of the Cuban Patriotic Council (JPC), I met

Dionisio Rodríguez Porta, a follower of the JPC. He was very descriptive of the events he shared, and I could see he was getting emotional as he unfolded the tragic story. Dionisio hailed from a small town in Pinar del Rio, the most western province of Cuba. He told me that during the mid-1970s there was a middle-aged black lady who became very popular in the town. She was a clandestine seamstress, eking out a living by making dresses, doing alterations, sewing and mending. She was an illegal entrepreneur since small, independent businesses are a forbidden activity in Cuba under the rigid Communist laws. The government prohibits private enterprises, no matter how small they may be, whether repairing shoes, mending clothes, shining shoes or selling goods or services. The state owns and controls every money-making enterprise.

Leonor was always helping people in her neighborhood. She was a good-natured person, often running errands for those in need, a natural leader and a noble lady. She was well known for her stand against the regime. She had been detained several times for her outspoken demeanor critical of abuses, food scarcity and rationing inequities. Many times while in line to get her allowance for certain foods, be it milk, meat, beans, flour or other essential staples, she would bitterly complain that the leaders of the so-called Neighborhood Vigilante Committees (card-carrying Communist Party members) were given priority in getting their allotments, even without using the rationing cards. They would walk right into the government stores without having to wait in line and obtain their goods while everybody else had to stay in line for hours. Every time she saw this happening she would protest loudly. She was brave and admired by her peers. Suddenly, one day it was noticed that she had disappeared; no one knew where she was. According to Dionisio, witnesses said that she had been forcibly taken while kicking and crying from her small apartment, located in a multiple-unit building, by two men. One was said to have been wearing a police uniform, and the other was in civilian clothes. They pushed her into a squad car and sped away. She was never seen again.

For months Leonor had adopted a routine of taking food scraps from her meals to feed a neighbor's little dog that became accustomed to waiting for her every evening at the same time, at the same place, under a porch by the sidewalk outside of its master's dwelling. About two days after Leonor's disappearance, Dionisio added, the dog sat at its habitual spot at the usual time and began howling with a mourning-like sound for about 15 to 20 minutes. The dog kept doing the same routine for several days. Out of curiosity, people began to gather around the little dog every evening to observe its unusual ritual. They were amazed at the sight of this creature mourning the absence of its protector.

The crowd grew larger every day. Since it was well known that Leonor had made a habit of feeding the little canine, there were conversations about the perception of death by dogs. Dionisio was part of that crowd. They came to the conclusion, based on the spread of the account of those who witnessed her removal and detention, that Leonor had been killed by the police and the dog was grieving her death, making a statement in its own way. The police did not like the idea of people gathering and talking to each other about the fate of Leonor. They began, with the help of goons, to disperse the crowd. A short time later, the dog was found shot to death by a bullet through its head. The entire episode was a pathetic display of the unconscionable system of oppression of the Castro satrapy.

The Culture of Survival

Cubans, out of necessity and fear, have cleverly developed what is popularly called the "culture of survival." Most people have learned that, to survive in a hostile and uncertain street environment where people distrust each other, they have to disguise their feelings about the revolution. They never know when they may be talking to a whistleblower, so they have adopted what is known as "two faces." On the surface they pretend to support Castro and Socialism. As demanded by the circumstances they would utter the coined slogan "Fatherland or Death" and reluctantly participate in the parades and "mass events" as required by the union leaders or other state organizations. On the other hand, below the surface, in the intimacy of their homes, the slogan becomes "To hell with Castro and Socialism" or "To the s---pile with Castro" ("Vaya a la mierda con Castro"). There is a routine in Cuba that everyone follows. When a husband leaves the house, his wife always reminds him to put on the mask, meaning the face of the pro-revolution person. This duality makes foreign journalists and pollsters ridiculously erroneous in reading the pulse of public opinion in Cuba. No one, except the valiant dissidents, ventures to speak ill of the revolution. The people have developed a natural distrust, a protective shield against potential government snitches. It is stupid of foreign journalists to ask questions about Castro or the revolution, thinking they are going to get a candid answer. My sympathies grow larger for the daring dissidents who openly defy the Communist tyranny against all adversities.

The culture of survival applies to other aspects of life under Communism. With the scarcity of food and just about everything else like apparels, appliances, cosmetics, soap, toothpaste, toothbrushes, shaving cream, razor blades and other essential items, people look for ways to get by. This could include engaging in permuting items or satisfying certain needs through the black market. Cubans are also very inventive and have come up with the dandiest homemade artifacts to substitute for things that are not easily available or affordable. As essential articles become evanescent, the culture becomes more creative. Even cooking recipes have been adapted to the necessities of life. Communism is a suffocating experience, but the instinct for survival does not vanish. There is a resolve to forge ahead in spite of all the adversity.

The grim reality the Cuban people have to confront and overcome in their own flesh and soul is that Communism is hostile to humanity. What an immense task to bear during an entire lifetime! We all must cogitate and sympathize with the tragic fate of an enslaved society and prevent, by all means possible, the morphing of our own free society into a similar disaster.

The "Coleros"

A new category of crime has surged in Cuba in recent years. "Los Coleros" is a derivative of the Spanish word cola, meaning queue or to be in line. The designation "coleros" applies in Cuba to people who charge a fee for standing in line outside shops on behalf of the highest bidder. This new mode has become a routine as a result of the familiar long lines of people waiting to enter the state stores to purchase scarce food items or household and personal goods. The "coleros" come in early and hustle to sell the spot to someone who did not have the time to wait for hours in a line outside the shops. The distance the "colero" is from the store entrance determines the price charged for the position. At first sight, it doesn't seem that this practice constitutes a crime. However, under Socialism the procedure is considered a profit-making venture and, therefore, an illegal one.

"Coleros" are persecuted by the police and, if arrested, can be fined from $100 to $400 and given a jail term of from one month to one year. They are accused of "bad social conduct" and profiteering. The "coleros practice" is one more unconscionable effect engendered by the abominable Communist regime. In spite of the criminality assigned to this practice, they have found ways to disguise their activities by designing some gestures or hand language to indicate the spot they are holding is negotiable. It is, however, a very risky business conducted out of desperation.

Dividing the Provinces: A Machiavellian Scheme

Cuba before Castro had six provinces. They existed even during the time that Spain ruled over the island. The Constitution of 1940 officially recognized the provinces as Pinar del Rio, La Habana, Las Villas, Matanzas, Camagüey and Oriente. In 1976 Castro expanded the number of provinces to fourteen by changing the geographical demarcation of the island and creating eight additional provinces. The provinces became Pinar del Rio, La Habana, Metropolitan Habana (Ciudad Habana), Matanzas, Villa Clara, Cienfuegos, Sancti Spiritus, Ciego de Avila, Camagüey, Las Tunas, Granma, Holguin, Guantanamo and Santiago de Cuba.

Like everything he does, there was a Machiavellian purpose for this geopolitical division of the island. He wanted to exert a more drastic and absolute control over the country. By creating more provinces he positioned the military commands over smaller population centers to monitor more closely the existing and potential enemies of the regime, including members of his own armed forces. Spreading the generals and other top officers in his vast military apparatus into many other provinces not only rewarded some generals with provincial commands, but also diluted the core and strength of the troops in pre-existing military bases. This was a precautionary measure in case of internal defiance or unrest by military leaders, as happened when President Carlos Prío was deposed in 1952. Bear in mind that Castro did not trust anyone, not even his family or his close allies.

The splitting of the traditional provinces had another added incentive for Castro in his deliberate attempt to further break the back of the culture and the customs prevailing in Cuba before the Communist rule. Cubans were always proud of the province where they were born. There was no animosity between people of one province or another, just sort of a noble and ingenuous pride. Castro did not want Cubans to feel orgulous of any cultural tradition inherited from the past. He wanted to create a radically different society and did everything he could to crush all Cubans' previous heritage as part of a well-planned brainwashing operation. His aim was to disconnect Cubans from any vestiges of yesteryear.

The creation of additional provinces enlarged enormously the bureaucracy and the cost of government, further affecting the economy which has been a sordid failure from the beginning of the revolution, affecting primarily the poor Cuban population, but not the elite class within the Communist hierarchy. However, the lunatic dictator does not blink an eye when it comes to executing something that will serve his personal antics, whether he tortures and kills his enemies, or causes the nation to suffer and sink further into bankruptcy and despair.

14

SOCIALISM, COMMUNISM AND OTHER DISEASES. CLOSING THOUGHTS.

"Socialism can generally be introduced into a country in one of two ways: either by a 'Socialist Revolution' or by what I call 'Creeping Socialism.' The former is ruled out to occur in the United States. However, the latter can be incrementally attained if the liberals and radical left remain unbridled and unchallenged in our ambience."

Socialism and Communism

I HAVE IN some instances purposely used the words Socialism and Communism interchangeably, and would like to explain in simple terms the contemporary meaning of the two vocables. I will not get into the philosophical details about their origin, evolvement and history, or the intertwining of the two terms contained in the Communist Manifesto of 1848, as enunciated by Karl Marx and Friedrich Engels and interpreted by scholars throughout the years.

In practice, Socialism, as understood today, refers to a centralized system under which the state owns the various aspects of society dealing with private property, private enterprise, educational systems, and all the means of production and distribution of industrial products. The state controls the monetary policy, the judicial system, the legislative body, the intellectual property, the religious conformance, the consumption of goods, the providing of services, the means of telecommunications and news media, and the contracting of international transactions.

Communism, as it was applied in the former Soviet Union and its satellites and still pertains to a few countries today, including Cuba, is transformed into the political and ideological arm of Socialism under which a single party, the Communist Party, becomes an intrinsic part of the totalitarian government structure and its constitution. The party sets the basis for central economy planning. The system, in theory, is supposed to bring about the so-called predominance of the proletariat, which is a farce because the workers in a fictitious "classless society" become pawns of the state. As in the case of Cuba, the labor unions are still permitted, but only as an instrument of vigilance, control and indoctrination, serving the state rather than the workers. Laborers have no rights, are poorly paid and cannot ask for raises in salary because that would be considered counter-revolutionary. They cannot even request improvements in working conditions and, of course, are denied the right to strike. The workers become slaves of the central authority under the dictator's command, who is also the head of the Communist Party and carries the fraudulent title of "President of Cuba."

The utopian "classless society" leading to the last stage of Communism, a "stateless society" in which the economic goods were to be shared equally, as delineated by Marx and Engels, never materialized. It was only a mirage of the delusional mentality of Marx, Engels and their followers. On the contrary, as in the case of the former Soviet Union and now Cuba, as well as other countries that have contracted the disease, an elite ruling class is created composed of the top-ranking military brass, beginning with the dictator and the civilians in privileged positions. The elite class enjoys the spoils, luxuries and abundance denied to the rest of the population.

A pseudo-legislative body was instituted in Cuba under the flamboyant name of "National Assembly of the Popular Power," which serves as a rubber stamp for the ruler's wishes. There is even a "Supreme Court of Justice" composed of clowns dancing to the tune of the despot. This is the court that has, upon token appellations, consistently denied clemency to the victims of Castro's political persecution criminally executed by firing squads. There is no rule of law in Cuba.

Why do these useless and superfluous government bodies exist under a one-man rule? They are created as fronts to make it appear as a lawful government before international organizations such as the United Nations, and to promote the idea that there is an organized and popular society in Cuba to impress the free and democratic nations of the world.

Furthermore, under Socialism and following the tenets of the Marx theory, the traditional family nucleus has to be destroyed. Every individual becomes state property. The concept of God is crushed and atheism is implanted to erase all vestiges of spiritualism. Dialectical materialism replaces all ethics, dignity and the drive for individualism. The priority of matter over mind prevails. This in itself explains the cruelty of Socialism/Communism. It is based on a derailed mental attitude with no human perspective. Religion, initially, is placed under surveillance, with the aim of its gradual and complete obliteration as new generations are taught, from early childhood, that there is no God. Religion is counter to the atheistic and materialistic concepts of the Communist dogma. According to Marx and his followers, the moral foundation of society has to be dismantled and reshaped into the mold of the Communist framework. This is completely opposite to the natural aspirations of the human person since the early stages of civilization. It explains why Communism is only attained through an oppressive system whose foundation is fear, repression and slavery.

Opinions or thoughts not in conformance with the canons established under a Communist system are not permitted. The tyrannical regime does not allow deviations from the official dogma. Dissidents are harassed, persecuted, jailed or executed for expressing contrarian views to the established order. Liberals, radical leftists, neo-Socialists and other classifications are nonetheless abundant in democratic nations where free expression is allowed and protected.

Liberals and the Far Left

Liberals in countries like the United States are referred to as those who flirt with Socialism/Communism and serve, depending on their degree of radicalism, as tools of the Marxist-Leninist ideology, whether naïvely or intentionally. They normally favor additional taxes, more government control over industry and commerce, misleading and restrictive environmental policies, relaxing national security, a soft approach to terrorism, incremental social programs and entitlements at the expense of the taxpayers, further economic barriers, unrestricted illegal immigration, constraints on crude oil extractions on American soil, limitations on the construction and expansion of oil refineries, leniency for criminals (including sexual predators), no death penalty for heinous crimes, relaxing of moral values, appointment of liberal justices to the courts and other left-wing causes.

The oddity of liberals is that many are very rich and yet are trying to deter by their actions the drive, natural desire and motivation of individuals for self-improvement, personal responsibility, entrepreneurial opportunities and the development of a competitive climate for those who aspire to succeed in a free enterprise system. Government handouts are not going to solve and promote individual efforts. Instead they foster a mentality of dependency that is destructive and corrosive. Education, training, hard work and the fostering of individual empowerment are the venues for improvement and advancement in a free society. A free market economy, not the government, is the source for new jobs and growth.

Under a democratic government, the rights of the people are respected, not trampled. The government becomes the guardian of the civil society to safeguard its dynamic components, consisting of private enterprise, a free press, and all social, civic, political and cultural institutions. An environment of freedom inspires creativity, growth, new ideas and, most importantly, the recognition of human dignity as an essential element of life itself. If the natural structure of the civil society is broken, as it is in the case of a Socialist/Communist system, a climate of perversion and uncertainty prevails, human stability is disturbed, and the whole society is affected, thus opening the door to a tyrannical rule and eventual chaos.

The far left, radical left and neo-Socialists not only flirt with Socialism/ Communism, but additionally, as birds of the same feather, flock together with the practitioners of the Marxist-Leninist doctrine, serving as tools of their intentions. They are usually referred to as "useful fools," actively and openly promoting the Marxist line. It seems that these types do not learn from the lessons of history, nor do they feel compassion for the human rights abuses and the unimaginable misery perpetrated under the Communist system in every country where it is applied. They, like some extreme liberals, invariably and inexplicably favor tyrannical regimes like Castro's in Cuba and Chavez's in Venezuela. The blindness and warped minds of the radical leftists do not let them distinguish between reality and fiction. It is a syndrome born out of hate, insensitivity and disdain for humanity. They are determined to undermine the institutions of a free society to bring about its gradual disintegration.

A caution to our great American nation: beware of empty "charismatic leftist leaders" having no substance or demonstrable achievements – often hiding under the cloak of religion – promising the redemption of the poor through platitudes, hyperboles, pretentious pledges and Socialist initiatives. They make promises conducive to limiting free enterprise, freedom of expression, individual rights and personal determination, ultimately curtailing the capacity for growth and the motivation of individuals to carve out their own future. Their position clearly weakens the principles under which this nation was founded and grew to be the most powerful and progressive country in the world. They are surreptitiously sowing the seeds for the path to Socialism, the venom of society.

Socialism can generally be introduced into a country in one of two ways: either by a "Socialist Revolution" or by what I call "Creeping Socialism." The former is ruled out to occur in the United States. However, the latter can be incrementally attained if the liberals and radical left remain unbridled and unchallenged in our ambience.

Many of the liberal pundits are bent on discrediting the United States at every opportunity. They are disloyal and treacherous for reasons which defy common sense and rational thinking. What is most perplexing is that the ultra-liberals, far-left radicals, neo-Communists and other elements of the same ilk are attacking the very foundation of our nation – the foundation that sustains the democratic values which permit them to express their bitter and injurious criticism of the system that protects their right to free expression. They seem intent on destroying the environment of freedom and the free enterprise society under which many of them have thrived and built personal fortunes.

What is their objective? Is it a subconscious sense of guilt? And if in some way they feel guilty for being so rich, why don't they give it all up and become part of the have-nots they are hypocritically trying to defend? Would that make them feel better? Oh no, they wouldn't do that! Or is it that they are so selfish that they do not want others to grow and succeed under the same system that gave them the opportunity to be where they are now? Or perhaps they want to look "cute" or "different" by embracing extreme ideological causes to satisfy their egotistic vanity? This last assertion, in my opinion, seems to fit them perfectly. As we have seen, among them are famous movie actors and actresses, entertainers, celebrities, financial and business experts, politicians, journalists, university and college professors and other so-called intellectuals.

The danger is that most of their kind are in a position of public domain and can influence the thinking of the naïve and unprepared segment of the population, or those in the formative stages of ideological understanding. They can be mischievously persuasive and can contribute to the brainwashing of the mentally weak. They excel in praising our enemies and defiling America. This is not surprising because they all have something in common: their distaste for the United States. I suggest that they get a one-way ticket to Cuba and enjoy the "Communist Paradise" for the rest of their lives.

It is very obvious that some American scholars and grandstanding Hollywood celebrities – coincidentally partial to leftist causes – are given a lot of publicity by selectively picking and exposing human rights abuses in far away places, and there is nothing wrong with that. However, I have yet to see this same bunch denounce the Castro tyranny which is so close to our shores. Are they so shortsighted not to even see the unfolding human tragedy going on in Cuba for so many years? Or is it that they may be sympathetic to the repugnant Communist dictatorship? I would like to think that this is not the case.

Exposing the Tyrant

Castro's maniacal behavior has been demonstrated in every phase of his life, whether as a son, a student, a husband, a father, a brother, a friend or a tyrant. Communism and the dictatorial power that came with it have certainly befitted his endless, malicious conduct. The cruelty, suffering and grief that he has inflicted on the Cuban people have been manifested in many shapes and forms as exposed throughout the pages of this book. His path of destruction, hate and barbarism has given the world a true measure of his malice.

It is disgusting and repulsive to observe how Castro has perverted Cuban history to fit his diabolical design and to justify his hatred for the United States. What is equally nauseating is his use of lies as fodder to feed his apologists on the left in America and other countries.

I have dedicated many moments of my life to expose the Cuban tyrant for what he really is: a coward, a traitor, a hooligan, a fake, a liar and a cruel, heartless oppressor who eviscerated a well-developed nation. Whether he maintains his power after his very serious health problems reported during August 2006, or keeps his brother Raúl as the heir to the throne, or dies or survives doesn't make any difference at this moment in Cuba. The damage inflicted on the enslaved nation cannot be easily repaired. The suffering he has caused cannot be reversed. The innocent people he has killed cannot be revived.

Now concerning the speculation of the pundits as to whether one or the other of the two brothers is better or worse, the answer to this query is very simple. They are both worse (pardon my twisting of the English language), or as they commonly say, it boils down to "six of one or half a dozen of the other." Ultimately, in one way or another, the Communist tyranny will collapse and the Cuban people will regain their freedom. At this point I would like to share a simple verse I wrote reflecting the angst of the Cuban people:

Noble Dream

Oh, Cuba
Beautiful Cuba
Suffering Cuba
After years of repression
Cruelty, misery and pain
We long to see you
Free and democratic again!

World Evolution and Regression: Cuba an Example of the Latter

A perfect society has never existed in the world. Through the pages of history we have seen how people have constantly strived to improve or change conditions prevailing in tyrannical and even non-tyrannical systems of government. Religion has undoubtedly played an important role in the process by advocating faith in God, hope, love, moral values, understanding and the holding of society together. There are, of course, exceptions to this averment. For instance, some jihadist, extremist, fundamentalist Islamic groups deplorably promote hatred and the nihilistic murder of thousands of innocent people in many parts of our planet through terrorist activities, oftentimes using fanatical suicide bombers as weapons of destruction. These radical elements are determined to rule the world through a theocratic dictatorship. They represent today a treacherous menace to free society. Jihadists, lingering Communist dictators and other dysfunctional beings constitute forces of regression for the entire human race. The good news is that history has taught us deranged individuals of this kind will not prevail, and their diabolical intentions will lead them to eventual self-destruction.

Throughout the course of civilization, the mind has evolved to accept salutary changes and, conversely, the mind in some instances has been forcibly repressed to deter political, social and cultural evolution. We have witnessed how many countries have gone far in adapting to changes, while others have kept the status quo, and yet some have regressed like in the case of Cuba. It has been demonstrated over and over again that political, cultural and social tenets are not a constant, particularly in democratic societies where ideas can be openly enunciated and debated without fear of repression. Slavery, for instance, has been overcome in many countries. Minds have progressed to realize the wrong ways and take remedial action. Discrimination of some people against others because of race, religion, nationality or social status has been eliminated or attenuated in a variety of instances by people's adaptation to reality through education and human comprehension of what is right and wrong.

The advance of civilization has gone, and continues to go, through difficult and perilous times, including, but not limited to, violent struggles, famines, genocides, natural disasters, terrorism and wars. Science and technology have made strides beyond any imaginable expectations, impacting enormously on the quality of life. Through the centuries humanity has seen slavery of whites on whites, blacks on blacks, whites on blacks and slavery among other races. As inconceivable as it may seem, we still have slavery in certain regions of the world. Examples can be cited of black-on-black slavery and genocides in certain African countries like Uganda, Sudan, Somalia, Rwanda and Congo. However, we don't have to go that far to find such human rights inequities. We have a clean case of slavery in our own hemisphere only 90 miles from the tip of Florida. A contemptuous slaved society exists in Cuba imposed under sheer fear and systematic human rights abuses by the ominous Communist regime of Castro, the dinosaur of the Caribbean.

Closing Thoughts

Cuba will rise again from the ashes of a devastated land. I hope and pray that the spark of liberty, forever present in the hearts of the oppressed citizenry, will continue to guide and inspire its desire for redemption. It is only a matter of time before the people break away from the yoke of the corrupt despot. The heroic and persistent dissident movement is demonstrating that the struggle continues, in spite of persecution, torture and death. The intense desire to break the chains of slavery keeps burning like an everlasting flame. This will not be the first time a country under a brutal dictatorial siege has successfully rebelled against the forces of subjugation. There is a limit of endurance to human vilification and, in the case of Cuba, it has already reached its zenith. Cuba will be free again by the valorous effort of its population and the external support that is expected of the democratic nations of the world.

We are certain that the Cuban people, after liberation, will rise to the occasion and demonstrate their capability to return to a free enterprise system under a democratic environment. Systematically and following a comprehensive plan – already drafted by the leaders of the Cuban-exiled community and a trust of political, economic, public health and social experts – Cuba will regain its rightful place in the free world. Its people will be able to partake once again of the freedom, justice and human decency they have been denied for such a protracted period of time.

The imposition of a Communist system in Cuba by a merciless, mendacious and criminal dictator brings nightmares to a suffering population and to millions who escaped Cuba searching for freedom and justice, and who still care deeply about their country of origin and the families they left behind. The question that continuously pierces our brains and souls is, "Why?" It is inconceivable that a nation could be coerced into such brutal bondage maintained over a period of 48 long years. Yet there are still many who, surprisingly, are ignorant or have been misled about the process by which Cuba, so close to the United States of America, was forcibly converted to a country under a shameful servitude. The outside world is entitled to know the truth.

I trust this book, covering at large the various facets and magnitude of this incredible calamity, will open the eyes of the uninformed and cause them to comprehend its human dimensions. The Communist catastrophe hit Cuba with the force of a nuclear blast, wiping out a culture, family traditions, religious roots, a budding free enterprise structure, and the idiosyncrasies and dreams of a creative population. There is no better way to describe the totality of the cataclysm than *The Rape of a Nation!*

GOD SAVE CUBA! GOD BLESS AMERICA!

www.ingramcontent.com/pod-product-compliance
Lightning Source LLC
Chambersburg PA
CBHW060621290526
45793CB00001B/99